THE DOUBTERS' DILEMMA

EXPLORING STUDENT ATTRITION AND RETENTION IN
UNIVERSITY LANGUAGE & CULTURE PROGRAMS

THE DOUBTERS' DILEMMA

EXPLORING STUDENT ATTRITION AND RETENTION IN UNIVERSITY LANGUAGE & CULTURE PROGRAMS

MARIO DANIEL MARTÍN, LOUISE JANSEN, ELIZABETH A. BECKMANN

Published by ANU Press
The Australian National University
Acton ACT 2601, Australia
Email: anupress@anu.edu.au
This title is also available online at press.anu.edu.au

National Library of Australia Cataloguing-in-Publication entry

Creator: Martín, Mario Daniel, author.

Title: The doubters' dilemma : exploring student attrition and
                retention in university Language &
                Culture programs / Mario Daniel Martín,
                Louise Jansen, Elizabeth A. Beckmann.

ISBN: 9781760460440 (paperback) 9781760460457 (ebook)

Subjects: Educational evaluation--Australia.
                College student development programs.
                Universities and colleges--Sociological aspects.
                Language and culture--Study and teaching--Australia.

Other Creators/Contributors:
                Jansen, Louise, author.
                Beckmann, Elizabeth A., author.

Dewey Number: 379.1580994

All rights reserved. No part of this publication may be reproduced, stored in a retrieval system or transmitted in any form or by any means, electronic, mechanical, photocopying or otherwise, without the prior permission of the publisher.

Cover design and layout by ANU Press.

This edition © 2016 ANU Press

Contents

Illustrations vii

Tables. xi

Acknowledgements xv

1. Understanding the Problem: Student attrition and retention in university Language & Culture programs in Australia 1
   1.1. Why is it important to understand student attrition and retention? 1
   1.2. Attrition as a concern for university Language & Culture programs in Australia 5
   1.3. The impact of government, university and school policies on language teaching in Australia 8
   1.4. Historical perspectives from the teaching coalface. 11
   1.5. Research into attrition in university Language & Culture programs 14
   1.6. The LASP1 study 17
   1.7. The LASP2 study 18
   1.8. Implications of the LASP1 and LASP2 research. 21
   1.9. Attrition at the course level: Risk factors 22
   1.10. Learning anxiety as a specific risk factor in language learning 24
   1.11. Asking the difficult questions: Attrition as a research problem 25
   1.12. A reader's guide to this book. 28

2. Accounting for the Missing Students: Calculating retention rates in Language & Culture programs 31
   2.1. The importance of validity when calculating attrition and retention rates . . 31
   2.2. Calculating retention rates at ANU: The complexity of language enrolments 32
   2.3. The need for new ways of calculating language retention rates 42
   2.4. Further issues impacting the calculation of retention rates 47
   2.5. Do retention rates vary by discipline? 52

	2.6.	Late starters at advanced levels—Students who speak a language other than English (LOTE) at home 61
	2.7.	Summary... 71
3.	Splitting the Masses: Methodology and data analysis 73	
	3.1.	Phase 1 methodology 73
	3.2.	Implications of the Phase 1 findings from a methodological perspective . . 76
	3.3.	Beyond the dichotomy: Moving towards more effective statistical analyses 78
	3.4.	Phase 2 methodology 81
	3.5.	Summary... 99
4.	Some Detective Work: Comparing Committed Students, Quitters and Doubters 101	
	4.1.	Overview 101
	4.2.	A detailed interpretation of the cross-tabulated variables that characterise Committed Students, Doubters and Quitters............. 102
	4.3.	Summary.. 132
5.	The Road to Language Capital: Interpreting the findings 133	
	5.1.	Characterising the three student archetypes 133
	5.2.	Doubters as 'students at risk' 139
	5.3.	The concept of 'language capital' 140
	5.4.	The concept of language capital as a means of interpreting the classroom context... 142
	5.5.	Summary.. 148
6.	Where to from Here? Conclusions and suggestions 149	

Appendices: Online Questionnaires Used in the ANU Study

Appendix 1: Questionnaire 1. Language Retention Study:
First year students 2009....................................159

Appendix 2: Questionnaire: Continuing intermediate
and advanced level students 2009............................171

Appendix 3: Questionnaire: Discontinuing students 2009 185

Bibliography 197

Illustrations

Figure 1.1. Factors known to have a negative effect on student completion 5

Figure 1.2. Factors associated with course attrition, as identified from the literature 23

Figure 2.1. Comparison in the enrolment patterns of a Social Science major and two language majors 36

Figure 2.2. Apparent progression rates from Level 1 in 2008 to Level 3 in 2010 40

Figure 2.3. Comparison in the enrolment patterns of two Language majors when all students are considered and only the 2008 cohort of students is considered 41

Figure 2.4. Graphical representation of the figures used to calculate the Semester Level Retention Rate. The rate is calculated using only the levels of Language & Culture study shown. 45

Figure 2.5. Graphical representation of the figures used to calculate the Global Retention Rate. The rate is calculated using all three levels of Language & Culture study shown in all semesters. 45

Figure 2.6. Some factors affecting the calculation of retention rates 50

Figure 2.7. Retention rates based on 2008 Enrolment Year Student Cohort—Languages 51

Figure 2.8. Retention rates based on 2008 Enrolment Year Student Cohort—Languages compared with Sciences 54

Figure 2.9. Retention rates based on 2008 Enrolment Year Student Cohort—Languages compared with other disciplines 1 55

Figure 2.10. Retention rates based on 2008 Enrolment Year Student Cohort—Languages compared with other disciplines 2 56

Figure 2.11. Schematic representation of two types of undergraduate majors. 58

Figure 2.12. Comparison of enrolment patterns by language spoken at home and gender—All ANU languages 64

Figure 2.13. Comparison of enrolment patterns for international students who enrolled in first and second semester 2008— All ANU languages.................................. 66

Figure 2.14. Global Retention Rate for domestic and international students, discriminated by the type of LOTE spoken at home. Only students who enrolled in 2008 and report to speak a LOTE at home are considered. The figure provides load for all ANU languages studied. 68

Figure 2.15. Comparison of enrolment patterns for domestic and international students in general and domestic and international students who speak a Chinese language at home—All ANU Languages 70

Figure 3.1. The issue of learning to speak the language 79

Figure 3.2. Graphical representation of the Canonical Discriminant Functions—Full ANU study sample 97

Figure 4.1. Basic characteristics—Student characteristics. 104

Figure 4.2. Basic characteristics—Freedom to study languages. . . . 106

Figure 4.3. Basic characteristics—Perceptions of being forced to study or to discontinue studying a language 108

Figure 4.4. Reasons for studying the language 1. 110

Figure 4.5. Reasons for studying the language 2. 111

Figure 4.6. Family and peers 112

Figure 4.7. Previous exposure to language learning 114

Figure 4.8. Perceptions of difficulty of language studies........ 115

Figure 4.9. Difficulties in the language learning process........ 116

Figure 4.10. Perception of workload in learning the four
basic skills 118

Figure 4.11. Perception of teachers 119

Figure 4.12. Perception of the learning environment 120

Figure 4.13. The effect of grades/marks 122

Figure 4.14. Reasons to continue studying the language 1 123

Figure 4.15. Reasons to continue studying the language 2 124

Figure 4.16. Reasons to continue studying the language 3 126

Figure 4.17. Reasons to discontinue 1...................... 127

Figure 4.18. Reasons to discontinue 2...................... 129

Figure 4.19. Reasons to discontinue 3...................... 130

Figure 4.20. Reasons to discontinue 4...................... 131

Figure 5.1. Interest in learning the four language skills—
discriminated by grouping of languages................ 143

Figure 5.2. Perceptions of how well students report they
have learned the four language skills at the time of
the data collection. All students...................... 143

Figure 5.3. Perceptions of how well students have learned
the four language skills, discriminated by language
groups and propensity to discontinuation 144

Figure 5.4. Perceptions of how much students have learned
about the culture associated with the language and the
four language skills, discriminated by propensity to
discontinuation. All students........................ 145

Tables

Table 2.I. Language & Culture enrolments in 2009 discriminated by level and commencing/continuing status. 34

Table 2.II. Percentage of Late Starters in L&C and other ANU courses 2008–2010. 37

Table 2.III. Percentage of Advanced Starters in L&C and other ANU courses 2008–2010 38

Table 2.IV. Semester Level Retention Rate—All ANU languages. Only students who enrolled in 2008 are considered. Enrolment measured in EFTSL 44

Table 2.V. Global Retention Rate and Semester Level Retention Rate—All ANU languages. Only students who enrolled in 2008 are considered. Enrolment measured in EFTSL. 44

Table 2.VI. Languages taught at ANU in 2008, 2009 and 2010 48

Table 2.VII. Global Retention Rate for Languages and Sciences compared. Only students who enrolled in 2008 are considered 53

Table 2.VIII. Global Retention Rate for Languages and other groups of disciplines compared. Only students who enrolled in 2008 are considered 53

Table 2.IX. Semester Level Retention Rate for Languages and Sciences compared. Only students who enrolled in 2008 are considered 60

Table 2.X. Retention rates for students who report that they speak English at home. Only students who enrolled in 2008 considered—All ANU languages 62

Table 2.XI. Retention rates for students who report that they speak a LOTE at home. Only students who enrolled in 2008 considered—All ANU languages 62

Table 2.XII. Retention rates for female students. Only students who enrolled in 2008 considered—All ANU languages 63

Table 2.XIII. Retention rates for male students. Only students who enrolled in 2008 considered—All ANU languages 63

Table 2.XIV. Percentage of international students in each year and level—All ANU languages......................... 65

Table 2.XV. Percentage of students who speak a LOTE at home in each year and level—All ANU languages 67

Table 3.I. Languages represented in the focus group discussions (two students were enrolled in more than one language) 74

Table 3.II. Response rate for the two pilot questionnaire surveys (includes some repeat entries: students enrolled in more than one language course were allowed to complete a survey for each language).................... 75

Table 3.III. Classification of students' commitment to language study................................. 78

Table 3.IV. Chi-square analysis of variables in Figure 3.1 according to two different groupings of students 80

Table 3.V. Response rate of individual languages discriminated by level—Full ANU study sample. Students enrolled in 2009... 85

Table 3.VI. Reclassification of students' commitment to language study—Full ANU study sample.............. 87

Table 3.VII.a. Discriminant Function. Eigenvalues 89

Table 3.VII.b. Discriminant Function. Wilks's Lambda.......... 89

Table 3.VIII. Structure Matrix—Significant Variables—Full ANU study sample 90

Table 3.IX.a. Standardised Canonical Discriminant Function Coefficients (ranked by Function 1) 94

Table 3.IX.b. Standardised Canonical Discriminant Function Coefficients (ranked by Function 2) 95

Table 3.X. Classification Results[bc] for the Canonical
    Discriminant Functions 98
Table 5.I. Classification of students' commitment to language
    study used to characterise the student groups 134

Acknowledgements

This monograph is based on a collaborative research project undertaken at The Australian National University from 2008 to 2014. As noted in Chapter 1, section 1.2, one of the project's unique features was its collaborative nature across many internal institutional boundaries. A large number of staff participated in and helped to carry out the project. We wish to thank them for their commitment and generous contribution of their sparse time. Without them, the project would not have been successful.

During Phase I, the project was located in the Centre for Educational Development & Academic Methods (CEDAM), with Dr Gerlese Åkerlind as principal investigator. After administrative changes in CEDAM, the project was transferred to the College of Arts and Social Sciences School of Language Studies, with Dr Louise Jansen as principal investigator. Without the contribution of the many individuals involved, the project would not have been possible, and thanks are due to all of them. We acknowledge here:

Project team
- ** Gerlese Åkerlind, CEDAM (Project Leader, Phase I)
- * Louise Jansen, School of Language Studies (Project Leader, Phase II)
- * Mario Daniel Martín, School of Language Studies
- * Roald Maliangkaij, China and Korea Centre
- * David Marr, ANU Planning and Statistical Services Division

Wider project team
Research assistance
  Elizabeth Beckmann, CEDAM
- * Loan Dao, CEDAM

*   Sujatha Kalimili, CEDAM
       Maurice Nevile, CEDAM
       Nepali Sah, School of Language Studies

Consultation on Statistics
       Emlyn Williams, ANU Statistical Consulting Unit

Consultation on Languages and Cultures
       Ghassan Al Shatter, Centre for Arab and Islamic Studies
       Piera Carroli, School of Language Studies
       Louise Maurer, School of Language Studies
       Gabriele Schmidt, School of Language Studies
       Yanyan Wang, Southeast Asia Centre

Data Collection

       Ali Aldahesh, Centre for Arab and Islamic Studies
*   Ghassan Al Shatter, Centre for Arab and Islamic Studies
       Huda Al-Tamimi, Centre for Arab and Islamic Studies
*   Monica Aznarez, School of Language Studies
*   Richard Barz, Southeast Asia Centre
*   Peter Brown, School of Language Studies
*   Piera Carroli, School of Language Studies
       Chantal Crozet, School of Language Studies
*   Tim Hassall, Southeast Asia Centre
*   Hossein Heirani-Moghaddam, Centre for Arab and Islamic Studies
*   Shunichi Ikeda, Southeast Asia Centre
*   Mehmet Mehdi Ilhan, Centre for Arab and Islamic Studies
*   Louise Maurer, School of Language Studies
*   Elizabeth Minchin, School of Cultural Inquiry
*   Chintana Sandilands, Southeast Asia Centre
*   Gabriele Schmidt, School of Language Studies
*   McComas Taylor, Southeast Asia Centre
*   Bao Duy Thai, Southeast Asia Centre
*   Yanyan Wang, Southeast Asia Centre
*   Yogendra Yadav, Southeast Asia Centre

** Primary investigator in Human Research Ethics Protocol
* Co-investigator in Human Research Ethics Protocol

University authorities that funded, or supported funding requests, for different stages of the research

2008–2010
- Ian Chubb, Vice-Chancellor
- Kent Anderson, Director, Faculty of Asian Studies, CAP
- Andrew Hopkins, Acting Dean, CASS

2011–2014
- Howard Morphy, Director, Research School of Humanities & the Arts
- Jane Simpson, Head of School of Language Studies

2015–2016
- ANU Press Publication Subsidy Fund

We are extremely grateful to all the students in ANU Language and Culture programs who participated in the surveys and focus groups for this research. Without their co-operation and engagement, the work could not have happened.

1

Understanding the Problem: Student attrition and retention in university Language & Culture programs in Australia

> The more students learn, the more value they find in their learning, the more likely they are to stay and graduate ... the purpose of higher education is not merely that students are retained, but that they are educated. In the final analysis, student learning drives student retention. (Tinto, 2002, 4)

1.1. Why is it important to understand student attrition and retention?

What makes students decide to study a language at university? What makes those same students decide to continue or stop studying a language? As university academics and administrators supporting language and culture (L&C)[1] studies, how do we quantify these decisions

---

1   In this book, the term 'language and culture' or 'L&C' is used to encompass all higher education courses/units/programs in 'languages other than English' (LOTE) taught at universities, and explicitly includes the teaching of concepts and materials related to the cultures entwined with those languages. This terminology has been embraced by the Languages and Cultures Network for Australian Universities (www.lcnau.org) because it evidences the fundamental tenet that a language cannot be taught, or learned, effectively without reference to cultural contexts and competencies. For stylistic reasons, 'languages' is occasionally used in Tables and Figures, but always implies 'L&C'.

of students in ways that provide effective input into resourcing? How do we know if there are more students giving up on their L&C studies than on their studies in other disciplines, and whether this indicates a problem with L&C teaching? Is there anything that can, or should, be done to help students stay in L&C programs?[2]

These are questions that occupy all language teachers, policy makers and administrators at tertiary level, whatever the languages taught and whatever the institution. At the very least, universities should be able to measure accurately the rates at which students leave or stay in L&C majors. Ideally, universities should also understand exactly which factors—such as teaching style, workloads, or student characteristics—affect attrition and retention, and which are most influential.

Attrition is usually defined as the number of non-completing students (i.e. students who have not yet finished their program of study) who are enrolled in a specific university, school, discipline or program in a given year, but not enrolled in that same program the following year (Gabb, Milne and Cao, 2006, 3). Research into attrition (and its corollary, retention)—that is, examining the numbers and characteristics of students who withdraw from, or stay in, university study, and the reasons why they do so—has a long tradition in some countries such as the United States of America (USA, e.g. Pascarella and Chapman, 1983; Pascarella and Terenzini, 1991, 2005; Tinto, 1975, 1987, 1993, 2006; Wesely, 2010) but has only relatively recently become an area of interest in the United Kingdom (e.g. Jones, 2008; Ozga and Sukhnandan, 1997; Yorke et al., 1997), New Zealand (Zepke and Leach, 2006) and Australia (e.g. Foster, 2010; James, Krause and Jennings, 2010; Krause, 2005; McInnis, 2001; McInnis, Hartley, Polesel and Teese, 2000; Pitkethly and Prosser, 2001; Taylor and Bedford, 2004). The numbers involved are not insignificant: Pitkethly and Prosser (2001) calculated that about a third of all Australian students entering university at that time did not graduate, and that half of those who withdrew did so in their first year. The two

---

2   Throughout this book the word 'program' refers to a large group of courses or multiple majors that constitute a pathway to a certified award, such as a degree. 'Course' is used in the sense of a defined unit of university study, usually equivalent to a semester of face-to-face or online teaching. 'Major' refers to a cluster of courses that together indicate a defined level of expected learner competence.'Honours' refers to a one-year pre-doctoral research-orientated pathway.

fundamental questions asked by those who research student attrition at university are therefore 'How many students discontinue their studies before completing a degree?' and 'Why do students do this?'

Higher education administrators and budget planners have commonly used the very unsophisticated tool of raw enrolment numbers both as a measure of attrition and a surrogate indicator of a program's success. For example, the Australian Department of Education, Science and Training provided the first notable data set (1994–2004) for Australian higher education using 'simple measures of attrition at an institution level [whereby] the attrition rate plus the retention rate plus the completion rate for a given student population in a given year will equal 100 percent' (Lukic, Broadbent and Maclachlan, 2004, 2). The authors noted that, for methodological reasons, the rates included 'students who leave a course at one university and enrol the next year at another university ... [and] those students who leave university without completing their course, but who return later to the same university' (Lukic et al., 2004, 2). Using this measure, the Commonwealth Government reported an average attrition rate of 18 per cent for all students in Australian universities during the period 1994–2002, although considerable variation was noted across institutions and different student populations (Lukic et al., 2004). At The Australian National University, for example, attrition rates for first year students in that period were somewhat higher than the national average, and increased from 22 per cent to 24 per cent over the eight-year period.

Shaw (2008) has subsequently argued that, because this method of calculating attrition rates fails to allow for students who leave one university but enrol at another university the following year, the real national average attrition rate in 2002 was more likely to have been around 10 per cent. The rudimentary nature of such a measure of attrition is even more concerning when we remember that, as a critical outcome of the Nelson reforms in the early 2000s, attrition rates calculated in this way were used as performance indicators for the allocation of Learning and Teaching Performance Funds to universities (Gabb et al., 2006), despite the resultant data being relatively untrustworthy. A subsequent review of base funding did show that the government attrition rates used to measure and allocate university performance funding had indeed been misleading: in reality, about

10 per cent of students who had been counted as 'discontinuing' their higher education had actually transferred to another university (Lomax-Smith, Watson and Webster, 2010).

With this economic incentive, the paired parameters of attrition and retention became popular focal points for researchers in Australasian higher education in the early 2000s (e.g. McInnis and James, 2004; Taylor and Bedford, 2004; Zepke and Leach, 2006), especially with regard to the 'first year experience' (e.g. James et al., 2010; Krause, 2005; McInnis, James and Hartley, 2000; Nelson, Duncan and Clarke, 2009; Pitkethly and Prosser, 2001). These studies reported a clear need, from both economic and pedagogical perspectives, to identify students who are 'at risk' of withdrawing from individual courses, or from university study as a whole, especially in their first year of study:

> one wonders whether, if the institutions to which these potential dropouts belonged had known what they were thinking and feeling and why, things might have been done any differently to support them (Krause, 2005, 58).

Such identification requires an understanding of relevant student motivations. In a seminal work on retention, Tinto (1975) identified four factors of key importance: instruction, academic success, anxiety and motivation. Wesely (2010) explored the literature on these four factors in the specific context of foreign language teaching (from a US perspective). Overall, however, motivation remains little understood: while students provide many reasons for leaving university before graduating (Figure 1.1), Pitkethly and Prosser (2001, 186) argued that the factors most likely to affect students' failures or course withdrawals seemed related more often to the students' adjustment to the university context rather than to their difficulties with intellectual understanding of the relevant content, and hence have a local/national context that must be considered. Whether the motivations to give up study are the same for students in L&C programs is not clear: despite the new interest in university student attrition as an area worthy of empirical research, by the mid-2000s there was still little data available with respect to attrition of students in L&C programs, even in the USA (Wesely, 2010), and it is not clear how generalisable many research findings are to the special circumstances of L&C teaching.

- Wrong choice of program
- Poor quality of the student experience
- Inability to cope with the demands of the program
- Unhappiness with the social environment
- Matters related to financial need
- Dissatisfaction with aspects of institutional provision
- Problems with relationships and finance
- Pressure of work (academic and employment)
- Learning efficiency (students' general cognitive skills)
- Self efficacy (self reliance, locus of control, self directedness)
- Quality of instruction (perceptions of the quality of teaching)
- Course difficulty (in relation to available academic support and counselling)
- Interaction with academic staff
- Goal commitment (planning skills, motivation)
- Time for learning (planning and organising study programs)

Figure 1.1. Factors known to have a negative effect on student completion
Source: After Longden, 2006; Taylor and Bedford, 2004, 376; Tinto, 1975; Weston, 1998; Yorke, 1999.

1.2. Attrition as a concern for university Language & Culture programs in Australia

One could argue that the most striking characteristic of L&C programs in Australian universities is the relative scarcity of students. Although it is a complex statistic to calculate in any national or pan-national context, a snapshot of language teaching in Australian higher education in the early 1990s noted that just 2 per cent of higher education students were studying languages, with the highest proportion being in the Australian Capital Territory (Leal, Bettoni and Malcolm, 1991). Subsequent estimates suggested a relative increase in interest—Hajek (2001) reported 5 per cent of Australian university students studying at least one language, while Nettelbeck, Byron, Clyne, Hajek, Lo Bianco and McLaren (2007, 2) reported that 'fewer than 10% of first-year students undertake LOTE [language other than English] study of any kind … with overall languages enrolments stagnant over the 2005–2007 period while student cohorts increased'. While the most recent available Australian Government data, from 2013, does not refer specifically to L&C study, it suggests that fewer than 5 per cent of all students are studying in the broad field of Society and Culture (Australian Government Department of Education and Training, 2014).

The 2014 First Year Experience Study data from the University of Melbourne's Centre for the Study of Higher Education encourages some optimism: in both 2009 and 2014 (sample sizes 2,422 and 1,739 respectively), 23 per cent of the national first year respondents reported that they 'planned to, or were, studying a language as part of their course' (Baik, Naylor and Arkoudis, 2015). By way of international comparison, language studies were reported as accounting for 8.6 per cent of all 2009 course enrolments in US higher education institutions (Furman, Goldberg and Lusin, 2010, 5), and 8.1 per cent of all 2013 enrolments (Goldberg, Looney and Lusin, 2015), while Byrne (2005) reported that fully one third of tertiary students in Europe are studying languages as an assessable part of their degree.

The attrition rate of L&C students in Australian universities is of particular concern. In landmark research (detailed later in this chapter), Nettelbeck et al. (2007, 3) reported that:

> on average, one third of students beginning a LOTE at [an Australian] university do not complete more than one semester; a third of those remaining do not continue into second year; there is further attrition after second semester of second year, and of those completing second year, only two thirds continue into third year. Overall, fewer than 25% of students beginning a LOTE complete a third year.

Given this kind of data, and their lived experience of student attrition during a program, all L&C teachers in Australia at tertiary level—whatever the language they teach and whatever their institution—are likely at some point (usually when enrolments drop and their course is threatened) to ask themselves not only 'What makes students decide to study a language at university?' but also, perhaps even more urgently, 'What makes those same students decide to continue, or to stop, studying a language?'

Despite some key attempts in recent years to investigate these questions in a sector-wide context (e.g. Nettelbeck et al., 2007; Nettelbeck, Byron, Clyne, Dunne, Hajek, Levy, Lo Bianco, McLaren, Möllering and Wigglesworth, 2009), Australian research in this field has been very limited. On the basis of an extensive literature review, Lobo and Matas (2010, 39–40) argue that there is still an inadequate volume of research into student attrition in language learning courses, and that the research that does exist is patchy and poorly integrated into an overall theoretical framework. With no definitive data on whether the key influences on students' decisions about continuing or discontinuing language studies are related more to aspects of the teaching or the workload, or to the inherent or acquired characteristics of the students themselves, university language teachers have few evidence-based strategies with which to confront the harsh economic drivers that see languages with small overall enrolments or apparently high attrition rates relegated to minimal funding options or closure.

With attrition measures given sector-wide importance for decision-making around financial support, despite there being little evidence that attrition really is a measure of performance or quality, we should expect that, at the very least, universities are able to report accurately the rates at which students leave or stay in L&C programs. This was the goal set by the language-teaching academics at ANU in 2008, who decided to initiate an institution-wide research project to explore the issue of attrition and retention in all the L&C programs at ANU. (See Acknowledgements for details of participants in this research.) As no other Australian institution has conducted a study of such scope in breadth and depth, the research has become an important case study in this field, but one that has, until now, not been reported in its entirety, although there have been preliminary and selective presentations and publications (e.g. Jansen, Åkerlind and Maliangkay, 2011; Jansen and Martín, 2011; Jansen, Martín and Åkerlind, 2009; Jansen, Maliangkay, Martín and Åkerlind, 2009; Jansen and Schmidt, 2011; Martín and Jansen, 2011, 2012; Martín, Jansen and Beckmann 2015).

In this book, we remedy that omission by reporting in full the relevant methodologies, analytical processes and outcomes of the ANU case study, and thus provide other researchers with access to what is probably the most detailed and comprehensive institutional data set in the field. We also explain how we were able to use this data set to interrogate the motivations and constraints that influence tertiary students' decisions as to whether to continue or discontinue their L&C study. As we take the reader forward into understanding the context for this institutional case study, with detailed presentation, analysis and discussion of the research findings, we will start building the thesis of this book, namely that university language departments must become more aware that students at risk are found at all levels of L&C study (not just in first year or Beginner cohorts); that the 'language capital' of students plays a role in their propensity to continue their studies; and that policies that cater to the needs of *all* students are crucial to maximise retention through all levels of L&C programs.

1.3. The impact of government, university and school policies on language teaching in Australia

Before engaging the reader with the rationale and methodology of the ANU case study, however, we feel it is important to explain some aspects of the broader context of language teaching in Australian universities and their feeder systems (especially secondary schools). Australian government policies, along with societal and external factors, have clearly exerted significant influence on the levels of enrolment, retention and attrition in L&C programs in schools and universities (Clyne 1993, 1997; Djité, 2011; Kleinsasser, 2000; Leopold, 1986; Liddicoat, 2010; Liddicoat and Scarino, 2010; Lo Bianco and Gvozdenko, 2006; Nicholas, 2004; Pauwels, 2002; White and Baldauf, 2006). Djité (2011, 65) provides a thoughtful historical analysis of the way in which 'national sentiment and ideologies have ... dictated language policy in Australia over the last 30 years', and concludes that 'language policy in Australia continues to be a site for negotiation between the monolingual ethos and the urge for linguistic pluralism'. Two examples of influential late twentieth-century policies are the 1991 Australian Language and Literacy Policy (Australia, Department of Employment, Education and Training, 1991), and the 1994 report to the Council of Australian Governments (1994). The latter led directly to the National Asian Languages and Studies in Australian Schools (NALSAS) Strategy 1996–2002, which impacted on both the funding and the demand for Asian languages in schools and, as a knock-on effect, in universities.

Not surprisingly, many authors believe that the provision and uptake of languages in the Australian tertiary sector has been directly—and, most argue, negatively—influenced by the lack of effective language provision in the secondary (school) education sector (Group of Eight, 2007; Liddicoat, Scarino, Curnow, Kohler, Scrimgeour and Morgan, 2007, 38–41; Liddicoat and Scarino, 2010; Lo Bianco, 2009, 48–51). Despite multiple strategic federal and state/territory government policy changes, each indicating a willingness to address the issue of language study at secondary level, there appears to have been no increase in the last 20 years in the proportion of Year 12 students studying a language (Liddicoat et al., 2007, 38–41; Lo Bianco, 2009, 48–51), which is the indicator most commonly used as a surrogate for the extent of language study at secondary level. In contrast to the 10 per cent of Australian Year 12 students studying a foreign language in 2006 (Lo Bianco, 2009, 49), about 60 per cent of senior secondary students in Europe in 2009/10 were learning two or more foreign languages (Education, Audiovisual and Culture Executive Agency, 2012). In the words of the Group of Eight (research-intensive) universities: 'decades of policy neglect and inaction mean Australian school students now spend less time learning a language than students in all other OECD countries' (Group of Eight, 2007, 1).

What has led to this somewhat parlous state of affairs? Martín (2004, 2005) and Lo Bianco (2009) argue that the low levels of commitment to language study in Australia have resulted from various historical circumstances meshed with the characteristics of ethnic community relations, which have together discouraged the use of languages other than English in mainstream settings. Martín (2004, 2005) identifies three key twentieth-century influences: i) in the late 1940s and 1950s, newly created Australian universities often decided to waive knowledge of a language other than English (LOTE) as an entrance requirement; ii) in the 1960s, curriculum reforms reduced language provision in secondary schools; and, iii) since the late 1980s, the predominance of Australian government economic rationalist policies in higher education have not favoured the labour-intensive and small-enrolment nature of L&C courses. In evidence for the latter, for example, from 2001 to 2005 enrolments in L&C courses in Australian universities remained relatively stable, but fewer languages were taught, and there was an increasing reliance on casual, rather than permanent, language teaching staff (White and Baldauf, 2006).

In a more recent review of language offerings at Australian universities, Dunne and Pavlyshyn (2012, 15) argued that the 'apparent health' of tertiary language teaching in Australia, based on the total number of less commonly taught languages on offer, was 'illusory and potentially misleading', because the majority of those languages were only taught at ANU, and thus, in the author's words, and quite prophetically (Macdonald, 2015), 'vulnerable to changes in [that institution's] financial climate'.

Internal university policies also play an important role in encouraging student enrolments. In the USA, most tertiary institutions traditionally had compulsory language requirements for all undergraduate degrees (McGroarty, 1997, 80–83). Although this requirement has become less prevalent in recent years (Furman et al., 2010, 5), at least half of all US universities were still insisting on compulsory language study in 2010 (Lusin, 2012). This is especially true for institutions with highly competitive entry. For example, Yale College—a partner of ANU in the International Alliance of Research Universities (IARU)—requires all students to study a foreign language, regardless of their existing knowledge of that language or another (Yale College, 2015). At the University of California, Berkeley, (another IARU member), every student in the College of Letters and Science (but not in all Colleges) must demonstrate 'proficiency in reading comprehension, writing, and conversation in a foreign language equivalent to the second semester college level, either by passing an exam or by completing approved course work', although this can be achieved through evidence of appropriate high school study (University of California, Berkeley, 2015). It is notable that, following increases in aggregate US higher education enrolments in all languages consistently from 1980 to 2009, there was a decrease in the period between 2009 and 2013 (Goldberg, Looney and Lusin, 2015), the same period during which compulsory requirements were becoming less common or less rigorous (Furman et al., 2010, 5).

By contrast, no Australian university has compulsory language requirements for all undergraduate degrees on offer, although a limited level of compulsion may occur in some degree programs. At ANU, degrees with compulsory language study accounted for just 10 per cent of the total student load in 2008 and 2009 (the relevant period for the case study): this proportion has decreased even further in the light of subsequent reforms in relevant degree structures.

1.4. Historical perspectives from the teaching coalface

The changes and difficulties experienced in Australian university language departments in the mid to late twentieth century is perhaps best encapsulated by the personal case study of Professor Keith Leopold, who detailed his own experiences in the German department at the University of Queensland over a period of some 40 years (Leopold, 1986). Identifying many factors that impacted on course structure, teaching approaches, workload, and standards—all of which significantly influenced what he called the 'struggle for students'—Leopold (1986, 9) described the outcome of his long-term perspective from the coalface: 'as the stress on numbers has become greater and greater, finances have become tighter and tighter, [and] the utilitarian aspects of education have moved more and more into the foreground'. Leopold (1986) especially noted the significant stresses on staff that derived specifically from the widening range in the language competence of beginner students. Some 30 years later, our experience is that many university language teachers still identify very closely with Leopold's concerns.

In the same time frame, but methodologically in diametric contrast to Leopold's very personal analysis, an extensive set of relevant research data was collected by Bowden, Starrs and Quinn (1989). Through diverse methods, including a national survey, interviews, and observations, these authors examined the attitudes of Australian university academics who were teaching LOTE on aspects such as students' entry skills, streaming, student workload, curricula, course structures, students' expectations, the use of audio-visual media, teaching specialisations, language-teaching methodologies, and the status of language teaching. Most of the university language departments in the study complained of difficulties with staffing levels, which impacted on the feasibility of implementing appropriate approaches to teaching (Bowden et al., 1989).

The diversity in background knowledge and skills of students starting L&C study has long been an issue for university teaching departments. Bowden et al. (1989) found that first year students showed great diversity in their previous experiences of learning a second language, which was attributed to inadequate language provision in the secondary sector. The researchers concluded that teaching staff could no longer expect all students to have specific skills or capabilities on entry, and that budgetary constraints made it difficult to provide enough staff to meet the consequently varied and divergent needs of these students (Bowden et al., 1989). Smaller departments in particular have to balance the learning benefits and staff costs of finely tuned streaming versus the need to ensure adequate assistance to individual students in more broadly streamed, and thus staffing-effective, placements (Bowden et al., 1989, 132). Dealing with this by streaming students according to their level of language attainment on entry (i.e. placing language-competent first year students into second or third year L&C classes) has, in our experience, met with only limited success, because of budget constraints that impact on the required class sizes and teaching methods.

In addition, since the mid-1980s, most Australian institutions have had more students enrolling in languages at Beginner Level (Level 1) than at other entry points (Hawley, 1982; Nettelbeck et al., 2007), because of the reduction of language teaching in high schools. Naturally, this has implications for undergraduates' potential levels of achievement: for example, Australia's Group of Eight research-intensive universities—which includes ANU—openly acknowledge that students who start out as beginners at university are unlikely to achieve a sophisticated level of language competence in three years of classroom-based study alone (Group of Eight, 2007, 4).

At this stage, readers may be wondering why this chapter is referring extensively to research that dates back more than 25 years. The sad truth is that there is still a disappointing relevance to this data, and to the conclusion reached by Bowden et al. (1989, 129), namely that 'tertiary language teaching bristles with sensitive and contentious issues … subject to conflicting opinion and practice'. At least four of the key issues highlighted all those decades ago by Bowden et al. (1989) are still highly relevant in Australia today.

First, problematic degree structures are still making it difficult for students to combine the study of a language with other subjects: despite some universities implementing changes that improve the situation (e.g. Diploma of Languages at several universities; the creation of flexible double degree opportunities at ANU;

and the degree curriculum changes at the University of Melbourne and the University of Western Australia), degree structures remain a key barrier to L&C studies in many universities.

Second, the increasing number of international students enrolling in higher education who wish to study their own first language, or another language that they have previously studied or spoken, has increased still further the range of entry skill levels among students, with a consequent emphasis on the need for ever more effective placement tests and streaming. This aspect is crucially important to learning outcomes: Bowden et al. (1989, 131) found high levels of dissatisfaction among first year students who were placed in unstreamed classes, not least because complete beginner students were reluctant to speak their 'new' language in the presence of more advanced students.

A third issue that remains highly topical is the disparity between the expectations of students and those of teachers and university administrators. Bowden et al. (1989, 139) found 'a close correlation between the level of student satisfaction with the course, and the level of [oral] fluency achieved' in all the language departments they visited. Students were strongly in favour of communicative approaches to language teaching: most reported a desire to *speak* the language of study, while relatively few wanted to *read* literature in that language (Bowden et al., 1989, 141). The researchers concluded that Australia was 'witnessing a major shift in orientation away from a traditional humanist view of university language teaching … towards a very pragmatic emphasis on practical communicative competence' (Bowden et al., 1989, 145).

Leal et al. (1991) soon confirmed this perception in a government-sponsored Australia-wide review, revealing with concern that outcomes sought by students did not always correspond to those sought by teaching staff. While heads of departments focused first on students' linguistic and reading performance, and next on their cultural knowledge, a large majority of students were primarily seeking a high level of oral/aural proficiency, with an appreciation of the relevant society and culture being quite a secondary objective:

> although … third year students were happy or very happy with their courses, they did not hesitate to propose changes in the curriculum … [most frequently] a request for more oral input into the mode of teaching (38%). As in most past surveys, oral command of the language was what students most wanted to achieve (Leal et al., 1991, 120).

The 'contest' between spoken and other forms of language learning remains a concern of curriculum designers today.

The final issue identified by Bowden et al. (1989) that is still highly relevant today concerns student perceptions that workloads are different in different languages (for example, that European languages require relatively less effort than Asian languages). The researchers found students reporting that they had withdrawn from L&C courses with (perceived) heavy workloads because the students felt that such workloads would prevent the attainment of the relatively high marks needed to assure scholarships and jobs.

In closing this section, we note with disappointment that key issues about L&C teaching in universities that were raised some 25 years ago by Leopold (1986) and Bowden et al. (1989)—degree structures unsupportive of L&C study; high diversity in student cohorts; curriculum design conflict from the perspective of students and staff around the relative importance of spoken and written language; and perceptions of workload—are still highly relevant, empirically identified in the findings of the ANU case study (considered in depth in Chapter 4) as well as in other studies described below.

1.5. Research into attrition in university Language & Culture programs

Despite an increasing focus on retention and attrition as surrogate measures of performance, including as funding indicators (Gabb et al., 2006), until the late 2000s there was virtually no systematic research on L&C courses in Australian universities, and only a little relevant research focused on the school sector. While school and university perspectives are by no means equivalent—school students are often strongly influenced by their parents, and schools are affected by state and territory government policies as well as national ones—language-teaching staff in universities have often been able to relate anecdotally to some of the findings and conclusions of school-focused studies.

For example, there was interest in the research by Curnow and Kohler (2007) on why high school students continued studying a language: the most important reasons were academic achievement, personal interests, and relationships, with other notable factors including bonus schemes that rewarded language study in university entry schemes; students having travelled to, or having connections with, a country where the target language was spoken; and the influence of friends. Important reasons for discontinuing study included the lack of availability of their preferred language; the perception that learning languages gave rise to a relatively higher workload than learning other subjects; and the belief that language learning was not meaningful, because other subjects carried more value (Curnow and Kohler, 2007).

Another schools-focused discussion worthy of note is the more philosophical, rather than empirical, review of language education in Australia's schools by Scarino (2012). Noting the complexity of measuring language-learning outcomes among individual students and cohorts, especially in the light of the 'highly diverse teaching, learning and assessment practices and diverse expectations about learner achievements' created by the diverse policy contexts across Australia, Scarino (2012, 240) identified the need nationally for a 'curriculum and assessment framework that acknowledged the diversity of student achievements' to provide baseline and reference points for monitoring and planning.

In university-based language education, the continuing lack of reliable and valid data on any aspect of tertiary L&C programs (Leal et al., 1991; Murray, 2010), let alone on the key aspects of retention and attrition (Lobo and Matas, 2010), means that even informal findings from universities have been valued. One such study, given much attention at the time, was the internal review of the University of Melbourne's Diploma in Modern Languages (DML), documented (but not published) by Rover and Duffy in 2005. The DML was a supplementary program that allowed undergraduate students to study a language in addition to their degree. The internal review was triggered by high discontinuation rates (about 60 per cent of enrolled students) occurring in the early 2000s. The review examined six of the program's languages (French, German, Italian, Chinese, Japanese and Indonesian) through semi-structured individual interviews with 13 staff and 50 current or past students, across wide-ranging topics, including students' motivations for enrolling, their learning experiences during the program, and, where applicable, their reasons for discontinuing. The qualitative data collected in this way were complemented by internal statistical data.

The findings showed that the DML was regarded positively by both staff and students, even when those students had withdrawn from the program (Rover and Duffy, 2005). Students reported many reasons for enrolling in the DML, including (in descending order of frequency) wanting greater 'flexibility' in their degree; 'continuing language study' (beyond the Year 12 certification level); 'learning a language' (for beginners); and the 'opportunity to learn two languages'. Students most commonly left the program in its earlier stages: although there were many reasons given, the most common were 'high workload', 'wrong placement level', and 'personal reasons' (Rover and Duffy, 2005).

While it was clear in the mid-2000s that strategically designed and evidence-based policies were crucial to the quality of future language teaching in the higher education sector, it was equally obvious that Australia lacked valid and reliable empirical data on which to base such policies. In consequence, the Australian Academy of the Humanities decided to fund first one, then a second, national investigation into Beginner (Level 1) courses in university L&C programs. These Australian Research Council Linkage Learned Academies Special Projects (LASP) studies delivered broadly scoped and wide-reaching findings, including specific consideration of issues related to retention and attrition, documented in two reports referred to hereafter as LASP1 (Nettelbeck et al., 2007) and LASP2 (Nettelbeck et al., 2009).

The timing of these two LASP studies—which respectively involved data collection in 2007 and 2008, and reports in 2007 and 2009—largely paralleled the in-depth institutional case study being conducted from 2008 to 2009 at ANU on the nature of retention in L&C programs. This coincidence of timing meant that ANU language-teaching staff were contributing to LASP1, and facilitating the involvement of ANU students in LASP2, at the same time as supporting the institutional research reported in this book.

We ask readers to recognise that this concurrency means that the LASP findings were not available when the ANU data collection research was being planned, implemented and analysed. Nevertheless, the fact that the LASP2 data were being collected in the same year as those of the second phase of research at ANU meant that the ANU research team was able to support its fellow researchers by maximising the collection of LASP2 data at ANU, thus ensuring that the ANU case study—focused in depth on one institution—would complement and give more resonance to LASP2, which was focused on many institutions. Bearing this timing in mind, we will now review the methodologies, findings and implications of the LASP1 and LASP2 research, as well as some more recent research on retention strategies for L&C at the course level, again unknown to the ANU researchers at the time (e.g. Lobo and Matas, 2010, 2011; Hanley and Brownlee, 2013), before delving deeply into the ANU institutional case study in future chapters.

1.6. The LASP1 study

The LASP1 research provided an audit survey of Beginner (Level 1) courses in L&C university programs Australia-wide, derived from an intense study of 10 universities and at least 10 distinct languages (Nettelbeck et al., 2007). Data collection methods included questionnaires, classroom observations and interviews with staff 'interlocutors' (but notably, *not* with students: their voices did not come into play until LASP2). Unfortunately, the LASP1 report did not identify all the languages that it had covered, but it did identify a focus on six languages with increasing enrolments, and four languages with decreasing enrolments (Nettelbeck et al. 2007, 12). With respect to retention and attrition, LASP1 requested and analysed retrospective longitudinal enrolment data over five semesters from two cohorts, namely those students who had started studying in a Beginner[3] L&C course in Semester 1 (February) 2005 and those who had started in Semester 2 (July) 2006.

---

3   We use the nomenclature of Beginner, Intermediate and Advanced courses to denote Level 1, 2 and 3 courses respectively. These are usually expected to equate to first, second and third year enrolments at university, but—as we explain in detail in later chapters—this form of contextualisation actually creates an excessive oversimplification that hinders, rather than helps, an understanding of the complexities involved.

The authors noted that determining attrition was 'particularly arduous because many institutions merge Beginners' streams with others at various points', so that the research required 'close analysis of actual class lists as distinct from enrolment numbers' (Nettelbeck et al., 2007, 14). Moreover, while some of the 10 institutions surveyed could provide such detailed source data, others could not. Nevertheless, the authors believed that 'sufficient data was collected overall … to make some important observations' (Nettelbeck et al., 2007, 14).

The key LASP1 findings (Nettelbeck et al., 2007, 14) relevant to the theme of this book were that:

- retention from Beginner (Level 1) to Advanced (Level 3) courses averaged just 25 per cent for the 2005 cohort, with a similar pattern found in the 2006 cohort
- retention rates varied considerably among institutions and
- retention rates varied considerably within institutions for different languages.

Why were some three quarters of students who started an L&C course at university giving up on those L&C studies before completing their degree? The staff interlocutors who were surveyed suggested four reasons for the high attrition rates, namely that many students:

- had problems with the (perceived) heavy workload
- were frustrated with their slow progress
- were experiencing timetabling problems and/or
- were starting a language as an elective in later years (Nettelbeck et al., 2007, 15).

With such high attrition rates in L&C programs Australia-wide finally revealed, the LASP1 researchers identified an urgent need for a large-scale national study, which was soon realised in LASP2 (Nettelbeck et al., 2009).

1.7. The LASP2 study

The LASP2 research essentially involved a follow-up study of 11 universities: the original 10 universities examined in LASP1, plus one more. Like LASP1, the focus of LASP2 was Beginner (Level 1) students.

The data collection focused on a semi-longitudinal student survey to explore retention strategies and the use of technology-enhanced language learning, via two hard-copy questionnaires completed by 2,968 students in Semester 1, 2008 and 1,810 students in Semester 2, 2008 (Nettelbeck et al., 2009). The questionnaires contained 14 structured questions—with mostly predetermined response choices—regarding students' academic profile, language background, intended length of study and motivations. (It is important to note here that, although LASP2 sought a longitudinal dimension to its data analysis, this was not possible in terms of statistical validity, as the surveys did not control for individual student identity in the two sets of responses.)

Among a wealth of results, the LASP2 study had seven key findings of particular relevance to this book's theme: four of these findings identified factors that are potentially confounding for those studying student attrition, while the remaining three findings related to student motivation, data collection issues and policy recommendations (Nettelbeck et al., 2009).

The first relevant LASP2 finding—and one which confirmed data from LASP1—was that many first year L&C students are late enrolments, 'taking up a language too late in their studies to be able to complete a major or even a minor sequence in the language' (Nettelbeck et al., 2009, 11). Whereas traditional measures of L&C attrition assume that all students begin language study in their first year at university, no less than half the students who responded to the LASP2 surveys reported starting a language *after* their first year of study at university. Although even short-term language learning has significant value—as Nettelbeck et al. (2007) had argued in the LASP1 report—there are significant implications for course and program planning and design if students are enrolling later than expected in their university career (Nettelbeck et al., 2009). We draw readers' attention to this issue, and will explore the full import of 'Late Starter' language students in Chapters 2 and 5, where we present a detailed analysis of the Late Starter phenomenon as explored in the ANU case study.

A second important LASP2 finding from our perspective was that even Beginner (Level 1) classes contain mixed levels of proficiency: indeed, among the so-called Beginner students surveyed in LASP2, just 38 per cent actually had no previous background in the target language, while most Beginners had diverse previous language-learning experiences, including a 'not insignificant number ... who had successfully completed [that language at school in] year 12' (Nettelbeck et al., 2009, 12). As identified decades earlier by Leopold (1986) and Bowden et al. (1989), the impact of such mixed proficiency groups in Beginner classes was problematic for teachers, potentially creating 'perceptions of disadvantage', and hence negative impacts on motivation, among genuine Beginners (Nettelbeck et al., 2009, 12). In addition, cross-cultural, related-language issues were evident: for example, some 30 per cent of students enrolling in Beginner Spanish had previously studied French, which might confer some familiarity advantage, while about half the students who were enrolled in Beginner Japanese identified themselves as native Chinese speakers, which might confer some advantage in terms of character recognition (Nettelbeck et al., 2009, 12). This situation again arose in the context of the ANU case study, and is explored in detail in chapters 2 and 4.

The LASP2 study also found a mismatch between students' expectations of workloads and the reality—or, rather, students' perceptions of reality—with many students reporting that their L&C workload was 'higher than expected' (Nettelbeck et al., 2009, 19), again echoing the earlier research findings by Bowden et al. (1989). Perceiving the workload as high was not a clear disincentive, however: many students reported that they would be studying the language for longer than they had originally planned because they had found the learning 'more interesting' and/or the teaching 'better', than expected (not because they had experienced 'less work than expected' or other reasons). Finding students apparently pleasantly surprised by the quality of language teaching at university, Nettelbeck et al. (2009, 19) concluded that 'high attrition does not appear to be caused (and may in fact be mitigated) by perceived quality of teaching or course interest'.

Crucially, LASP2 respondents valued language speaking skills most highly, followed by understanding (Nettelbeck et al., 2009, 19). This finding—again consistent with previous research (e.g. Bowden et al., 1989; Leal et al., 1991)—has profound implications for course design. Unfortunately, as Nettelbeck et al. (2009, 19) explained—and again echoing the research findings of 20 years earlier—'the dominant motivations [of students] could hardly be clearer, [but] the degree to which [these motivations] are taken into account in course planning and design is less evident'.

1.8. Implications of the LASP1 and LASP2 research

Both LASP studies were unequivocal in their call for action as a result of their research findings. The LASP1 authors identified 'an urgent need for governments and universities alike to recognise languages as a strategic and essential sector and to support them accordingly' (Nettelbeck et al., 2007, 6).

This view was reiterated by the LASP2 report's primary recommendation:

> That universities, at the policy level, give explicit and urgent recognition of the strategic importance of the study of languages and cultures; and that they develop appropriate strategies and provide adequate resources for the promotion and effective maintenance of these studies (Nettelbeck et al. 2009, 6).

A direct outcome of these recommendations—and a policy action of great significance with regard to L&C programs in Australian higher education—was the creation in 2011 of the Languages and Cultures Network for Australian Universities (LCNAU; see www.lcnau.org; Hajek, Nettelbeck and Woods 2013). This network, which aims to raise the profile of language educators and public awareness of the cultural, strategic and economic importance of language education in, and for, Australia, is already having an impact as a central voice and focus for research outcomes and policy development (John Hajek, pers. comm., 2014).

Of even more significance to the central theme of this book, both LASP1 and LASP2 researchers identified the lack of accurate data as a significant hindrance to the calculation of realistic rates of attrition in university L&C programs. The LASP1 authors placed the onus for better data collection onto universities, recommending the 'creation of processes to ensure that universities collect data in a readily accessible form on the LOTE experience of their students, including formal secondary training and background experience'

(Nettelbeck et al., 2007, 6). The LASP2 authors focused more on the complexities of collecting accurate and useful data on comparative L&C enrolments in Australian universities, and recommended that 'the university sector ... work towards a uniform and nuanced definition of what constitutes attrition, and that the relevant faculties generate and make readily available comparative statistics about attrition in languages and other humanities and social sciences areas' (Nettelbeck et al., 2009, 6). This crucially important issue is one that we address in depth in Chapter 2, in the context of the ANU case study, where we report on an innovative approach to calculating retention rates based on detailed institutional and collected data.

1.9. Attrition at the course level: Risk factors

So far, the findings described in this chapter have largely focused on research at the university or program level. For students, of course, the decision to discontinue their formal L&C studies generally occurs during a specific course. For this reason, Lobo and Matas (2010, 2011) looked specifically at attrition at the level of an individual L&C course (i.e. students withdrawing from a course before its end), by investigating the reasons why students withdrew from a first-year *ab-initio* (Beginner/Level 1) Spanish course at an Australian university. The authors' approach was prognostic/remedial rather than diagnostic/explanatory: instead of aiming to explain attrition from the perspective of the students who had left the course, the authors attempted first to identify students at risk of withdrawing, and then to provide an intervention that would reduce that risk (Lobo and Matas, 2010, 155–161; 2011, 305–306). Through an extensive review of the Australian and international literature on attrition and retention focused on first year students, the authors identified 17 key factors known to influence the likelihood of a student *not* completing a course (Figure 1.2, which can be seen to be an extension of Figure 1.1; Lobo, 2012). The authors next developed a student 'risk' questionnaire based on these factors, phrasing questions such that responses could be scored, and totals ranked, to provide cut-off values that identified an individual student's risk of withdrawing before the end of the course in one of three categories ('very little risk', 'fair risk' and 'high risk'). To add a qualitative dimension to the scoring, some students were also interviewed.

1. UNDERSTANDING THE PROBLEM

1. Students' expectations and perceptions of university life and study (of the course, degree or programme, the people and the university itself)
2. Social and academic student integration
3. Teaching and learning styles
4. Assessment strategies used in courses
5. Lack of student mentoring
6. Students' living arrangements (on campus, with friends, at home, among others)
7. Student age
8. Student gender
9. Work and issues with employment
10. Financial concerns
11. Student lack of preparation for university life and study
12. Family responsibilities and obligations
13. Dissatisfaction with the university
14. Academic difficulties
15. Health and personal reasons
16. Course or Program unsuitability
17. Learning anxiety (in particular foreign language learning anxiety)

Figure 1.2. Factors associated with course attrition, as identified from the literature
Source: After Lobo and Matas (2010, 14–40).

With this knowledge of the risk factors of attrition, and the information from their students' risk questionnaires, the researchers then developed a two-page 'First Year Student Guide' specifically designed 'to facilitate the social inclusion and academic connection of [each] student' (Lobo and Matas, 2011, 311). This guide, which provided students with relevant information about how to study and the university's support services, was given to students after they had completed the risk questionnaire, and then followed up with class discussions half-way through the semester. Remarkably, given the 85 withdrawals from the previous year's cohort, no student from the 'Guide' cohort withdrew from the course. From this outcome and student feedback, the authors argue that their approach to maximising retention was successful, although they acknowledge that both survey and guide require validation with a larger sample (Lobo and Matas, 2011, 312).

1.10. Learning anxiety as a specific risk factor in language learning

Although the literature reviewed by Lobo and Matas (2010) suggests many generic reasons why a student may discontinue his or her enrolment in a first year course (Figure 1.2), three factors appear particularly relevant to language learners. These are i) the perception of a high (and higher than expected) workload in the course; ii) the student having 'less serious' reasons for enrolling in the course (for example, thinking that language learning would be 'fun', and so being less prepared for the realties of workload and assessment); and iii) the important notion of students being burdened by 'foreign language learning anxiety' or 'second language anxiety' (Lobo, 2012).

While learning anxiety is by no means unique to languages (it has also been identified as a problem faced by students of mathematics and science, capable of negatively impacting on performance—Ashcraft and Kirk, 2001; Ma and Xu, 2003; Sherman and Wither, 2003; Nunez-Pena, Suarez-Pellicioni and Bono, 2013), it is notably the only risk factor specific to the language-teaching context (Lobo, 2012, 207). 'Second language anxiety'—defined as 'the feeling of tension and apprehension associated with second language contexts, including speaking, listening and learning' (Onwuegbuzie, Bailey and Daley, 1999, 222), and closely linked to performance in oral examinations or other forms of language production in the classroom—is considered one of the major factors in foreign language attrition (e.g. Horwitz, 2010; Horwitz, Horwitz and Cope, 1986; Scovel, 1978; Wesely, 2010). Lobo and Matas (2010, 127) found language anxiety—primarily derived from concern about an oral interview assessment task—was a key factor reported by students who withdrew from the Spanish L&C course under study. This anxiety was associated with perceptions that other students were better at languages, and that the classes were too fast-paced, perceptions that all contributed to a feeling of inadequacy in class (Lobo and Matas, 2010, 102–110). However, the situation is not simple: some students who reported anxiety related to speaking, listening, and especially the oral interview nevertheless persisted in their studies, to the admitted bemusement of the researchers (Lobo and Matas, 2010, 124).

It may appear somewhat surprising that the relative level of learning anxiety among individual students is *not* an effective predictor of the likelihood of those students continuing or discontinuing their language study. The ANU findings give some insights to the relevant differences in student characteristics that may in future provide this kind of predictive capacity for teachers: these findings also suggest why the Student Guide produced by Lobo and Matas (2011) had its excellent outcome in reducing attrition.

1.11. Asking the difficult questions: Attrition as a research problem

We began this chapter with a list of questions about student attrition that concern university L&C teachers. As we have seen, some significant attempts have been made in recent years to tackle these questions (e.g. Nettelbeck et al., 2007, 2009; Lobo and Matas, 2010, 2011). While the relevant research is still far too limited to provide trustworthy answers across the sector, it does show that raw enrolment numbers provide extremely crude measures of attrition in university L&C programs. Nevertheless, such raw data are still commonly used by administrators and budget planners as surrogate indicators of a program's success, and, critically, may be used as performance indicators to guide the allocation of institutional and government funding, as occurred from 2006 to 2009 nationally with the Learning and Teaching Performance Funds (Gabb et al., 2006).

The need for a more effective approach to calculating and understanding retention in L&C programs was crystal clear to L&C teachers at ANU in the mid-2000s. The apparently low retention rates being experienced across the 18 ANU L&C programs on offer at that time—especially in terms of students discontinuing after Beginner level—was a key discussion point among teaching staff. This led to the establishment of an internally funded research program to explore in detail the best ways of calculating and comparing student retention rates, and the motivations of students in making decisions about their L&C studies, using ANU as a case study. This was not just an opportunistic choice of institution, but a strategic one: ANU has long had a tradition of teaching many L&C programs, and was not only identified as teaching the greatest diversity of languages of any university included in the LASP1 research (Nettelbeck et al., 2007), but also as the only university teaching many of Australia's less commonly taught languages (Dunne and Pavlyshyn, 2012).

In designing the case study, the research team was mindful of two perspectives that had not yet been voiced, but have subsequently been well expressed by other researchers. First, we understood the overall complexity of researching L&C education. In the context of a review of languages in the school sector, Scarino (2012, 244) explained this complexity:

> In the Australian context of languages education, descriptions that do not take into account acknowledged differences across languages, across groups of students with diverse linguistic and cultural backgrounds and affiliations with the target language, and across program conditions such as time-on-task, are too generalised to be meaningful and of value to the diverse users.

We also understood that this complexity would be increased, rather than lessened, with our focus on retention.

Secondly, we understood, in the more recent words of Hanley and Brownlee (2013), that 'investigating questions of attrition and student motivation in tertiary language programs is not simply a matter of asking students why they do or do not continue in their area of study'. We thus approached the concept of student retention in university L&C programs not just as an educational issue but also as a social phenomenon, and thus deliberately set out to collect data on our students' social characteristics through institution-wide surveys of L&C students in 2008 and 2009, with our approaches designed to maximise response rates, and—again as Hanley and Brownlee (2013) later reinforced—to avoid inadvertently allowing results to be skewed by methodological defects.

The research was thus designed as a highly structured case study that would generate valid and reliable empirical data to enlighten our understanding of attrition and retention in the context of a specific institution, while also suggesting appropriate methodologies for future studies on a broader scale.

Our approach was strongly influenced by Bourdieu's concluding comments in the methodological appendix to his seminal work, *Distinction*:

> The epistemological obstacles which social science has to overcome are initially social obstacles. One of these is the common conception of the hierarchy of the tasks which make up the sociologist's job, which leads so many researchers to disdain humble, easy yet fertile activities in favour of exercises that are both difficult and sterile. Another is an anomic reward system which forces a choice between a safe thesis and a flash in the pan, pedantry and prophecy, discouraging the combination of broad ambition and long patience that is needed to produce a work of science. Unlike the sometimes illuminating intuitions of the essay form, the sometimes coherent thesis of theoreticism and the sometimes valid observations of empiricism, provisional systems of propositions which strive to combine internal coherence and adequacy to the facts can only be produced by a slow, difficult labour which remains unremarked by all hasty readings. These will only see repetitive reaffirmations of theses, intuitions or already known facts in the provisional conclusion of a long series of totalizations, because they ignore what is essential, namely, the structure of the relations between the propositions (Bourdieu, 2010 [1984], 513).

We thus sought to collect comprehensive data that we could subject to patient analysis as we sought 'internal coherence'. In addition, our work focused on students being at the heart of language teaching, and their experiences and 'individual differences' (Dörnyei, 2005) as learners being at the heart of language-teaching research. In so doing, we hoped to advance the ideas on student motivation presented by Joe Lo Bianco, Professor of Language and Literacy Education at the University of Melbourne Graduate School of Education:

> Ultimately language learning is the preoccupation of individual students, in the same way as language teaching is the preoccupation of language teachers. In recent policies, written with the hand of diplomats, trade officials and other elites, there has been far less consideration of the practical issues involved in schooling, and therefore a tendency towards stressing accountability and imposition of numerical targets, with less focus on capacity-building, acknowledgment of the learner population, issues of motivation, resource constraints, personal aspirations, experiences and motivation, identity issues and family background. All too often it is assumed that the motivations learners have available to them are the prospects of employment and other material advantage that attach to language learning.

> This outsider perspective on motivation is less tenable today in light of the powerful shifting of emphasis towards the internal perspective and experience of learners, and on the quality of micro-school experiences in influencing motivation, persistence and interest among language students … This research is important to language education planners because it shows that even in the face of negative attitudes students might inherit from the wider society, or from their parents, about languages being unimportant, or that 'everyone speaks English', micro-motivation effects (good teaching, concrete perceptible sense of achievement, success) can override negativity and sustain student interest. Here policy is practice, in the hands of individual teachers and schools (Lo Bianco, 2009, 27).

Accordingly, rather than to present any particular policy or strategy solution ourselves, our focus in reporting the ANU case study research in this book is to present detailed data and analytical methodologies that we believe will be highly relevant to the development of any future evidence-based language policies intended to increase student participation and retention in university L&C programs.

1.12. A reader's guide to this book

The ANU case study had three data-related aims. First, it sought to document the nature and rates of student retention and attrition in ANU L&C programs, and, for comparative purposes, in other discipline areas taught at ANU. Second, the study sought to explore ANU students' motivations for, and experiences of, studying a language at university. In particular, the researchers investigated students' motivations for continuing, discontinuing, or thinking about discontinuing/deferring their language studies. Third, the case study was designed to identify the incentives or disincentives that influence students either to continue language studies to the completion of an undergraduate degree major,[4] or to discontinue those studies before completing a major. In addition, the researchers' awareness of the potential for generalisations from the institutional findings to inform future sector-wide policies related to increasing the

---

4   At the time of this research, an ANU undergraduate student seeking to complete an L&C major had to complete either seven or eight courses, usually at a load of one course per semester. Students aiming to complete a major in three years usually enrolled in additional L&C courses in their final semester of study (generally the second semester in any given year).

rates of student retention in L&C higher education programs led to a realisation, during the analyses of the collected data, that what was required was a reconceptualisation of the concept of attrition with regard to L&C programs.

In presenting the methodologies, analytical processes and outcomes of the ANU case study, therefore, this book positions the significant findings of this single-institution research in the broader context of retention and attrition of university language students Australia-wide, and suggests some implications of these findings in terms of future research and policies. Through Chapter 1, readers should now have a good grasp of some of the key issues relevant to research into attrition in L&C programs in Australian universities. Chapter 2 takes readers into the contentious world of calculations, as we explore how meaningful retention rates can best be computed, and compare rates for L&C programs with those of other disciplines. The chapter introduces a novel and comprehensive approach to calculating retention rates from student data that universities already collect. Using ANU data, we will show how this approach negates the potential distortions of having several cohorts active at the same time, while respecting the specific and unusual nature of L&C enrolments and allowing fair comparisons with other disciplines.

In Chapter 3, the reader will meet the 'Doubters' of the book's title for the first time, as we explain the rationale and detail of the single-institution research methodology, and the analytical approach we adopted in dealing with the student survey data. The crucial impact of this approach was that it demonstrated unequivocally that the simple dichotomous classification traditionally used in retention studies—that is, comparing those who continue studies (Continuers) to those who stop studies (Discontinuers)—did not explain the core issues at the heart of the discussion of retention in L&C programs. Even with in-depth statistical analyses, this simple dichotomous classification did not provide satisfying explanations of attrition, because we simply could not find statistically significant differences between Continuers and Discontinuers in terms of students' background, motivations, perceptions or behaviour related to their L&C studies. The chapter takes readers on the researchers' journey in seeking a new, data-based approach to the grouping of students. The reader will here meet the four descriptively named groups into which students were clustered in terms of their characteristics—Committed Students, Doubters,

Reluctant Quitters and Voluntary Quitters—and understand why the nature of the ANU data required a merging of the latter two categories into an inclusive grouping of Quitters (essentially equivalent to 'Discontinuers').

In Chapter 4, the three functional groupings—Committed Students, Doubters and Quitters—come to the fore, as we explore how they differ across a range of demographic, attitudinal and educational variables. As we describe the intergroup differences between the three, we show just how different are their reasons for continuing or discontinuing L&C studies.

In Chapter 5, we take this characterisation of the three student archetypes further, as we interpret the empirical research findings in a way that provides an overarching explanation of the differences among the groups. This is where we develop our argument based around the construct of 'language capital', and show how the students categorised as Doubters are easily identifiable as the students that other retention studies classify as those most 'at risk' of discontinuing. The chapter also includes an exemplar discussion of students' perceptions about learning spoken language as an illustration of the capacity of the language capital construct to explain the empirical findings commonly found in studies of L&C students.

Chapter 6 brings the book to its conclusion by presenting an overview of the findings from the single-institution case study, and suggests ways in which the methodologies and the construct of language capital could benefit researchers and those developing language policies in the future.

2
Accounting for the Missing Students: Calculating retention rates in Language & Culture programs

2.1. The importance of validity when calculating attrition and retention rates

Retention rates are only useful as tools of comparison and discussion when they are realistic, replicable and consistent. This chapter is designed to give readers a deeper understanding of the concept of 'retention rates' and the ways in which they have typically been calculated. Using data from the case study institution (ANU), we consider in detail the processes and limitations of calculating retention rates, and the diverse issues that are relevant in the calculation of retention (i.e. the proportion of students who remain in a course of study) versus the calculation of attrition (i.e. the proportion of students who leave a course of study). Attrition can occur naturally (i.e. the student completes the program of study) or by choice (i.e. the student continues to study at the same university, but no longer chooses to study in that discipline area; or the student leaves the university). We focus particularly on the shortcomings of current methods of calculation, and describe how these led us to develop some new concepts and methods of calculating retention, the latter being presented in sufficient detail to allow full replication of our approach in future research.

The main difficulty with calculating retention rates is that one of the key components of measuring retention, the measure of attrition, is very difficult to determine for specific disciplines. The Australian Government department responsible for higher education calculates attrition for a given university essentially on the basis of the formula:

Retention + Attrition + Completion = 100%

(Lukic et al., 2004; see Chapter 1).

Attrition, consequently, is defined as the number of non-completing students who were enrolled in a particular university in a given year, but not enrolled in the following year, that is:

Attrition = 100% − Completion − Retention.

A similar formula could in theory be used to calculate attrition for disciplines or programs (Gabb et al., 2006, 3). However, whereas it is easy to identify enrolment at a university or in a specific program, enrolment in majors or disciplines (L&C or others) is difficult at many universities, including ANU, because there is no requirement for students to 'declare a major'.

2.2. Calculating retention rates at ANU: The complexity of language enrolments

Our first attempt at obtaining an overall ANU-wide retention rate from 2008 to 2009 was to use the centrally provided enrolment lists (see Chapter 3) to calculate the proportion of students who were enrolled in an L&C course in 2008, but were not enrolled in such a course in 2009. Dividing the latter by the former yielded a 54 per cent retention rate.

However, while this method gives a simple estimation of retention from 2008 to 2009, it does not fully address attrition. First, the 46 per cent of students enrolled in 2008 who were not enrolled in 2009 actually comprise a combination of three subgroups:

1. Those students who had discontinued L&C studies but had continued to study at ANU (i.e. were enrolled in studies in non-L&C programs);
2. Those who had completely discontinued studying at ANU (i.e. were no longer enrolled in any ANU courses, but had not completed their degree program); and
3. Those who were no longer enrolled in any ANU courses because they had completed their degree program.

Disappointingly, it was not possible to access the information needed to assess the component of overall attrition that related specifically to groups 2 and 3. Moreover, the simple calculation described above excluded students who were not enrolled in an L&C course in 2008, but who did commence L&C study in 2009 at a level other than Beginner (an issue to which we will return shortly). To ensure reliability and validity in the calculations, therefore, a more comprehensive method of determining retention and estimating attrition was needed.

To reveal the complexity of language enrolments at ANU more fully, the analysis focused on all enrolment data for 2009 across the whole university, focusing on the proportion of ANU students who were enrolled in L&C courses, and distinguishing whether they were enrolled in Level 1 (Beginner) or higher-level courses (Table 2.1). These calculations showed that, in 2009, L&C courses accounted for 6.4 per cent of the total ANU student load, and 6.6 per cent of the Level 1 (Beginner courses) student load. This relatively simple approach allows for a comparison of ANU and other universities in regards to the proportion of L&C enrolments. ANU was at the lower end of the universities surveyed by LASP1, where the proportion varied from 5 per cent to 12 per cent, with about half the universities having less than 10 per cent of their students studying languages (Nettelbeck et al., 2007, 11). The LASP1 study also found that, among the universities surveyed, more than 50 per cent of L&C enrolments were in Level 1/Beginner courses (Nettelbeck et al., 2007, 11). By contrast, students who were enrolled in Level 1/Beginner language courses at ANU in 2009 constituted some 39 per cent of the student load in L&C courses.

Table 2.1. Language & Culture enrolments in 2009 discriminated by level and commencing/continuing status

Level	Commencing ANU degree	Continuing ANU degree	Total	Per cent Commencing	Per cent Continuing
Beginner (Level 1) Language & Culture courses	119.9	63.9	183.8	65.2%	34.8%
Non-Beginner (Level 2 and 3) Language & Culture courses	89.5	261.3	350.8	25.5%	74.5%
Total Language & Culture Load	**209.4**	**325.2**	**534.6**	**39.2%**	**60.8%**
Level 1 ANU Load	2,118.6	687.4	2,806.0	75.5%	24.5%
Levels 2 and 3 ANU Load	574.4	4,962.0	5,536.4	10.4%	89.6%
Total ANU Load	**2,693.0**	**5,649.4**	**8,342.4**	**32.3%**	**67.7%**
Per cent of Language & Culture in Level 1 Load	5.7%	9.3%	6.6%	All enrolment figures are given in EFTSLs (Equivalent Full-Time Student Load). Usually 1 EFTSL = 8 students enrolled in a single subject	
Per cent of Language & Culture in Level 2 and 3 Load	15.6%	5.3%	6.3%		
Percentage of Language & Culture courses at ANU	7.8%	5.8%	6.4%		

Source: Derived from 2009 enrolment data provided by the ANU Statistical Unit.

Given the complexity of the data (Table 2.1), and the lack of data about students' majors in the university statistics, it seemed appropriate to adapt the principles of the 'Student Progress Ratio', a method of aggregating student load widely used in higher education (under various names) to study student progression (Gabb et al., 2006, 5). This requires calculation of a ratio based on the student load (measured in Equivalent Full-Time Student Load, or EFTSL) at a given level of study divided by the student load enrolled in the same discipline at a previous level. In seeking a suitable methodology with which to calculate language retention rates, we began by comparing the enrolment figures in two different types of language majors over three successive years (2008 to 2010) in the normal major progression of core language courses (Beginner, Intermediate and Advanced) with those of a Social Science major. We chose the 'Language 1' major to be representative of languages which are taught widely in high schools, whereas the 'Language 2' major was representative of languages not in this category. To make the comparison easier, the student load was converted into a percentage value, that is, the 2008 enrolments were considered equivalent to 100 per cent for all three majors (Figure 2.1.a). The apparent progression through each major was then compared to the proportion of students who started studying at ANU in those three consecutive years (Figures 2.1.b to 2.1.d). The differences in the figures illustrate the impact of two phenomena, namely 'Late Starters' and 'Advanced Starters'.

2.2.1. Late Starters

Late Starters were identified by Nettelbeck et al. (2007, 15) as those students who start studying a language in their second or subsequent years of university study: they are thus non-first year students in 'first year' (Beginner level) L&C courses. Students may choose this path for various reasons, including a change in their chosen major; an L&C course being taken as an elective; a change in degree programs to one that requires compulsory or advised language study; or personal interest. This issue is not trivial, as data analysis shows the notable magnitude of the Late Starters phenomenon. Figures 2.1.b to 2.1.d show the students from 2008–2010 classified according to their status as commencing students (that is, students who commenced a degree in that year) and continuing students (that is, students who were already enrolled in a degree before that year). For all three majors

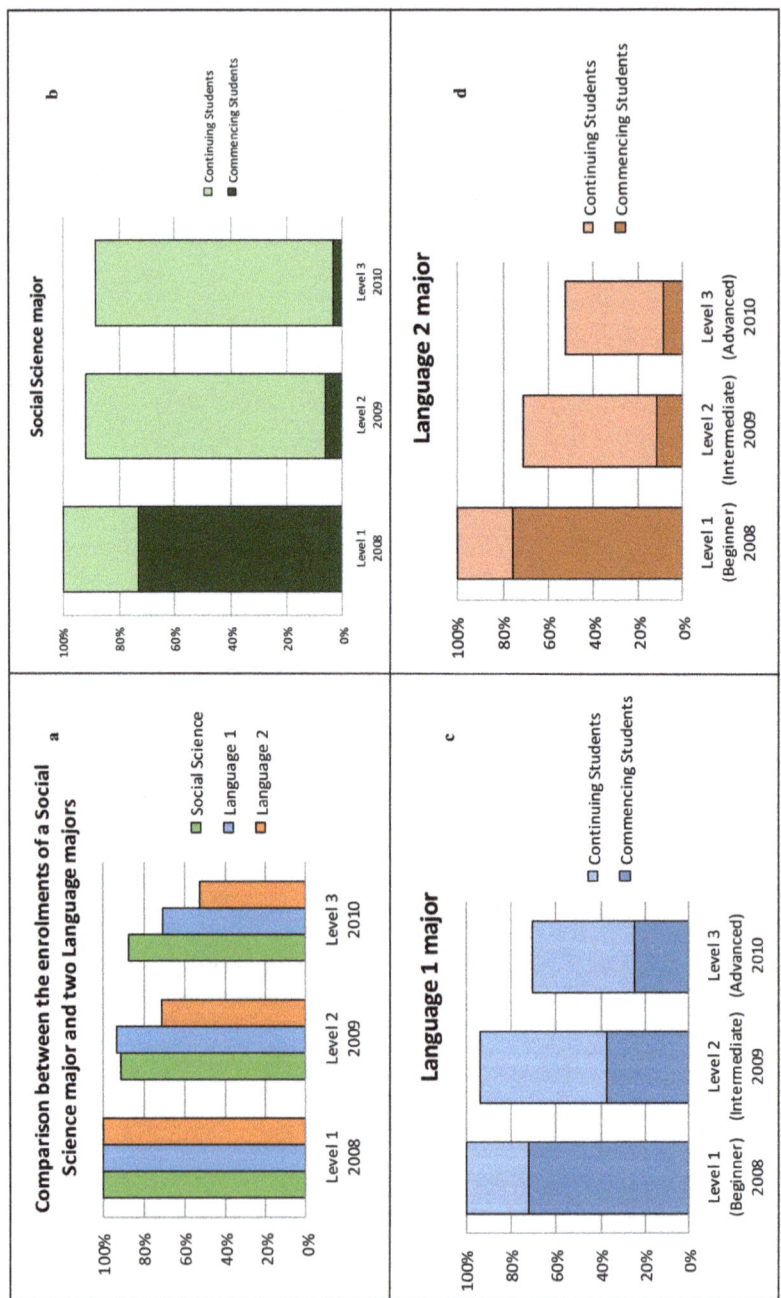

Figure 2.1. Comparison in the enrolment patterns of a Social Science major and two language majors

Source: Derived from 2008–2010 enrolment data provided by the ANU Statistical Unit.

(Social Science, Language 1 and Language 2), more than 25 per cent of the students are Late Starters, that is, students who are attending introductory courses in these disciplines in their second, third or even fourth year at university (see the first column of the three graphics in Figures 2.1.b to 2.1.d, that is, the column that corresponds to Level 1/Introductory/Beginner courses in 2008).

Any attempt to measure the retention/attrition rate of students with regard to the completion of L&C majors is thus significantly confounded by the presence of Late Starters (because students who start languages in their second or third year of a degree program rarely spend additional time at university simply to complete a full L&C major sequence, which lasts at least three years). While the 2008–2010 data shows that this is not a phenomenon restricted to languages (Late Starters were also involved in the Social Science major; Figure 2.1.b), it is more prominent in L&C courses than in non-L&C ANU courses. For example, 32.6 per cent of students in Level 1/Beginner L&C courses were Late Starters, compared with 21.6 per cent in other ANU Level 1 courses (Table 2.II).

Table 2.II. Percentage of Late Starters in L&C and other ANU courses 2008–2010

Courses	2008	2009	2010	Average 2008–2010
L&C courses	31.3%	34.8%	32.3%	32.6%
Other courses	18.1%	24.0%	22.6%	21.6%
All ANU	19.0%	24.7%	23.2%	22.3%

Source: Derived from 2008–2010 enrolment data provided by the ANU Statistical Unit.

2.2.2. Advanced Starters

The LASP studies (Nettelbeck et al., 2007, 2009) were restricted to Level 1/Beginner students. As a result, these studies did not discover a second phenomenon that can confound the calculation of retention rates in L&C programs, namely the presence of 'Advanced Starters'. These are students who enter university with a previous knowledge of the language they are choosing to study, and, following a placement test, are placed in Level 2 (Intermediate) or Level 3 (Advanced) courses. In other words, these are students who start a language major sequence at a relatively advanced level compared to Beginner students.

The relative proportion of Advanced Starters in the majors compared in Figure 2.1 shows that this is a phenomenon that is more prominent in languages than in the Social Science major. In Figure 2.1, the second and third columns (corresponding to Level 2 and Level 3 courses) show more commencing students in 2009 and 2010 in the L&C majors than in the Social Science major. Whereas one might expect that Language 1, which is taught widely in schools, might have many students arriving at university with sufficient knowledge to start studying the language at a post-Beginner level, it is notable that even Language 2—much less commonly taught in schools—also has many Advanced Starters. By comparison, the Social Science major shows fewer Advanced Starters, which reflects the relatively low number of students who could effectively start Level 2 or Level 3 Social Science courses without having completed Level 1 prerequisites. (For example, these could be students transferring with completed Level 1 courses from another university.) Overall, 24.1 per cent of all students enrolled in ANU L&C courses in 2008–2010 were Advanced Starters, compared to 8.8 per cent in all other courses ANU-wide (Table 2.III): in other words, there are almost three times as many Advanced Starters in L&C courses than in other courses.

Table 2.III. Percentage of Advanced Starters in L&C and other ANU courses 2008–2010

Courses	2008	2009	2010	Average 2008–2010
L&C courses	20.6%	25.5%	26.0%	24.1%
Other courses	8.5%	9.4%	8.6%	8.8%
All ANU	9.3%	10.4%	9.7%	9.8%

Source: Derived from 2008–2010 enrolment data provided by the ANU Statistical Unit.

2.2.3. Shortcomings in a simplistic view of retention

The two phenomena described above can significantly distort retention rates as the apparent progression of students from Level 1 to Level 3 courses is composed of a mix of students who began their degrees in different years. Figure 2.2 shows the contrast between considering the apparent student progression without taking into consideration the phenomena described above (Figure 2.2.a), and how this progression can be conceptualised when the year in which students started their degree is considered (Figure 2.2.b and c). The figure shows this for a language that is widely taught in schools (i.e. Language 1 in Figure 2.1). Specifically:

- Figure 2.2.a (which corresponds to Figure 2.1.c) shows the apparent progression of students across the three core language courses from 2008 to 2010.
- Figure 2.2.b shows that a majority of Level 3 students in 2010 for this language (in fact 69 per cent of students enrolled at Level 3) are Advanced Starters, that is, students who began studying the language in 2009 or 2010.
- Figure 2.2.c shows that the apparent retention rates are significantly reduced when only the 2008 cohort of students is considered, i.e. when both Late Starters and Advanced Starters from other student cohorts have been excluded from the calculation.

As the distortions illustrated in Figure 2.2 are, to a considerable extent, caused by the phenomenon of Advanced Starters, they come to bear particularly strongly in majors in languages that are taught widely in schools, such as the Language 1 major illustrated in Figure 2.2. We therefore contrast in Figure 2.3.a the retention rates for Language 1 with those of Language 2, a major in a language not widely taught in schools (Language 2 in Figure 2.1). In this figure, where both Advanced Starters and Late Starters are included, the Language 1 retention rate appears clearly higher than the retention rate of Language 2.

Figure 2.3.b shows the apparent progression of students across the three core language courses from 2008 to 2010 when only the 2008 cohort of students is considered. In this case, the Language 2 retention rate is higher than the retention rate of Language 1. This is because only the 2008 cohort is considered, and both Late Starters and Advanced Starters from other cohorts have been excluded from the calculation.

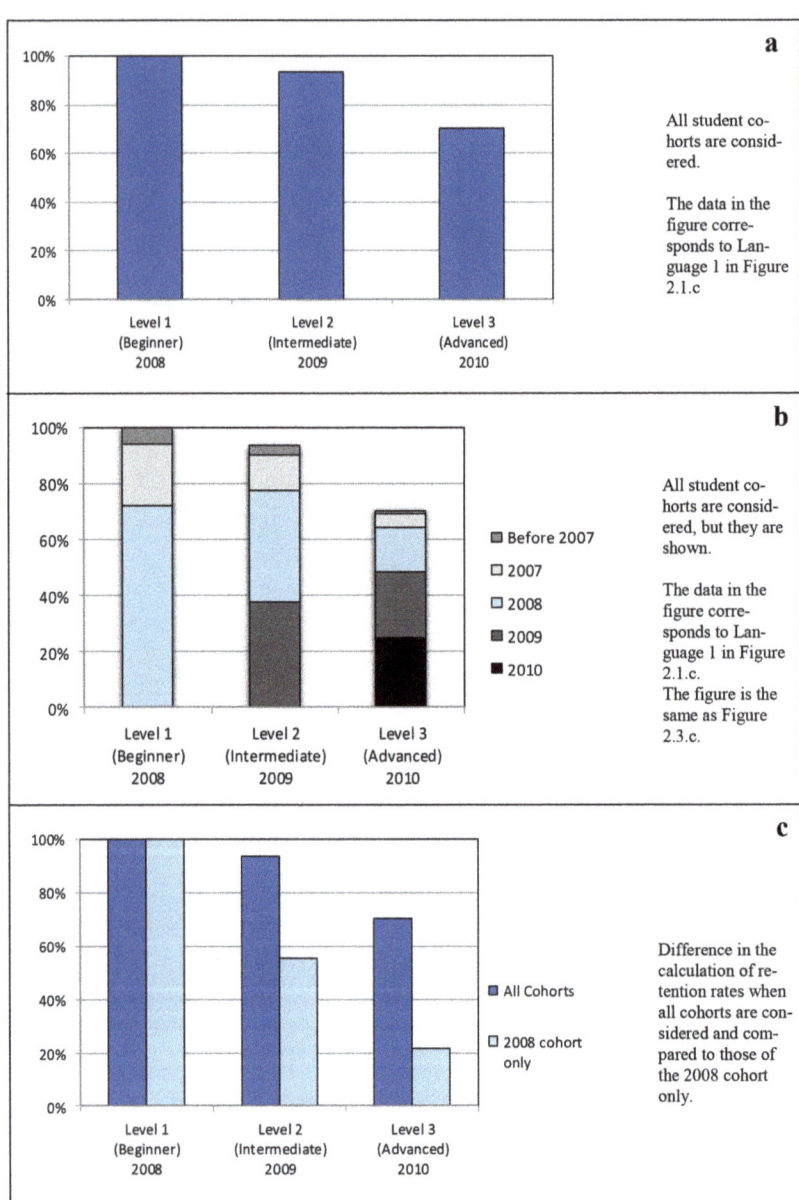

Figure 2.2. Apparent progression rates from Level 1 in 2008 to Level 3 in 2010

Source: Derived from 2008–2010 enrolment data provided by the ANU Statistical Unit.

2. ACCOUNTING FOR THE MISSING STUDENTS

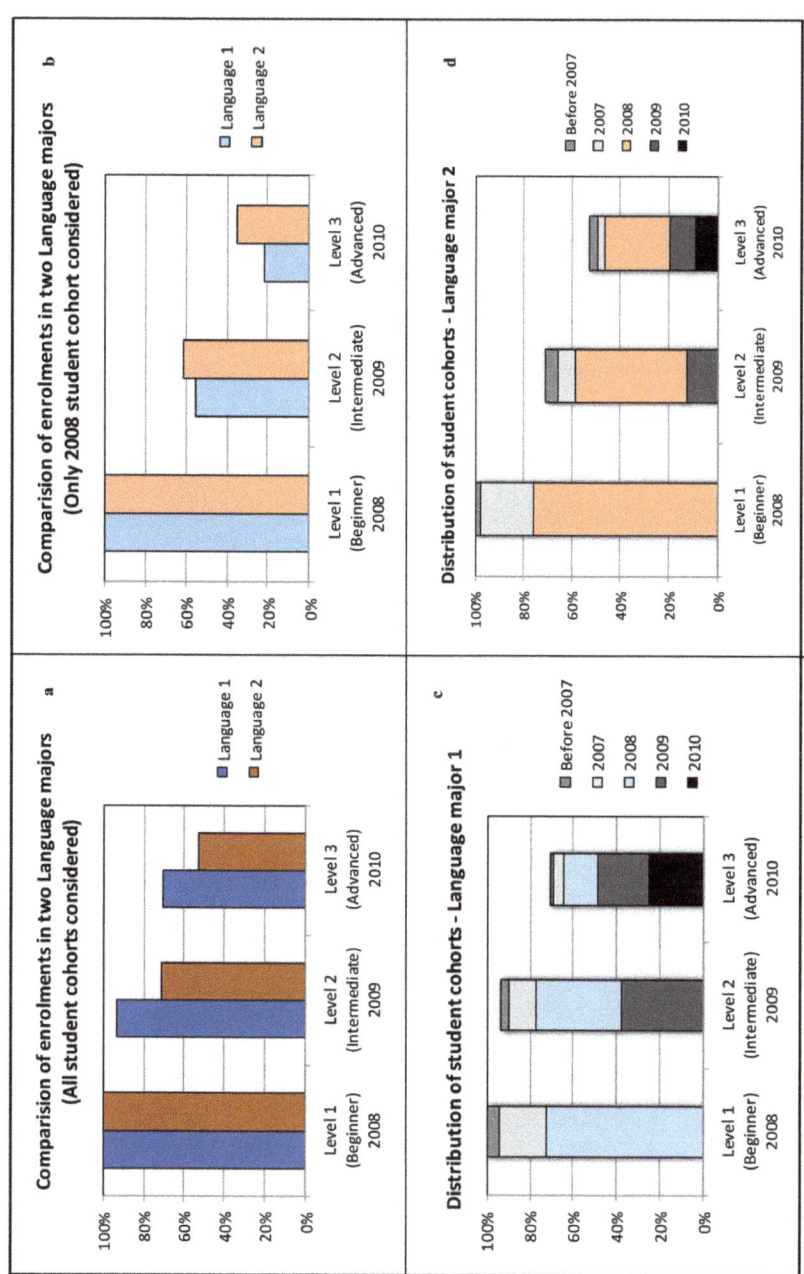

Figure 2.3. Comparison in the enrolment patterns of two Language majors when all students are considered and only the 2008 cohort of students is considered

Source: Derived from 2008–2010 enrolment data provided by the ANU Statistical Unit.

Figures 2.3.c and 2.3.d help us to understand the apparent contradiction when contrasting the two ways of exploring retention rates. Figure 2.3.c (which is identical to Figure 2.2.b) shows that a significant proportion of Level 3 students in 2010 for Language 1 are Advanced Starters, that is, students who began studying the language in 2010 (in fact 35 per cent of students enrolled at Level 3). In the case of Language 2 (Figure 2.3.d) Advanced Starters who began studying in 2010 at Level 3 are not so numerous proportionally (they account for only 17 per cent of Level 3 students).

We hope that by now the reader can see the considerable differences in calculated retention rates that occur depending on whether Late and/or Advanced Starters from different cohorts are considered or not. Indeed, we have demonstrated that it can be quite misleading to adopt the traditional way of looking at retention in majors, that is, to consider simply the number of students enrolled in one year compared with the number enrolled in the prerequisite course in a previous year. In other words, in L&C programs, unlike most other disciplines, the level at which students are enrolled does not necessarily correspond to the same year of their degree. Students in Level 1/Beginner courses thus cannot be assumed to be commencing (first year) students, because some commencing students enrol directly in Level 2 and 3 courses. Similarly, continuing students (i.e. students who have been enrolled at the university in previous years) will not always be those enrolled in Level 2 and Level 3 L&C courses, but may be also those enrolled in Beginner/Level 1 courses. This deeper analysis leads inexorably to the conclusion that a more accurate way of calculating retention rates is essential if they are to be trustworthy tools for reporting and planning.

2.3. The need for new ways of calculating language retention rates

To approximate the calculations that Nettelbeck et al. (2007, 12–13) carried out with respect to Beginner students, enrolment data for all university courses was obtained from the ANU Statistical Unit. The courses were classified according to their level (the year in the degree at which students would normally take them), and the enrolment data (measured in EFTSL) were converted for analysis by the statistical package SPSS®, taking into consideration several additional variables as well as level, such as cohort (year and semester of enrolment), part-time/full-time status, gender, domestic/international, etc. These data were used to calculate a Semester Level Retention Rate, restricting the calculation to the normal progression of Beginner/Level 1 students, Level 2 students and Level 3 students only for those students who began their degree in 2008 as Beginners. This approach filters out the distortions, discussed in the previous section, when multiple cohorts are considered simultaneously. As retention rates are then calculated semester by semester, this approach thus draws a more refined picture than the more commonly used Year Level Retention Rates, where the data of the two semesters are combined.

Included in these calculations were *all* L&C courses, not just the sequence of core language courses, as most languages have additional courses that parallel the core courses but focus on literature, film linguistics, etc., taught in the target language. The retention rate for each semester was thus calculated by dividing the total number of students enrolled in this semester by the number of Level 1 students enrolled in Semester 1 at the Beginner level in 2008 (Table 2.IV). Both the actual EFTSL count and the percentages that define the Semester Level Retention Rate have been highlighted in the table. Subsequent tables in this chapter, where this rate or the source figures to calculate the Semester Level Retention Rate are used, have been highlighted with the same colour.

To account for the kinds of complexities found in student enrolments, and to extend the interpretive value of the Semester Level Retention Rate, we developed the concept of a Global Retention Rate, which allowed for the inclusion of both Late Starters within the 2008 cohort (i.e. those enrolling at Beginner level after their first year at university; in our case in 2009 and 2010) and Advanced Starters (i.e. those enrolling above Beginner level in their first year at university, in 2008 or later years).

To calculate the Global Retention Rate, we thus i) restricted the cohort of students to be analysed to those who enrolled at ANU in 2008; and ii) calculated the retention rate as the rate of enrolment in L&C studies in the sequence of six consecutive semesters from Semester 1, 2008, to Semester 2, 2010.

Table 2.IV. Semester Level Retention Rate—All ANU languages. Only students who enrolled in 2008 are considered. Enrolment measured in EFTSL

Semester and Year	Enrolment	Semester Level Retention Rate
Level 1 Sem 1 2008	70.0	100.0%
Level 1 Sem 2 2008	60.1	85.9%
Level 2 Sem 1 2009	40.8	58.3%
Level 2 Sem 2 2009	35.2	50.3%
Level 3 Sem 1 2010	23.5	33.6%
Level 3 Sem 2 2010	25.7	36.7%

Source: Derived from 2008–2010 enrolment data provided by the ANU Statistical Unit.

Table 2.V. Global Retention Rate and Semester Level Retention Rate—All ANU languages. Only students who enrolled in 2008 are considered. Enrolment measured in EFTSL

Semester	Level 1	Level 2	Level 3	Total All Levels	Global Retention Rate
Sem 1 2008	70.0	18.1	7.6	95.7	100.0%
Sem 2 2008	60.1	18.4	9.8	88.3	92.3%
Sem 1 2009	22.8	40.8	16.8	80.4	84.0%
Sem 2 2009	13.3	35.2	17.4	65.9	68.9%
Sem 1 2010	7.3	20.3	23.5	51.1	53.4%
Sem 2 2010	4.1	14.4	25.7	44.2	46.2%
Total All Semesters	177.6	147.2	100.8	425.6	

Source: Derived from 2008–2010 enrolment data provided by the ANU Statistical Unit.

2. ACCOUNTING FOR THE MISSING STUDENTS

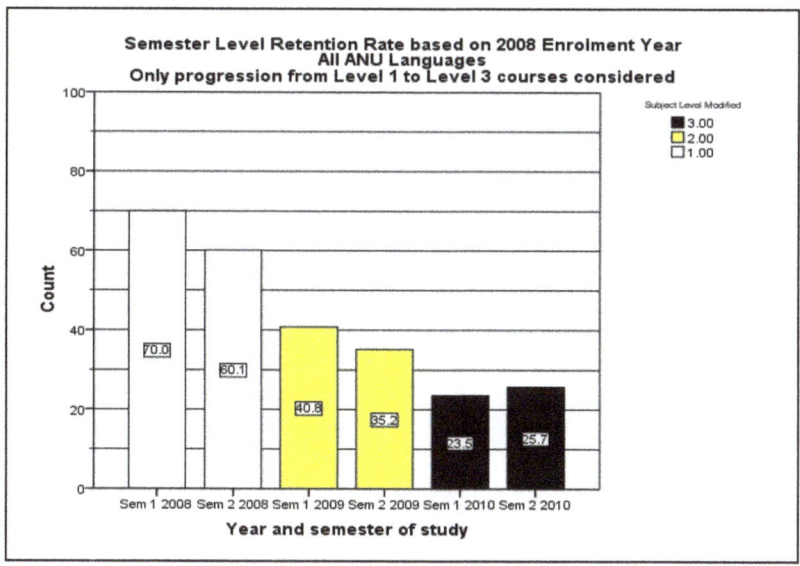

Figure 2.4. Graphical representation of the figures used to calculate the Semester Level Retention Rate. The rate is calculated using only the levels of Language & Culture study shown.

Source: Derived from 2008–2010 enrolment data provided by the ANU Statistical Unit.

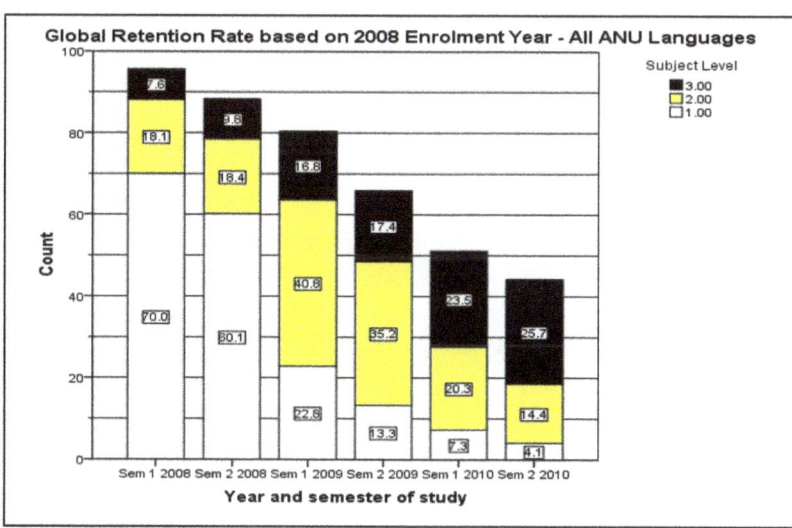

Figure 2.5. Graphical representation of the figures used to calculate the Global Retention Rate. The rate is calculated using all three levels of Language & Culture study shown in all semesters.

Source: Derived from 2008–2010 enrolment data provided by the ANU Statistical Unit.

The main difference between this approach and the traditional approach (of looking at sequences of consecutive courses in the major) is that all students from a cohort enrolled in all levels are taken into account, that is the progression perspective is switched from the progression in consecutive courses through the major to the progression of students through semesters. This approach made possible the calculation of a Global Retention Rate (Table 2.V), which includes all students of the 2008 cohort (not only those who follow the normal progression of enrolment by level in the three years under consideration but also Late and Advanced Starters within the 2008 cohort). The Equivalent Full-Time Student Load (EFTSL) per semester for all ANU languages at each level, from Semester 1, 2008 to Semester 2, 2010, is shown in Table 2.V (columns 2 to 4).

The Global Retention Rate for a given semester is calculated by dividing that semester's total language enrolment at all levels by the total language enrolments at all levels in Semester 1, 2008. The Semester Level Retention Rates (Table 2.IV) are highlighted in Table 2.V, as these are the source semester figures for the calculations of these rates. The differences in retention rate calculations between the Semester Level Retention Rates and the Global Retention Rates for all ANU languages is evident in the final columns of Tables 2.IV and 2.V: the source student load figures used to calculate these two rates are also shown in Figures 2.4 and 2.5.

We believe that this new measure of Global Retention Rate is a potentially very useful analytical tool because it addresses the contextual complexity that arises from students entering L&C studies at different levels. While the simpler Semester Level Retention Rate only takes into consideration the apparent normal progression of students from Level 1 to Level 3 from 2008 to 2010 across the core courses in the L&C majors, the more comprehensive Global Retention Rate, in contrast, takes into account both Late and Advanced Starters in the 2008 cohort as well. This has, of course, consequences when apparent retention rates are calculated. Comparing Tables 2.IV and 2.V, we can see that the apparent student retention rate for Semester 2, 2010 (the second semester of the third year of study of the 2008 cohort) is almost 10 per cent higher if the Global Retention Rate is used (46.2 per cent) instead of the more commonly used Semester Level Retention Rate (36.7 per cent).

Another factor influencing the rates is the number of L&C courses a particular student is enrolled in for a particular semester of study. When the student loads for Semester 1, 2010 and Semester 2, 2010 are compared, the load for the latter is actually slightly higher than the load for the former (Figure 2.4). This apparent anomaly appears to be a consequence of the degree structure at ANU: an L&C major requires seven or eight courses, and students aiming to complete a major in three years usually take additional L&C courses in their last semester of study, which is generally the second semester of any given year. This leads to the apparent increase in numbers of students in Semester 2, when it in fact reflects students doing more than one L&C course in that semester (see also section 2.4). Both Global Retention Rate and Semester Level Retention Rate are cohort-based measures. While they do more effectively address some of the potential distortions found with traditional, simpler measures of retention, they nonetheless contain distortions of their own. These are discussed in detail, with reference to some methodological issues, in the following section. Nevertheless, we believe that both the Global Retention Rate and Semester Level Retention Rate illuminate pertinent issues relevant to retention in L&C programs, and, importantly, provide analytical tools that offer insights into the apparent low level of L&C retention rates as generally presented in the literature and sector debate.[1] We will return to these issues in section 2.5, where we use the Global Retention Rate and Semester Level Retention Rate to compare retention rates for languages with those of other disciplines.

2.4. Further issues impacting the calculation of retention rates

In the LASP1 study, Nettelbeck et al. (2007, 14–15) found that retention rates in Australian L&C programs vary according to the specific language involved. However, they did not consider the influence of Late Starters and Advanced Starters in their calculation of retention rates. While it would be useful and interesting for us to compare the individual retention rates found by LASP1 with those

---

1 Except when otherwise indicated, all the figures and tables presented in the rest of this chapter contain rates that have been calculated using our reorganisation of the data provided by the ANU Statistical Unit, processed with SPSS®.

of individual ANU language programs, and include the influences explored above, we cannot do so for reasons of confidentiality (i.e. we cannot report on individual disciplines or administrative units at an identified university). In order to compare the ANU retention rates in L&C courses with those for groups of cognate disciplines at ANU, we aggregated the 21 Asian, Classical, European and Middle Eastern languages taught at ANU in 2008, 2009 and 2010 into the groupings shown in Table 2.VI. Notably, this aggregation does not coincide with any administrative unit existing at the time.

Table 2.VI. Languages taught at ANU in 2008, 2009 and 2010

Name of group	Languages included in this group
East Asian & Pacific Languages	Burmese, Cantonese, Chinese (Mandarin), Classical Chinese, Indonesian, Japanese, Javanese, Korean, Laotian, Melanesian Pidgins & Creoles, Thai, Tetum, Vietnamese
European & Classical Languages	Classical Greek, French, German, Italian, Latin, Spanish
Middle Eastern & Central Asian Languages	Arabic, Hindi, Persian, Russian, Sanskrit, Urdu, Turkish

Source: ANU Undergraduate Handbooks.

As noted above, the rates defined in the previous section are cohort rates, based on course enrolments rather than on individual students' enrolment information, and our method of calculating rates is similar to the Student Progress Ratio (Dobson and Sharma, 1993), as it determines student progression by aggregating student load. However, our rates are restricted to one cohort of students, namely those commencing a degree at ANU in 2008. Our rates are still apparent retention rates, but the distortion produced by the different cohorts of students starting L&C studies at different times in multiple cohorts is reduced. We have chosen to use these rates here because they permit comparison with the progression rates used in Nettelbeck et al. (2007), and because they allow comparison of L&C retention rates with those of other groups of disciplines. However, despite the improvements achieved by considering the 2008 cohort only, and including Advanced and Late Starters, there are still inevitable distortions remaining because of the aggregation of students in such calculations. For example, when a student discontinues studying a language in one semester, but chooses to study another language in the following semester, this would still be counted as studying languages in the calculations reported in Tables 2.IV and 2.V.

There are four additional factors that make the chosen apparent Global and Semester Level Retention Rates still not as accurate as computations that used individual student data.

- **Second semester entry:** Students who commenced their university studies in second semester 2008 were not necessarily able to start L&C studies in their semester of initial enrolment. Such students increase the number of Late Starters in the first semester of the following year (as shown in Figure 2.6.a, comparing the second and third bars).
- **Mode of study:** Part-time students affect the apparent retention rate, as they do not necessarily follow the path of studying languages in every semester under consideration. As Figure 2.6.b shows, the data include a component of part-time students. Similar influences can be found when considering combined degree students, students who enter university through associated degrees, cross-institutional enrolments and students who transfer from other institutions.
- **International students:** International students also appear to start L&C studies in their second or third years of study at university. This is shown in Figure 2.6.c, where it can be seen that the international student load for 2009 is higher than the load for 2008 in both semesters, and that the international student load for both semesters in 2010 is higher than the load for Semester 2, 2009. We will explore the situation of international students and students that speak a LOTE at home in section 2.6, because this has an influence on the perceptions of other students.
- **Varying pathways:** Similar irregularities can be found for different student pathways in language majors. For example, the load for Middle Eastern and Central Asian languages increases in second semester 2009 because the summer course study in Jordan is included (evident in Figure 2.6.d and even more obviously in Figure 2.7.d).

THE DOUBTERS' DILEMMA

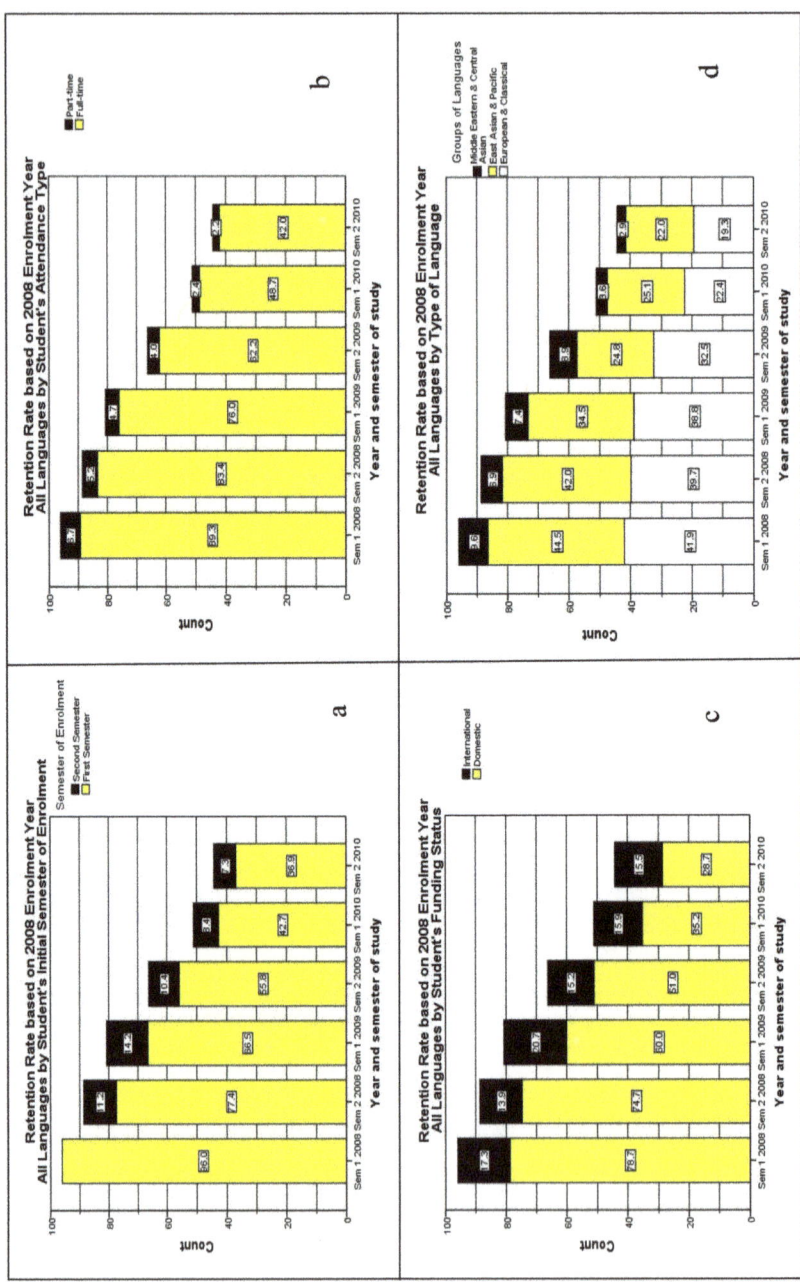

Figure 2.6. Some factors affecting the calculation of retention rates
Source: Calculated based on enrolment data provided by the ANU Statistical Unit.

2. ACCOUNTING FOR THE MISSING STUDENTS

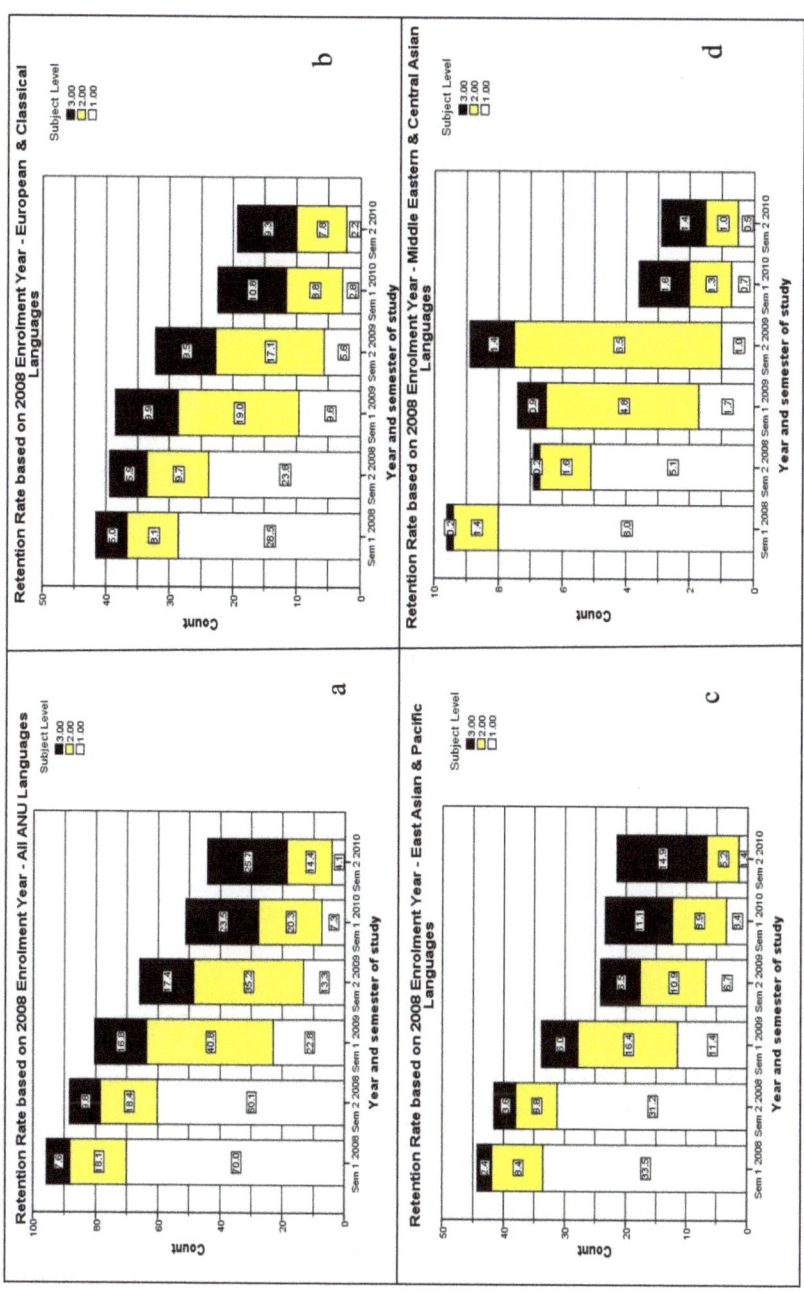

Figure 2.7. Retention rates based on 2008 Enrolment Year Student Cohort—Languages

Source: Calculated based on enrolment data provided by the ANU Statistical Unit.

In spite of all these remaining systematic distortions in rate calculations, the application of the retention rates as defined in section 2.3 is not only a significant advancement over the traditional way of calculating retention rates, but can also provide useful information when comparing L&C programs with other disciplines.

2.5. Do retention rates vary by discipline?

As previously explained, confidentiality concerns prevented us from calculating retention rates for individual ANU L&C programs, so instead we developed an approach that allowed comparisons of retention rates across ANU discipline areas. First, we compared L&C programs with the discipline grouping 'Physical and Natural Sciences', and specifically with two teaching areas ('Mathematics, Statistics, Econometrics & Mathematical Finance' and 'Physics, Astronomy & Chemistry') that had patterns of sequential courses in their majors similar to those found in L&C programs. Although the Global Retention Rates for all sciences were approximately similar to those for all languages, the 'East Asian & Pacific Languages' and 'European & Classical Languages' groups (as defined in Table 2.VI) performed better on this index than the grouping 'Mathematics, Statistics, Econometrics & Mathematical Finance' (as can be seen by comparing the columns corresponding to these disciplines in Table 2.VII). Similarly, all L&C groupings performed better than the grouping 'Physics, Astronomy & Chemistry' (Table 2.VII). These patterns can also be seen graphically in Figure 2.8, where the actual count of the student loads are shown. While the tables compare percentages, in the figures the important features to compare are the overall shape of the figure as a whole, the slope of the reduction of load across semesters, and the relative size of different levels of student load shown in the bars.

We also compared Global Retention Rates for all ANU L&C programs with those for diverse groupings of ANU disciplines. As can be seen in the relevant columns in Table 2.VIII, Global Retention Rates for L&C were lower than those for 'English & Creative Arts' and other humanities and social science disciplines, and even lower than groupings such as 'Computer Science & Engineering' or 'Management & Commerce'. These patterns can also be seen graphically in Figures 2.9 and 2.10. For some of these disciplines, the comparisons are not that meaningful, simply because the majors require courses in other disciplines as prerequisites (for example, Mathematics courses are prerequisites for the Computer Science and Engineering majors).

2. ACCOUNTING FOR THE MISSING STUDENTS

Table 2.VII. Global Retention Rate for Languages and Sciences compared. Only students who enrolled in 2008 are considered

Semester	All Languages	East Asian & Pacific Languages	European & Classical Languages	Middle Eastern & Central Asian Languages	All Physical & Natural Sciences	Mathematics, Statistics, Econometrics & Mathematical Finance	Physics, Astronomy & Chemistry
Sem 1 2008	100.0%	100.0%	100.0%	100.0%	100.0%	100.0%	100.0%
Sem 2 2008	92.3%	93.1%	94.7%	71.9%	90.0%	94.7%	67.4%
Sem 1 2009	84.0%	77.7%	92.5%	77.1%	83.3%	78.8%	49.0%
Sem 2 2009	68.9%	55.2%	77.4%	92.7%	61.0%	63.1%	35.2%
Sem 1 2010	53.4%	52.1%	53.8%	37.5%	55.2%	46.2%	29.5%
Sem 2 2010	46.2%	47.9%	46.4%	30.2%	51.7%	36.7%	21.8%

Source: Calculated based on enrolment data provided by the ANU Statistical Unit.

Table 2.VIII. Global Retention Rate for Languages and other groups of disciplines compared. Only students who enrolled in 2008 are considered

Semester	All Languages	English & Creative Arts	Area Studies, International Relations & Political Science	Sociology, Anthropology & Archaeology	Biology, Zoology & Environmental Sciences	Computer Science & Engineering	Management & Commerce
Sem 1 2008	100.0%	100.0%	100.0%	100.0%	100.0%	100.0%	100.0%
Sem 2 2008	92.3%	105.2%	97.9%	108.9%	118.1%	117.5%	134.0%
Sem 1 2009	84.0%	88.5%	81.4%	98.9%	101.9%	102.3%	111.3%
Sem 2 2009	68.9%	81.5%	73.3%	113.9%	88.4%	107.9%	113.5%
Sem 1 2010	53.4%	67.9%	80.1%	71.8%	80.0%	85.3%	113.7%
Sem 2 2010	46.2%	61.8%	63.5%	70.7%	73.1%	77.9%	90.0%

Source: Calculated based on enrolment data provided by the ANU Statistical Unit.

53

THE DOUBTERS' DILEMMA

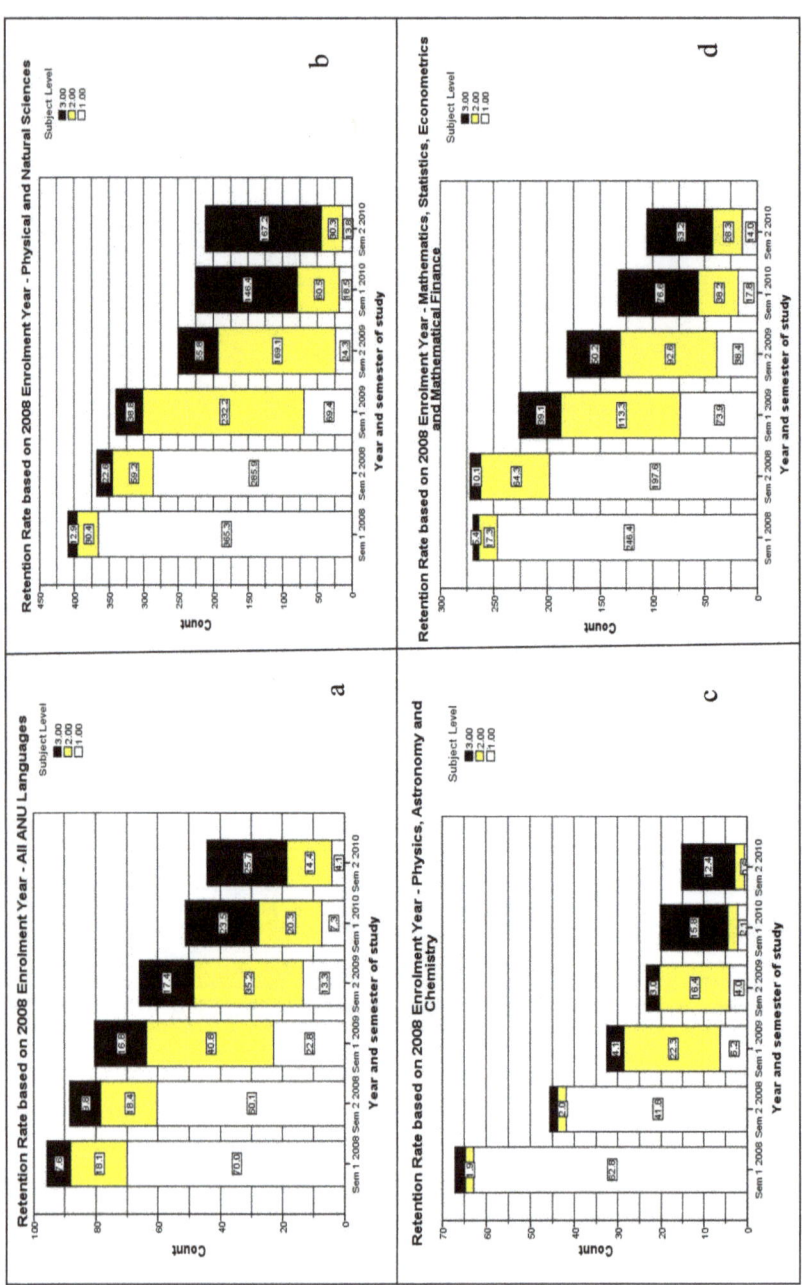

Figure 2.8. Retention rates based on 2008 Enrolment Year Student Cohort—Languages compared with Sciences

Source: Calculated based on enrolment data provided by the ANU Statistical Unit.

2. ACCOUNTING FOR THE MISSING STUDENTS

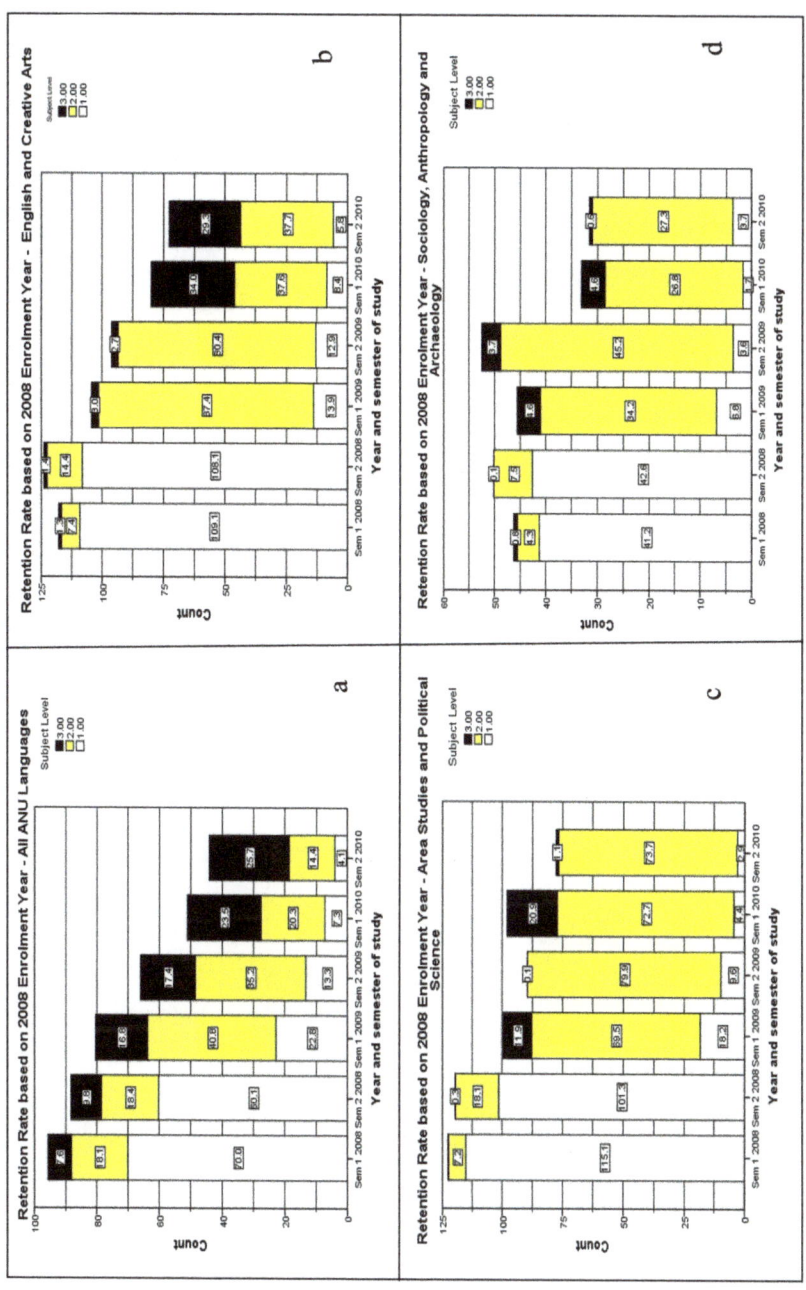

Figure 2.9. Retention rates based on 2008 Enrolment Year Student Cohort—Languages compared with other disciplines 1

Source: Calculated based on enrolment data provided by the ANU Statistical Unit.

THE DOUBTERS' DILEMMA

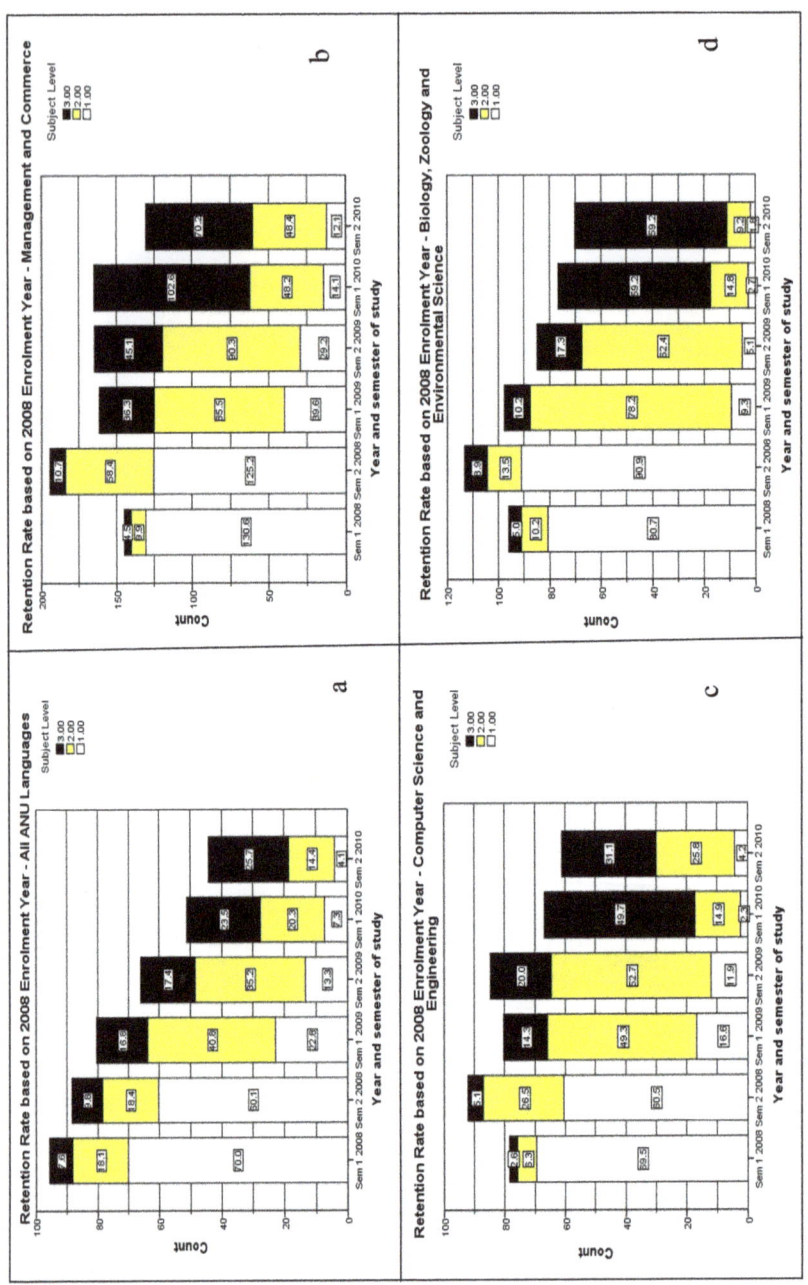

Figure 2.10. Retention rates based on 2008 Enrolment Year Student Cohort—Languages compared with other disciplines 2

Source: Calculated based on enrolment data provided by the ANU Statistical Unit.

We also believe that the lower rate of retention in L&C courses is partly a reflection of the cumulative structure of L&C majors compared with majors in other disciplines, and partly an outcome of the type of content available to students (itself a manifestation of the language of instruction in those disciplines). Clearly, the diverse structures of the relevant major within a degree, or of the degrees themselves, also play a significant role in retention rates, by influencing students' decision-making with respect to continuing or discontinuing L&C study. This represents a key impacting factor in the different retention rates, so is worth expanding on.

We can conceptualise a language major as a string of connected and related courses, which build on previous courses from Beginner level (Figure 2.11.a), and therefore create a crucial set of prerequisites for those students who wish to study L&C at an advanced level. Consider a student who wishes to study Advanced Persian I: before being able to enrol, she must either show that she has successfully completed four semesters of compulsory Introductory and Intermediate Persian courses, or she must be able to demonstrate (usually through a placement test) an equivalent background in Persian (for example, through study elsewhere). If the student arrives at university with a particular interest in engaging with Persian literature, she may have to study for four or five semesters simply to attain the language skills needed to engage effectively with complex literary texts. While there will of course normally be some exposure to literary texts in conjunction with language studies in Beginner and Intermediate courses, in general in-depth literature study is not possible unless and until students have begun to master the relevant language skills.

In contrast, if the same student were to arrive at university with an interest in English literature, and wanted to complete an English major, she could immediately choose from three or four introductory courses on different aspects of English literature, and an array of later year (Level 2 and 3) courses (Figure 2.11.b). Notably, this would be the case even if the student's first language was not English: the level of English proficiency required to study in Australia would normally allow her, even in the first year of a degree, to be viewed at the equivalent level of language mastery of an Advanced Persian I student. Furthermore, even if the student of Persian had attained sufficient mastery of the language to engage with complex texts, the range of subject choices would remain much more limited than for the student of English, simply because L&C programs are typically unable to provide a wide range of electives. This deficit is a direct outcome of the need for L&C programs to devote a significant proportion of their comparatively impoverished resources to meet the needs of Beginner and Intermediate students.

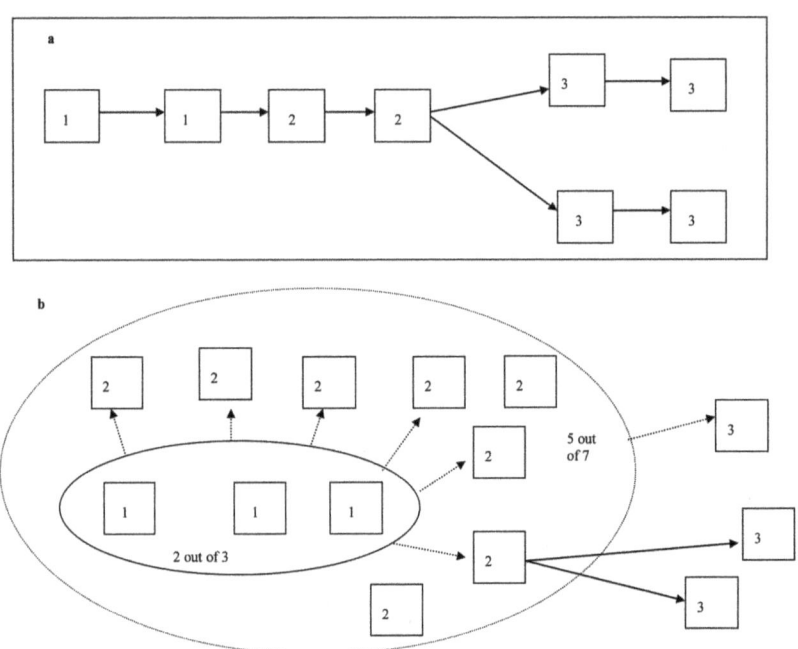

Figure 2.11. Schematic representation of two types of undergraduate majors

Source: Based on an analysis of the structure of ANU majors.

The differences in degree structures between L&C and other programs are similarly influential. For example, a student enrolled in the ANU general Engineering degree can choose from a (limited) set of Engineering majors and, after having completed the basic Level 1 courses, may select from a wide variety of elective Engineering courses. In contrast, an ANU L&C student has far fewer electives from which to choose, and many of the so-called elective options in the degree program are actually taken up with courses directed at achieving mastery of the language itself. Although this situation may be alleviated somewhat by enrolment in the ANU Bachelor of Languages or Bachelor of Arts, which have a high proportion of electives, in general universities have only a limited capacity to provide advanced courses that are taught in a target language and cater to the full spectrum of students' interests.

How do these structural differences influence retention rates? Sciences, like Languages, have majors that comprise a sequence of correlated courses, and require a long process of mastering basic knowledge before the more interesting content can be accessed (Figure 2.11.a). When we compare Languages with Sciences using the more restrictive Semester Level Retention Rate (Table 2.IX), we find that they are quite comparable, with some Languages performing even better than the two selected groupings of Science disciplines.

We can conclude then that the perceived lower retention rates in Languages are structurally conditioned by the shape of the disciplinary major at ANU and by the relatively few students who enter university with sufficient language proficiency to allow them to start their L&C studies at later-year levels (Level 2 or Level 3 courses). The latter situation appears to be a consequence of the relatively low provision of language teaching at secondary level in Australia (Chapter 1, section 1.3). It is not a coincidence that retention rates for Languages are comparable to those in the Sciences, as these disciplines have similarly structured majors: both require commitment to progressive study over several semesters. Increasingly, it is becoming apparent that inadequate high school science teaching is creating similar issues for tertiary sciences as has happened with languages, that is, allowing students to enter university without a solid foundation in the relevant discipline. One could argue that this factor too is contributing to the similarity of retention rates.

Table 2.IX. Semester Level Retention Rate for Languages and Sciences compared. Only students who enrolled in 2008 are considered

Level & Semester	All Languages	East Asian & Pacific Languages	European & Classical Languages	Middle Eastern & Central Asian Languages	All Physical & Natural Sciences	Mathematics, Statistics, Econometrics & Mathematical Finance	Physics, Astronomy & Chemistry
Level 1 Sem 1 2008	100.0%	100.0%	100.0%	100.0%	100.0%	100.0%	100.0%
Level 1 Sem 2 2008	85.9%	93.1%	83.5%	63.8%	78.3%	74.7%	66.6%
Level 2 Sem 1 2009	58.3%	49.0%	66.7%	60.0%	63.6%	42.9%	35.5%
Level 2 Sem 2 2009	50.3%	32.5%	60.0%	81.3%	46.3%	35.0%	26.1%
Level 3 Sem 1 2010	33.6%	33.1%	37.9%	20.0%	40.1%	29.0%	25.2%
Level 3 Sem 2 2010	36.7%	44.5%	32.6%	17.5%	45.8%	23.9%	19.7%

Source: Calculated based on enrolment data provided by the ANU Statistical Unit.

2.6. Late starters at advanced levels — Students who speak a language other than English (LOTE) at home

Our data exploration below will show that the group we designate as Late Starters includes not only those students who enrol in Beginner L&C courses when they are close to completing their degrees, but also those students who enrol in Advanced L&C courses at that stage. This phenomenon was not discovered in the LASP1 and LASP2 studies (Nettelbeck et al., 2007, 2009) simply because both studies were restricted to Beginner level. The ANU case study found that international students and domestic students who speak a LOTE at home tend to enrol directly in L&C courses at Advanced levels after they have commenced their university studies. In general, we will also explore whether retention rates in L&C programs are significantly influenced by the number of enrolled students who speak a LOTE at home.

In Chapter 1 (section 1.7) we noted the LASP2 finding that some 50 per cent of students at Beginner level in Japanese reported speaking Chinese at home (Nettelbeck et al., 2009, 12). In our analysis, we questioned whether this was a relevant finding, worthy of consideration or merely an incidental one. Unfortunately, while the ANU study included a demographic question that allowed us to distinguish between domestic and international students, the LASP2 survey did not, so direct comparison was not possible. Nevertheless, given that Chinese students constitute about 27 per cent of all international student enrolments (the largest group Australia-wide by far: Australian Bureau of Statistics, 2011), we decided to explore the issue using the Global Retention Rate and Semester Level Retention Rate calculations described in this chapter. To make the analysis clearer, we compare the variable classifying students according to the language spoken at home (English/LOTE) with an unrelated variable traditionally associated with differences in retention rates for L&C studies, namely student gender.

Table 2.X. Retention rates for students who report that they speak English at home. Only students who enrolled in 2008 considered— All ANU languages

Semester	Level 1	Level 2	Level 3	Total All Levels	Global Retention Rate	Semester Level Retention Rate
Sem 1 2008	51.5	12.7	4.6	**68.8**	*100.0%*	*100.0%*
Sem 2 2008	45.5	13.9	5.3	**64.7**	*94.0%*	*88.3%*
Sem 1 2009	11.1	29.4	11.2	**51.7**	*75.1%*	*57.1%*
Sem 2 2009	6.8	26.4	11.1	**44.3**	*64.4%*	*51.3%*
Sem 1 2010	4.1	13.9	14.2	**32.2**	*46.8%*	*27.6%*
Sem 2 2010	2.6	9.6	14.4	**26.6**	*38.7%*	*28.0%*
Total All Semesters	**121.6**	**105.9**	**60.8**	**288.3**		

Source: Calculated based on enrolment data provided by the ANU Statistical Unit.

Table 2.XI. Retention rates for students who report that they speak a LOTE at home. Only students who enrolled in 2008 considered— All ANU languages

Semester	Level 1	Level 2	Level 3	Total All Levels	Global Retention Rate	Semester Level Retention Rate
Sem 1 2008	18.5	5.4	3.0	**26.9**	*100.0%*	*100.0%*
Sem 2 2008	14.6	4.5	4.5	**23.6**	*87.7%*	*78.9%*
Sem 1 2009	11.7	11.4	5.6	**28.7**	*106.7%*	*61.6%*
Sem 2 2009	6.5	8.8	6.3	**21.6**	*80.3%*	*47.6%*
Sem 1 2010	3.2	6.4	9.3	**18.9**	*70.3%*	*50.3%*
Sem 2 2010	1.5	4.8	11.3	**17.6**	*65.4%*	*61.1%*
Total All Semesters	**56.0**	**41.3**	**40.0**	**137.3**		

Source: Calculated based on enrolment data provided by the ANU Statistical Unit.

2. ACCOUNTING FOR THE MISSING STUDENTS

Table 2.XII. Retention rates for female students. Only students who enrolled in 2008 considered—All ANU languages

Semester	Level 1	Level 2	Level 3	Total All Levels	Global Retention Rate	Semester Level Retention Rate
Sem 1 2008	42.6	12.2	4.2	59.0	100.0%	100.0%
Sem 2 2008	37.1	12.3	5.7	55.1	93.4%	87.1%
Sem 1 2009	14.1	26.2	10.7	51.0	86.4%	61.5%
Sem 2 2009	7.3	22.3	11.2	40.8	69.2%	52.3%
Sem 1 2010	4.1	13.9	16.0	34.0	57.6%	37.6%
Sem 2 2010	2.7	9.8	17.1	29.6	50.2%	40.1%
Total All Semesters	107.9	96.7	64.9	269.5		

Source: Calculated based on enrolment data provided by the ANU Statistical Unit.

Table 2.XIII. Retention rates for male students. Only students who enrolled in 2008 considered—All ANU languages

Semester	Level 1	Level 2	Level 3	Total All Levels	Global Retention Rate	Semester Level Retention Rate
Sem 1 2008	27.4	5.9	3.4	36.7	100.0%	100.0%
Sem 2 2008	23.0	6.1	4.1	33.2	90.5%	83.9%
Sem 1 2009	8.7	14.6	6.1	29.4	80.1%	53.3%
Sem 2 2009	6.0	12.9	6.2	25.1	68.4%	47.1%
Sem 1 2010	3.2	6.4	7.5	17.1	46.6%	27.4%
Sem 2 2010	1.4	4.6	8.6	14.6	39.8%	31.4%
Total All Semesters	69.7	50.5	35.9	156.1		

Source: Calculated based on enrolment data provided by the ANU Statistical Unit.

THE DOUBTERS' DILEMMA

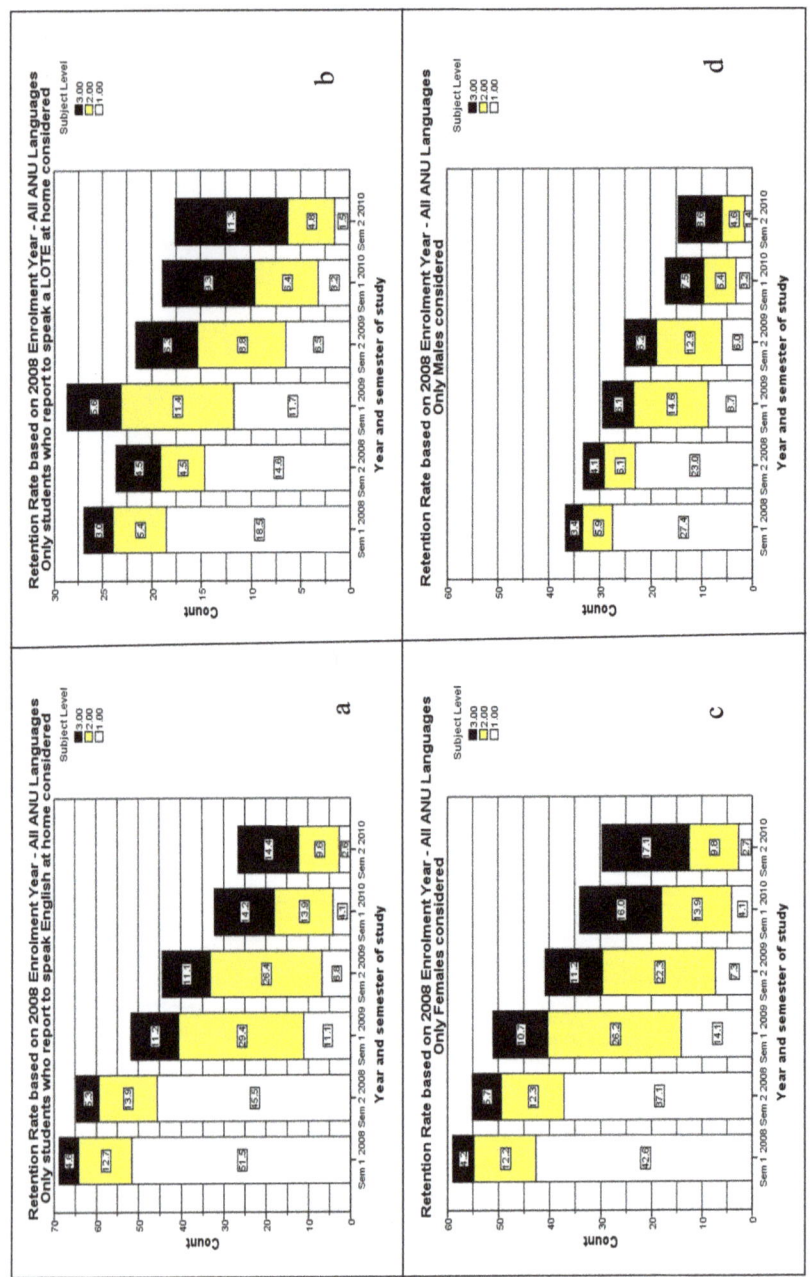

Figure 2.12. Comparison of enrolment patterns by language spoken at home and gender—All ANU languages

Source: Calculated based on enrolment data provided by the ANU Statistical Unit.

We calculated the load enrolment data and the retention rates (Global Retention Rate and Semester Level Retention Rate) for all students enrolled in ANU L&C programs who either speak English at home (Table 2.X) or speak a LOTE at home (Table 2.XI). We also calculated the corresponding Global Retention Rate and Semester Level Retention Rate for female and male students in our data (Tables 2.XII and 2.XIII respectively). All these data are summarised in Figure 2.12. When the retention rates for these four groups of students (i.e. speak English at home, speak a LOTE at home, female, male) are compared, the enrolment pattern of LOTE students (Table 2.XI) shows two anomalies. First, the Global Retention Rate increases to 106.7 per cent in Semester 1, 2009. Second, the Semester Level Retention Rate decreases from Semester 1, 2008 to Semester 2, 2009, but then increases again in 2010, with a pronounced increase from Semester 1, 2010 to Semester 2, 2010. Notably, the latter increase is much greater than the few percentage points we might expect (as shown in the cases of non-LOTE students, males and females), because of the impact of ANU students who choose to take more than one Level 3 course in their final semester to complete requisite language majors (as previously noted).

To investigate these anomalies further, we undertook an extensive analysis of enrolment data, and found two major contributing factors: the enrolment behaviour of international students and the specific LOTE spoken at home.

Table 2.XIV. Percentage of international students in each year and level—All ANU languages

Semester	Level 1	Level 2	Level 3	Total All Levels
Sem 1 2008	19.4%	13.3%	17.1%	18.1%
Sem 2 2008	17.3%	9.2%	18.4%	15.7%
Sem 1 2009	41.7%	19.4%	19.6%	25.7%
Sem 2 2009	36.8%	16.5%	25.9%	23.1%
Sem 1 2010	39.7%	24.6%	34.0%	31.1%
Sem 2 2010	34.1%	30.6%	37.7%	35.1%
Total All Semesters	24.0%	18.5%	28.4%	23.1%

Source: Derived from 2008-2010 enrolment data provided by the ANU Statistical Unit.

THE DOUBTERS' DILEMMA

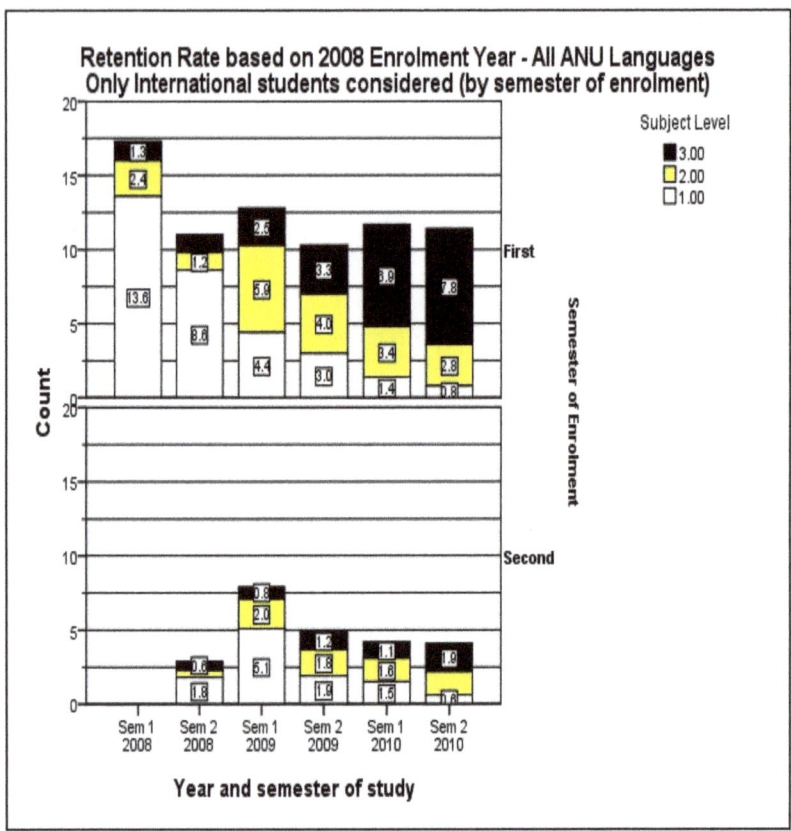

Figure 2.13. Comparison of enrolment patterns for international students who enrolled in first and second semester 2008—All ANU languages
Source: Calculated based on enrolment data provided by the ANU Statistical Unit.

The first anomaly—an increase in Global Retention Rate from 2008 to 2009 (Table 2.XI) is explained in part by the enrolment behaviour of international students. Some international students who start in the first semester of the academic year are actually enrolled in preparatory courses, and move into their degree program only in the second semester, while other international students actually arrive to study at ANU in the second semester ('mid-year entry'). In both situations, students without any knowledge of the language they want to study must wait to start L&C studies in Semester 1 of the following year (i.e. Semester 1, 2009 in this study), as borne out by the increase in enrolments in Semester 1, 2009 when compared to Semester 2, 2008 (as shown in Figure 2.13). We also believe that some international students, still adapting to studying in English in the Australian educational system, may even choose to start learning a new language only in their second or third year of study in Australia. This may explain the fluctuations in the percentages of enrolments of international students (Table 2.XIV).

The second anomaly—the increase in the number and proportion of LOTE-at-home speakers taking Level 3 courses in Semester 2, 2010 (Table 2.XV)—is likely to relate largely to the enrolment as Late Starters of those among these students who already have knowledge of the target study language, that is they commence study at post-Beginner level (either because they are native speakers of the target language or because they have previously studied that language before coming to Australia), but can also be influenced by the availability of parallel thematic courses at a higher level.

Table 2.XV. Percentage of students who speak a LOTE at home in each year and level—All ANU languages

Semester	Level 1	Level 2	Level 3	Total All Levels
Sem 1 2008	26.4%	29.8%	39.5%	28.1%
Sem 2 2008	24.3%	24.5%	45.9%	26.7%
Sem 1 2009	51.3%	27.9%	33.3%	35.7%
Sem 2 2009	48.9%	25.0%	36.2%	32.8%
Sem 1 2010	43.8%	31.5%	39.6%	37.0%
Sem 2 2010	36.6%	33.3%	44.0%	39.8%
Total All Semesters	31.5%	28.1%	39.7%	32.3%

Source: Derived from 2008-2010 enrolment data provided by the ANU Statistical Unit.

These explanations still do not reveal the whole story, however. When we examined the overall proportion of the 2008 cohort of students who spoke a LOTE at home more closely, considering all L&C students in all ANU programs, all years, and all levels (Table 2.XV), we found that the proportion of LOTE students was higher at Levels 2 and 3 in 2010. Indeed, the proportion of such students in the Level 3 classes in Semester 2, 2010 was significantly higher than that found in the Level 1 classes in Semester 1, 2008. Even assuming a 100 per cent retention of all LOTE students, these high percentages call for an explanation. We believe that this finding is a clear indicator not only that the retention rate of students who speak a LOTE at home is much higher than that of students who speak only English at home, but also that there are many such LOTE students who are Late Starters enrolling directly into Level 2 and 3 L&C courses (missing the Beginner level) in their third year of study at ANU. A comparison of the size of the level 3 enrolments for international students in Semester 1, 2010 (8.0) with the size of the level 2 enrolments in Semester 2, 2009 (5.8) shows that there is an increase in the number of international students that cannot be explained by the normal progression of students in a major (Figure 2.15b).

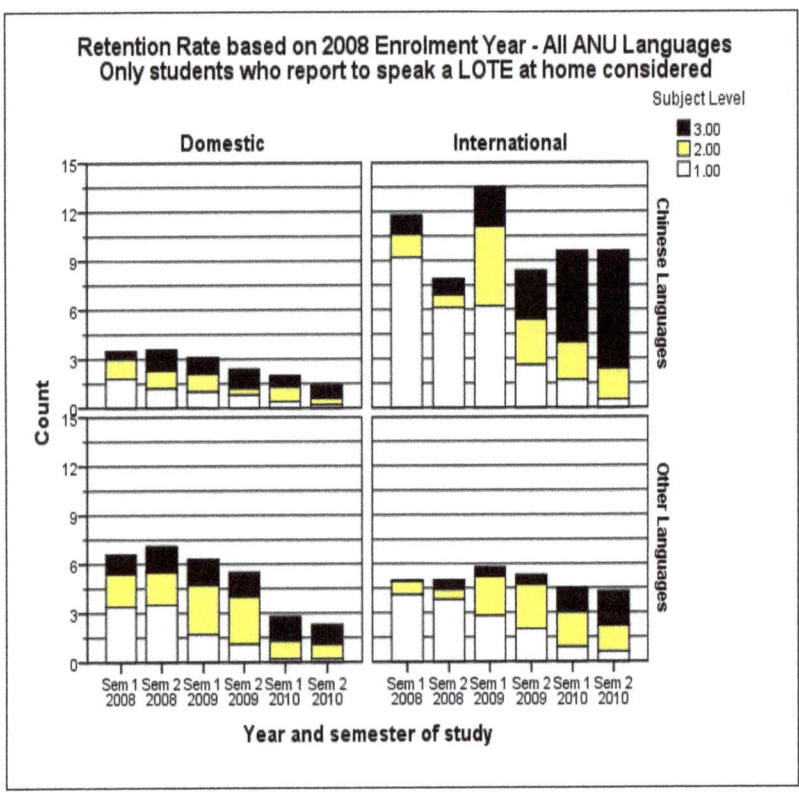

Figure 2.14. Global Retention Rate for domestic and international students, discriminated by the type of LOTE spoken at home. Only students who enrolled in 2008 and report to speak a LOTE at home are considered. The figure provides load for all ANU languages studied.
Source: Calculated based on enrolment data provided by the ANU Statistical Unit.

Moreover, a more detailed investigation, shown in Figures 2.14 and 2.15, shows that the Late Starter phenomenon associated with students who speak a LOTE at home could be explained by the enrolment behaviour of those international students who reported speaking a Chinese language at home (that is, not only major Chinese languages, such as Mandarin and Cantonese, but also others such as Chang Chow, Hunan, Kan and Hakka). A more detailed exploration (not shown here) found that these students enrolled in courses in Chinese-English translation, Classical Chinese and Cantonese as well as in diverse Level 3 (Advanced) courses in other languages.

Unfortunately, as our data were based on course enrolments and not individual student enrolments, we cannot calculate the proportion of students who had not previously studied a language at ANU but enrolled directly at Level 3. Nevertheless, the enrolment pattern for students who report speaking a Chinese language at home suggests that this behaviour may have a significant impact (Figure 2.14). After considering additional analyses related to this issue (Figure 2.15), we conclude that students who speak Chinese languages are likely to enrol in courses in other Asian languages at the Beginner level—which supports the LASP2 finding (Nettelbeck et al., 2009), and also likely to enrol in Level 3 courses and translation courses at an Advanced level. In fact, if Figures 2.15.b and 2.15.d are compared, it can be calculated that more than 75 per cent of international students enrolled in Level 3 L&C courses among the 2008 cohort are students who speak Chinese at home. Moreover, it is likely that this behaviour is typical of international students in general, that is, their first enrolment may occur at any level from Beginner to Level 3 and advanced translation. We therefore extend the finding by Nettelbeck et al. (2009) that students who speak a Chinese language at home are important contributors to enrolment anomalies beyond the Beginner level, and to note that other international students, and domestic Australian students who speak a LOTE at home, also contribute to these confounding influences on retention rates at all levels of L&C studies.

THE DOUBTERS' DILEMMA

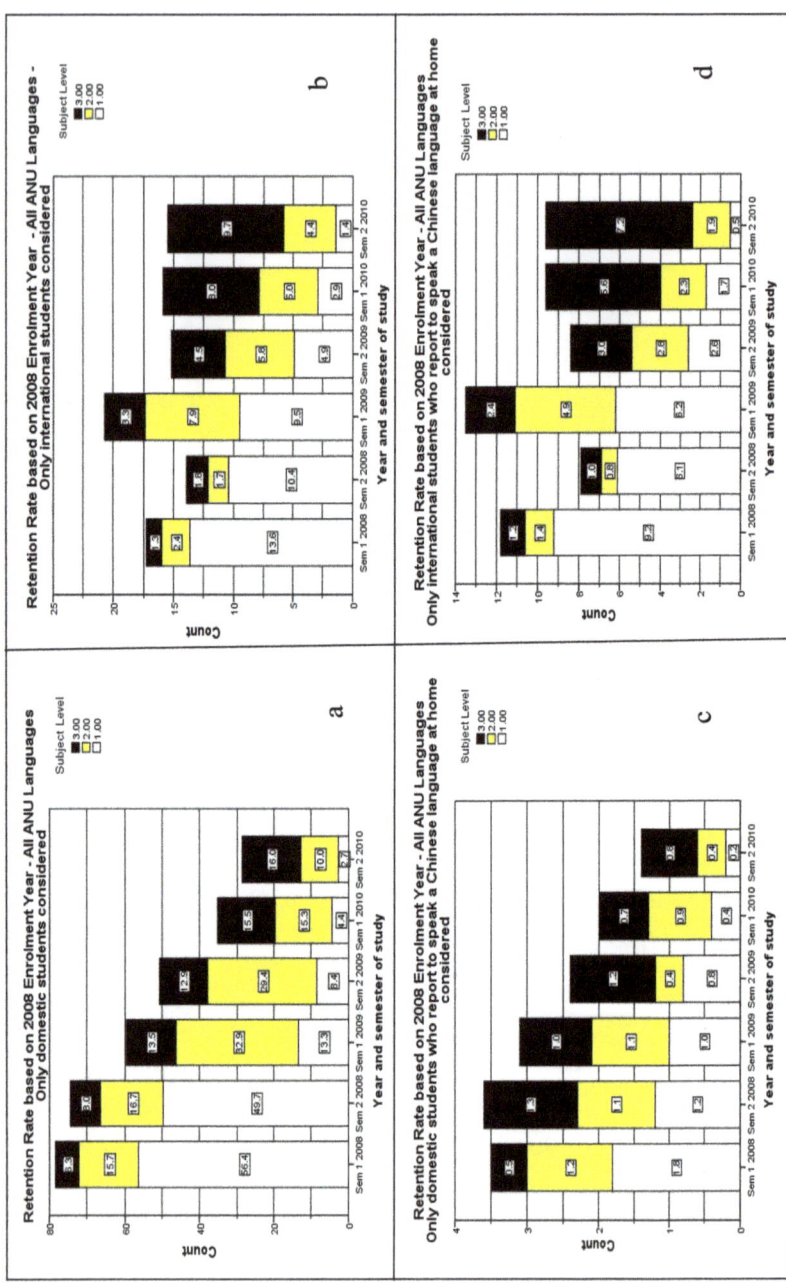

Figure 2.15. Comparison of enrolment patterns for domestic and international students in general and domestic and international students who speak a Chinese language at home—All ANU Languages

Source: Calculated based on enrolment data provided by the ANU Statistical Unit.

In other words, our data shows that students who begin studying a language when they are close to completing their degrees includes not only those students who enrol in Beginner L&C courses (which we designate as Late Starters), but also those students who enrol in Advanced L&C courses at that stage of their degrees. This also means that Advanced Starters are not only first year students who begin their major at an Advanced level, but also students who are close to completing their degree who begin to study L&C courses at advanced language levels. While this is obviously an important finding in relation to the calculation of retention rates, it is also important when thinking about how domestic students are influenced in their thinking about discontinuing. We know that, with regard to Year 12 language examinations, students from English speaking backgrounds feel that the presence of LOTE native speakers impacts negatively on their grades (Lo Bianco, 2009, 50–52; Orton, 2008, 27–29), and these attitudes are almost certainly also found among tertiary students. We will come back to this issue in Chapter 5 when we discuss the issue of mixed levels in advanced courses.

2.7. Summary

In this chapter, we have reported a new, more reliable way of calculating retention rates—the Global Retention Rate—based on the principles of the Student Progress Ratio. Using this measure we have been able to calculate retention rates for L&C programs from 2008 to 2010 and we have compared the rates of the 2008 student cohort to those of other disciplines at ANU. Unfortunately, we have not been able to do similar calculations for attrition rates because we lack the necessary data, namely completion rates and information on students who discontinue university studies at ANU altogether (section 2.4). We were also able to explore the situation of LOTE and international students using the new calculations.

We found that the retention rates for languages, traditionally conceived as low, are in fact comparable to those in disciplines with similar structures in their majors, such as the sciences. We also found that retention rates in languages are influenced by the phenomena of Late Starters and Advanced Starters more than in other university disciplines. Finally, we generalised the findings of Nettelbeck et al. (2009) regarding international students who have Chinese as a mother tongue, and showed that their influence goes beyond the enrolments at Beginner levels.

3

Splitting the Masses: Methodology and data analysis

3.1. Phase 1 methodology

3.1.1. Planning the data collection

An exploratory data collection was conducted in 2008. We refer to this as Phase 1, because we did a more comprehensive data collection later, which we call Phase 2. There were two steps in Phase 1: i) Focus-group student interviews, to provide background information and help inform the development of the data collection instruments; and ii) an online questionnaire, to focus and expand on quantitative aspects of the study.

The online questionnaire targeted two groups of students: 'Continuers' (i.e. students who had enrolled in a Beginner L&C course in 2007 and had continued their study in 2008); and 'Discontinuers' (i.e. students who had enrolled in a Beginner L&C course in 2007 and had discontinued their study of that language in 2008). To ensure that the privacy of individual students was protected, a core research group based in the university's evaluation and academic development unit (Centre for Educational Development and Academic Methods) carried out all data collection and analyses. The online questionnaires were hosted on the university's dedicated online survey system, ANU Polling Online (APOLLO©).

3.1.2. Questionnaire design

In developing the questionnaires, we used some questions from previous studies on student retention and motivation as a starting point, and further elaborated them into four categories:

1. Background information, including previous experience of languages and demographic information;
2. Reasons for studying a language at university;
3. Experience of language study at university; and
4. Reasons for discontinuing language study (only asked of Discontinuers) or reasons for continuing language study and, where applicable, for *thinking about* discontinuing or deferring (only asked of Continuers).

We were able to supplement the collected survey data with ANU internal institutional data on program of study, age, gender, grades obtained in language courses, enrolment category (full-time or part-time, domestic or international), and language spoken at home.

Table 3.I. Languages represented in the focus group discussions (two students were enrolled in more than one language)

Language	No. of Students
Arabic	3
Chinese	11
French	8
German	1
Hindi	1
Indonesian	4
Japanese	7
Korean	1
Spanish	9
Turkish	1
Not mentioned	8

Source: Phase 1 Focus Groups Data.

3.1.3. Data collection

The data collection process was trialled in April 2008. Students who were studying a language at ANU at that time were asked to participate in focus groups through an invitation flyer distributed by lecturers in language classes. Four focus groups were held, with a total of 52 participants (both first and second year students), representing at least 10 languages (Table 3.I). The primary purpose of these focus groups was to test and refine the draft questionnaire, especially in terms of providing appropriate response options.

Table 3.II. Response rate for the two pilot questionnaire surveys (includes some repeat entries: students enrolled in more than one language course were allowed to complete a survey for each language)

	Continuing			Discontinuing		
	Enrolled	Responded	%	Invited	Responded	%
Arabic	39	14	36	26	12	46
Chinese	51	30	59	34	9	26
French	85	37	44	52	11	21
German	13	7	54	34	11	32
Hindi	12	1	8	4	1	25
Indonesian	21	3	14	13	4	31
Italian	18	3	17	28	4	14
Japanese	121	50	41	53	12	23
Korean	11	2	18	7	0	-
Persian	5	2	40	3	2	67
Sanskrit	1	0	-	5	2	40
Spanish	69	4	6	45	11	24
Thai	6	6	100	5	5	100
Turkish	4	0	-	2	1	50
Urdu	5	0	-		0	-
Vietnamese	4	0	-	3	2	67
Other, or not specified		4			3	
TOTAL	465	163	35	314	91	29

Sources: ANU Statistical Unit 2008 Enrolment Data and Phase 1 Questionnaire Data.

Formal data collection began in June 2008. All students who had continued into the second year of their language study in 2008 (Continuers) and all students who had discontinued their language study in 2008 (Discontinuers) were invited to complete an online questionnaire. To reach Continuers, flyers were distributed in class by the relevant lecturers. To reach Discontinuers, the relevant language convener sent personal emails to those students identified in this category. As an incentive to participate in the survey, both groups of students were told that they could choose to provide contact details (which would be kept separate from their responses) to go into a draw for three prizes (an mp3 player worth $300 and two book vouchers worth $100 each). In total, 254 questionnaires were completed, 163 by Continuers and 91 by Discontinuers, representing at least 16 languages (Table 3.II).

The response rates for students from different L&C programs varied from 0 to 100 per cent. Although the total response rate for Discontinuers was notably good for surveys of this type, no more than 12 students responded from any one language. This left little room to explore possible differences between languages, and instead required that we combine responses from several languages for most analyses.

While the Phase 1 findings are presented in some detail in section 3.3, it is important to discuss them at this point specifically in terms of their impact on the Phase 2 methodology, and in particular, on the statistical analysis of the Phase 2 data.

3.2. Implications of the Phase 1 findings from a methodological perspective

In brief, the most striking feature of the Phase 1 data was the *lack* of difference between Continuers and Discontinuers across the range of learning and motivational dimensions that we explored. Both groups reported similar backgrounds in pre-existing language knowledge, similar social relationships with second language speakers/learners, similar reasons for enrolling in *ab initio* language study and similar experiences of that study.

Two key differences did, however, hint at the underlying complexities. First, Continuers were more likely than Discontinuers to be at an earlier stage of their degree, and to have language study as a compulsory part of that degree. Continuers were also more likely to rate extrinsic or instrumental reasons (employment, degree requirements, life/work in a country of that language), more important than intrinsic reasons (such as interest in specific history/culture of the target language, or of languages in general) in their decision to study the language. Second, although no one reason for discontinuing language study was regarded as important by more than half the Discontinuers, some reasons were more common than others, and students' decisions to discontinue appeared to be characterised by a cumulative combination of reasons rather than one or two reasons alone. Moreover, almost all the most common reasons given for discontinuing were related, and correlated, to what can be summarised as 'performing unexpectedly poorly in the course'. At first glance, these findings appeared intuitively understandable: students who had poor experiences associated with their learning performance in a Beginner language course and no extrinsic reasons to continue were more likely to give up. However, the breadth and depth of the Phase 1 data allowed us to investigate the detail, and show that the 'obvious' was not so.

When we considered the quality of learning experiences and learning outcomes in more depth, we found that Discontinuers and Continuers reported *equivalent* experiences of teaching and learning, and *equivalent* learning outcomes from their Beginner course. What were we to make of this apparent paradox? One possible explanation was that students were influenced not so much by their reasons for *discontinuing* but rather by their reasons for *continuing*: that is, all students may experience similar pressures to discontinue, but some experience more pressures to continue. Evidence for this viewpoint included our finding of a higher proportion of compulsory language study amongst Continuers, and the greater importance ascribed to instrumental reasons for language study by Continuers (as previously described).

Overall, then, the Phase 1 study raised more questions than it provided answers, and showed the deep complexity underlying the deceptively simple concepts of attrition and retention. Although we had learned much about students' backgrounds and motivations in general, our exhaustive exploration of the Phase 1 data with conventional statistical techniques showed virtually no significant differences between students who decided to continue with L&C studies and those who did not. It thus became obvious that for us to feel confident that we understood why students discontinued L&C programs at ANU, and what we could do about it, not only did we need more data, and not restricted to students who have completed a Beginner L&C course only, to increase sample sizes, but we also needed a much more sophisticated way of analysing and interpreting that data.

3.3. Beyond the dichotomy: Moving towards more effective statistical analyses

Our Phase 1 study had been based on the assumption that there would be clear differences between students who continued their L&C studies and those who did not. So when our use of conventional statistical techniques failed to identify clear characteristic differences between Continuers and Discontinuers, we decided to explore the data beyond that basic dichotomy. Considering the respondents as a whole, one additional discriminatory characteristic available to us was the qualitative description of the students' reasons for continuing or discontinuing their language studies. We used this data to devise a new classification based on students' commitment to language study, and their circumstances. Initially, we used a cross-tabulation of commitment to language studies and the Continuer/Discontinuer dichotomy (Table 3.III) to derive four new categories, which we labelled Committed Students (committed Continuers), Doubters (less committed Continuers), Reluctant Quitters (committed Discontinuers) and Voluntary Quitters (less committed Discontinuers).

Table 3.III. Classification of students' commitment to language study

Commitment to language studies	Continuing Students	Discontinuing Students
High	**Committed Students** Did not think of discontinuing and continued	**Reluctant Quitters** Had no choice but to discontinue (wanted to continue)
Low	**Doubters** Thought of discontinuing but continued (or had to continue)	**Voluntary Quitters** Discontinued (Thought of discontinuing and had discontinued)

Source: Extrapolated from an analysis of Phase 1 Questionnaire Data.

Our exploration of the data grouped in this way certainly showed important differences among the four groups, but also, somewhat surprisingly, demonstrated unexpected similarities between some subgroups.

3. SPLITTING THE MASSES

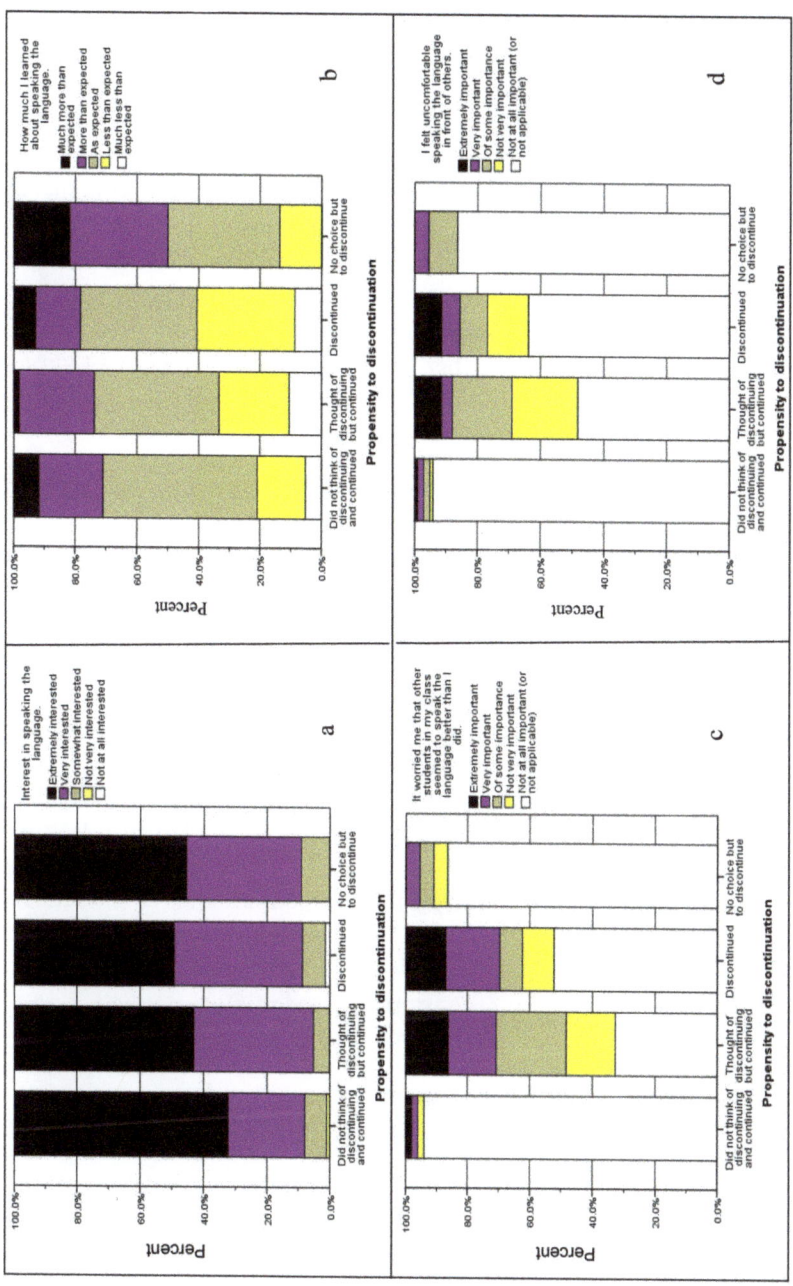

Figure 3.1. The issue of learning to speak the language
Source: Phase 1 Questionnaire Data.

To illustrate this, we will look at the data related to a topic that will be discussed later, namely the issue of learning to speak the language (Figure 3.1). When exploring the answers for the four groups, we found that all four groups showed a very strong interest in acquiring spoken language (Figure 3.1.a). However, the two groups characterised as Committed Students (did not think of discontinuing) and Reluctant Quitters (had no choice but to discontinue) reported that they had learned more spoken language than they had expected in their courses, while the Doubters (thought of discontinuing but continued) and Voluntary Quitters (discontinued voluntarily) reported that they had learned less of the spoken language than they had expected, and less than the other two groups (Figure 3.1.b). These subgroups belonged to different categories in our dichotomous Continuing/Discontinuing analysis.

These results suggested another hypothesis, namely that an important factor influencing students to abandon their L&C study might be their failure to achieve their learning expectations in terms of *spoken* language. This hypothesis was supported by the finding that Doubters and Voluntary Quitters were more likely (than Committed Students and Reluctant Quitters) to identify two additional reasons that reflected language anxiety: 'worrying that other students seem to speak better' and 'feeling uncomfortable to speak the language in front of others' (Figures 3.1.c and 3.1.d). At this point in analyses of the Phase 1 data, it became clear that the lack of statistically significant differences between Continuers (comprising the Committed Student and Doubter subgroups) and Discontinuers (comprising the Voluntary Quitters and Reluctant Quitters subgroups) might be a consequence of the internal diversity and spread within the Continuer and Discontinuer groups. To examine this possibility more fully, we decided to explore the data set in greater detail with other statistical techniques.

Table 3.IV. Chi-square analysis of variables in Figure 3.1 according to two different groupings of students

Question	Continuing / Discontinuing	4 groups
Interest in speaking the language	5.756	10.632
How much I learned about speaking the language	4.908	14.315*
I felt uncomfortable speaking the language in front of others	3.201	54.635**
It worried me that other students in my class seemed to speak the language better than I did	5.928	84.302**

* significant at the 0.05 level **significant at the 0.001 level
Source: Phase 1 Questionnaire Data.

Conventional statistical analyses had not identified many significant differences between Continuing and Discontinuing students. For example, there were no statistically significant values coming from Chi-square analysis of cross-tabulated variables (from Figure 3.1.a–d) with the traditional Continuing/Discontinuing dichotomy (Table 3.IV, column 2), whereas the four group classification proposed in Table 3.III (Table 3.IV, column 3) did show significant differences among groups for variables such as 'It worried me that other students in my class seemed to speak the language better than I did' or 'I felt uncomfortable about speaking the language in front of others'. This motivated us to explore retention and attrition with a more detailed classification of students than the initially proposed Continuer/Discontinuer dichotomy.

Given the complexity of the Phase 1 data, we were particularly keen to apply a data reduction statistical technique called Discriminant Analysis (Keckla, 1980), which allows researchers to examine the combination of predictors that best separate the groups with regard to a specific dependent variable. (More details provided in section 3.4.3). In our case, we trialled the use of the variable related to relative commitment (propensity to discontinue) that is, the variable that gave rise to the four groups of students described above (Table 3.III). Unfortunately, the Phase 1 data did *not* meet the basic assumption of the statistical procedure. Nevertheless, we now recognised a way in which to discriminate usefully among groups of respondents beyond the Continuer/Discontinuer dichotomy: with the much larger data set to be collected in Phase 2, we potentially had a more effective statistical tool to help us explore attrition and retention in more depth.

3.4. Phase 2 methodology

3.4.1. The Phase 2 data collection instruments

Like Phase 1, Phase 2 was aimed at investigating retention and attrition in L&C programs at ANU and placing the results in the broader context of all Australian universities. Building on the Phase 1 questionnaire, three Phase 2 questionnaires were developed and implemented using the same ANU Apollo© online survey software. The three versions of the questionnaire (Appendices) were respectively administered to:

1. students who were enrolled in Beginner courses in 2009 (110 questions; Group 1)
2. students who were enrolled in post-Beginner courses that is, Intermediate or Advanced in 2009 (125 questions; Group 2)
3. students who had been enrolled in at least one L&C course in 2008, and had since discontinued (111 questions; Group 3).

The questionnaires for Groups 1 and 3 each had four groups of questions:

1. background information (basic academic and demographic characteristics)
2. reasons for studying the language
3. experience of language study
4. reasons for discontinuing or deferring language study, or thinking about discontinuing.

The questionnaire for Group 2 students (Continuers) had an additional section on 'reasons for continuing'. Again, the questions were mostly close-ended (predetermined answers) but some had options for further details. Most questions required answers on a five-point scale (i.e. 'not at all important'; 'not very important'; 'of some importance'; 'very important', and 'extremely important').

There were two important differences between the Phase 1 and Phase 2 questionnaires. First, while Phase 1 questionnaires were limited to students who had completed a Beginner level course in the previous year, Phase 2 questionnaires were aimed at all students studying languages at ANU, to look holistically at the complex phenomenon, that is, to include students who enter or discontinue L&C studies at different levels (as explored in sections 2.2 and 2.6). Second, the Phase 2 questionnaire included additional questions to allow easier identification of the four subgroups identified in the analysis of the Phase 1 data (where the difference between Reluctant Quitters and Voluntary Quitters was gathered from answers to open-ended questions).

3.4.2. Target respondents, data collection and response rates

The target students for Phase 2 were those enrolled in a Beginner or later year ANU L&C course in Semester 1, 2009 (as at 31 March, the census date for the Australian Government's Higher Education Contribution Scheme), as well as those who had been enrolled in an ANU L&C course in Semester 1, 2008 at any level, but who had subsequently discontinued their L&C enrolment. To identify the Phase 2 sample, we obtained ANU Student Administration Office records of all students enrolled in any language course in 2008 and 2009.

According to these records, 854 students were enrolled in Beginner level language courses in 2009, and 1,354 were enrolled as continuing students in Intermediate and subsequent courses. This group of 2,208 students was considered the Phase 2 sampling universe (indicating the number of enrolments for all L&C courses, rather than the precise number of students, as some students were enrolled in more than one course). From the same records, we identified 1,033 students as having discontinued L&C studies in 2009 (that is, they had been enrolled in at least one L&C course in 2008 but were not enrolled in an L&C course in 2009). As we could not confirm the number of students who discontinued their study in each language course, we took the total number of discontinued students as our sampling universe.

The Phase 2 data were collected online (again using the Apollo© web-based interface) between May and September 2009. As required by our approved ANU Human Research Ethics Protocol, full information was given with the survey instrument about the objectives of the survey, the confidentiality of the personal information provided, and the time frame. Having had success obtaining good response rates in Phase 1 by using mp3 devices and book vouchers as participation incentives, we again used these incentives in Phase 2. Continuing respondents were recruited via in-class announcements, supported by postings on individual course sites within the ANU Learning Management System. Reminder emails were sent to students' ANU email addresses. Where possible, students were given time to complete the questionnaires during a scheduled class in a classroom with IT facilities. All students who had discontinued L&C studies, as indicated by university records and manual comparisons of 2008 and 2009 enrolment lists, and who had a valid ANU email address recorded by Student Administration, were emailed and offered the opportunity to participate in the online survey. To augment this approach, we also encouraged students enrolled in L&C studies in 2009 to contact known student peers who had discontinued L&C studies.

For ethical and privacy reasons, we could only attempt to contact discontinued students via extant ANU email addresses (not personal email addresses). As we do not know what proportion of students who graduate or leave the university before completing their studies are likely to check their ANU emails, one frustration in this kind of research is that we must assume that all non-respondents have chosen not to respond (and thus include them in calculating response rates), whereas it is more likely that many students who have discontinued studies at a university (whether because they have graduated or because they have left the university before completion) no longer check their university email addresses and therefore have effectively never received the invitation to participate. Unfortunately, we have no means of even estimating the proportion of our contacted sample for whom this was the case. Our calculated response rates should therefore be considered minima rather than accurate values.

Of the 2,208 enrolled students that we invited to participate in the Phase 2 survey, 1,283 responded, across a range of L&C programs (Table 3.V), comprising:

- 432 students enrolled in a Beginner level course (51 per cent of all enrolled students)
- 520 students enrolled in a more advanced course (38 per cent of all enrolled students)
- 321 students who had been enrolled in a language course in the previous year (2008), but had since discontinued their language study (31 per cent of all enrolled students).[1]

A total of 38 responses were excluded from the data set because they were invalid or incomplete. Courses in the Classics program, which did not participate in Phase 1 of the study, did participate in Phase 2.

---

1   These are not shown in Table 3.V because we can only calculate the response rate for the whole group and not for individual languages.

Table 3.V. Response rate of individual languages discriminated by level— Full ANU study sample. Students enrolled in 2009

Language	Beginner Students			Post-Beginner Students 2009		
	Enrolled 2009	Responded	% Response	Enrolled 2009	Responded	% Response
Ancient Greek	8	6	75.0	23	20	87.0
Arabic	47	18	38.3	84	34	40.5
Chinese	102	65	63.7	237	84	35.4
Classics	37	8	21.6	23	2	8.7
French	172	82	47.7	221	100	45.2
German	57	47	82.5	89	36	40.4
Hindi	10	1	10.0	20	4	20.0
Indonesian	34	11	32.4	56	25	44.6
Italian	36	20	55.6	49	17	34.7
Japanese	190	32	16.8	241	62	25.7
Korean	15	15	100.0	31	9	29.0
Latin	14	12	85.7	24	17	70.8
Persian	7	5	71.4	15	4	26.7
Sanskrit	9	3	33.3	10	1	10.0
Spanish	103	93	90.3	196	95	48.5
Thai	13	12	92.3	18	1	5.6
Others	8	8	100	40	29	72.5
Total	854	432	50.6	1,354	520	38.4

Sources: ANU Statistical Unit 2008 Enrolment Data and Phase 2 Questionnaire Data.

3.4.3. Phase 2 data analysis

When the online surveys were completed, responses were downloaded in SPSS® format for recoding and analysis. Existing variables were recoded and some new variables computed to suit the planned data exploration. We merged the data from two of the surveys—the second or later year continuing students in 2009 and the discontinued students—as these students comprised our interest group. Realising that we would indeed need to move beyond the basic dichotomy of Continuer/Discontinuer, as we had foreseen from our experience with the Phase 1 data, we revisited the categorisation of students into four groups through the use of a dependent variable that indicated the propensity to discontinue (as explained in section 3.3). In contrast to the manual classification undertaken in Phase 1, in Phase 2 this variable was calculated from three direct survey variables—namely the student's present status (Continuer or Discontinuer), the reason for discontinuing (for Discontinuers), and whether the student reported having seriously thought about discontinuing. This classification, essentially based on each student's 'commitment' to language study and their personal circumstances (Table 3.III), created the same variable with four categories that we used in the exploration of Phase 1 data:

- Committed Students (those who had continued L&C studies and had not thought of discontinuing)
- Doubters (those who had thought about discontinuing but had decided to continue)
- Voluntary Quitters (those who wanted to discontinue and had done so)
- Reluctant Quitters (those who reported wanting to continue but had actually discontinued).

However, although the new variable (propensity to discontinue) allowed for the classification of all students, we found that there were too few cases in the Reluctant Quitters for the relevant analyses to be carried out. This was the outcome, we believe, of the great difficulty in contacting students who are no longer members of an enrolled class, and may even have left the university, as discussed previously. As a result, we felt compelled to combine the Reluctant Quitters with the Voluntary Quitters into a new collective category called simply Quitters (i.e. those who had discontinued L&C studies, the old Discontinuers category). The classification of students for the analysis, then, corresponded to the distribution in Table 3.VI.

Table 3.VI. Reclassification of students' commitment to language study—Full ANU study sample

Commitment to language studies	Continuing Students	Discontinuing Students
High	**Committed Students** Did not think of discontinuing and continued	**Quitters** Discontinued. Include both: 1. Wanted to continue, but had had no choice but to discontinue (Reluctant Quitters) and 2. Thought of discontinuing and had discontinued (Voluntary Quitters)
Low	**Doubters** Thought of discontinuing but continued (or had to continue)	

Source: Extrapolated from an analysis of Phase 2 Questionnaire Data.

As with Phase 1, we first used conventional statistical methods to investigate the possibility of significant differences between characteristics and responses of Continuers and Discontinuers. Although the larger sample size did allow us to find more differences between the groups than we had in Phase 1, we still could not discover any reliable way of clearly differentiating the two groups. We also used factor analysis to try to find a bottom-up classification of the variables that described reasons for discontinuing L&C studies (reported in Jansen and Schmidt 2011). This factor analysis focused on a sub-sample of the Phase 2 data that pertained to reasons for 'discontinuing' and 'thinking about discontinuing'. The sample comprised 671 students who had either discontinued their language studies, or declared that they had seriously considered discontinuing. The two groups were combined when a statistical comparison confirmed that they were very closely related. Analysis identified four underlying factors, weighted fairly equally, which could be summarised as follows: 'having difficulties with language learning' (factor 1); 'negative learning experiences, often contrary to expectation' (factor 2); 'practical, external reasons' (factor 3); and 'affective reasons' (factor 4).

Although the results were useful for other purposes, as we will see in Chapter 4, the student classification issue was not illuminated further with this procedure when the continuing/discontinuing dichotomy was used to explore the results. However, when we used the three group classification that corresponded to Table 3.VI, we found no less than 49 variables that showed significant differences among the three groups, and 24 additional variables that showed significant differences between subgroups. Traditional data analysis would have stopped here, postulated that the three-way classification of students should be the basis of analysis, and carried out a detailed analysis of the differences between the groupings based on the rankings of the variables that had shown significant differences between the groups. To have done this, however, would have overlooked the implication that what these significant differences show is the individual relationship of a particular variable with the variable that classifies student's commitment to language studies, without taking into consideration the overall relationship of all the variables that describe the sample. To justify more conclusively that this classification of students should be the basis of analysis, and to understand the phenomena in all their complexity, we again tried using the data reduction statistical technique of Discriminant Analysis (Keckla, 1980), which had been tested unsuccessfully with the Phase 1 data (see above, section 3.3).

3.4.4. Applying Discriminant Analysis to the Phase 2 data

Discriminant Analysis is the traditional data analysis method that allows researchers to examine the combination of predictors that best separate the groups under examination with respect to the dependent variable (Tabachnick and Fidell, 2005, 2.1.3.6). A Discriminant Function Analysis was used to explore the Phase 2 sample according to the three group classification of Committed Students, Doubters and Quitters (corresponding to Table 3.VI). The main aim was to ascertain the validity of using this three-way classification, which we named as the dependent variable 'propensity to discontinue'. Unlike factor analysis, where the aim is to explain the distribution of data based on a group of variables, Functional Canonical Analysis (FCA) postulates that there is a dependent variable (in this case the 'propensity to discontinue' variable), that explains the behaviour of the independent variables (in this case, all the responses to other survey questions). Like factor analysis, however, FCA uses the results of the analysis to suggest which factors or variables differentiate between the cases (in this case why some people have more or less propensity to discontinue language courses).

A total of 106 independent variables associated with the 'propensity to discontinue' dependent variable were suitable to be considered into the model. Based on the Analysis of Variance (ANOVA) function output, the model determined 79 variables significant in the analysis (with significance based on the Wilks's Lambda value, such that the smaller the Wilks's Lambda, the more important the independent variable to the discriminant function: Stevens, 2002, 287–289). Hence, only the variables with significant Wilks's Lambda values were considered for the final Discriminant Function Analysis. All remaining variables were dropped from the analysis, although we made an exception for the variable that classified gender and included it in the final model, because it is a variable traditionally associated with language proficiency, and was already linked to differences in our calculations of retention rates (Chapter 2, section 2.6). Hence, we ran the next step of the Discriminant Analysis with 80 variables.

Before the FCA test could be used, however, we needed to test two requisite assumptions—the homogeneity of covariance matrices, and multivariate normality—by running Box's M Test of equality of covariance matrices. In the case of the sample from the second survey, the Box's M Test of equality of covariance matrices proved to be not significant (with Box's M significance p>0.05), so we concluded that the three groups do not differ in their covariance matrices, which is the assumption we needed to run the Discriminant Analysis.

Table 3.VII.a. Discriminant Function. Eigenvalues

Function	Eigenvalue	% of Variance	Cumulative %	Canonical Correlation
1	11.514[a]	85	85	0.959
2	2.030[a]	15	100	0.819

a. First 2 canonical discriminant functions were used in the analysis.

Table 3.VII.b. Discriminant Function. Wilks's Lambda

Test of Function(s)	Wilks's Lambda	Chi-square	Df	Sig.
1 through 2	0.026	2835.61	46	0.000
2	0.33	864.688	22	0.000

Source: Discriminant Analysis of Phase 2 Questionnaire Data.

On computing a Discriminant Function, we noted that the dependent variable, propensity to discontinuation, has three groups, so the number of discriminant functions computed is two (Table 3.VII.a). The eigenvalues show how much of the variance in the dependent variable is accounted for by each of the functions. Wilks's Lambda shows each function is significant (Table 3.VII.b). The structure matrix (Table 3.VIII) shows the correlations of each significant variable with each discriminant function. The variables are ranked by their contribution to the first axis, the one which accounts for more variance. The correlations serve like factor loadings in factor analysis—that is, by identifying the largest absolute correlations associated with each discriminant function it is possible to gain insight into which variables are the most representative using the stepwise method of Discriminant Analysis, and to further select a smaller set of variables that allow to explain how people are classified by the two functions (Tables 3.IX.a and 3.IX.b). The standardised Discriminant Function coefficients in these two tables serve the same purpose as beta weights in multiple regressions: they indicate the relative importance of the independent variables in predicting the dependent. The standardised Discriminant Function coefficients were used to assess each independent variable's unique contribution to the discriminant function (Keckla, 1980, 52–58). The two key tables (Tables 3.IX.a and 3.IX.b) show the same 23 variables identified as contributing more weight to the variance of each axis in the structure matrix: in Table 3.IX.a, the variables are ranked by the first discriminant function, while in Table 3.IX.b the variables are ranked by the second discriminant function.

Table 3.VIII. Structure Matrix—Significant Variables—Full ANU study sample

	Function		Rank of Variables in	
Variables	F1	F2	Func 1	Func 2
I enjoy learning the language.	.732*	.088	1	42
I think knowing more than one language is important.	.657*	.171	2	26
I feel I am progressing well with the language.	.515*	-.100	3	36
I get good marks/grades.	.477*	-.050	4	52
I like the learning materials.	.473*	-.049	5	53
I like the way it is taught.	.472*	-.049	6	54
The workload is manageable.	.445*	-.058	7	48
It would be a shame to give up at this stage.	.367*	.210	8	23
I find the language easy to learn.	.348*	-.028	9	61
My family keeps encouraging me to study the language.	.281*	-.011	10	75

3. SPLITTING THE MASSES

Variables	Function		Rank of Variables in	
	F1	F2	Func 1	Func 2
I need to use the language in my work.	.244*	.016	11	70
My friends have also continued learning the language.	.216*	-.027	12	63
No better study alternatives are available.	.191*	.083	13	43
Other study commitments.	-.171	.335*	14	17
People are discouraging me from continuing language study.	-.168	.353*	15	15
Timetable clash.	-.127	.213*	16	22
I feel uncomfortable speaking the language in front of others.	-.123	.413*	17	10
I don't like the way the language is being taught.	-.122	.423*	18	9
I'm finding the workload too high.	-.116	.560*	19	1
I'm not enjoying the course content.	-.113	.488*	20	5
My expectations are not being met.	-.111	.403*	21	12
I'm not satisfied with my progress.	-.110	.504*	22	4
To participate in cultural activities of the language group.	.109*	-.064	23	45
To help me in my other studies.	.104*	.031	24	59
Paid work commitments.	-.099	.301*	25	18
Teaching/learning materials (including the textbook).	.099*	-.099	26	37
I'm not getting good marks/grades.	-.098	.440*	27	7
Not enough class time is spent on speaking the language.	-.098	.446*	28	6
I fell behind in my studies and can't catch up.	-.097	.384*	29	13
I'm interested in the history and culture of the language.	.094*	-.017	30	68
I'm finding the course too difficult.	-.094	.507*	31	3
I didn't think I would get to use the language outside university.	-.091	.345*	32	16
How interested were you in writing the language?	.078*	-.034	33	57
I'm thinking of terminating all of my studies.	-.078	.178*	34	25
Because of the reputation of this language at ANU.	.075*	-.068	35	44
My family encouraged me to study it.	.073*	-.014	36	74
Financial reasons.	-.069	.196*	37	24
It worries me that other students seem to speak better than I do.	-.065	.432*	38	8

	Function		Rank of Variables in	
Variables	F1	F2	Func 1	Func 2
To understand people and cultures outside of my own.	.065*	.016	39	71
How well I learned to write the language.	.063*	-.046	40	55
Sex of students.	-.062*	-.009	41	77
Number of language courses studied.	.060*	.015	42	72
Experience of previous language learning.	.059	-.113*	43	32
Class sizes are too big.	-.058	.406*	44	11
I do not fit in with other students in the course.	-.057	.365*	45	14
For employment reasons.	.053*	.019	46	66
Age of respondents.	-.052*	.006	47	78
How interested were you in reading the language.	.046*	-.028	48	62
Because I had previously studied the language.	.045*	-.016	49	69
Enjoyment of language learning.	.044	-.094*	50	39
I thought it would be an easy subject.	-.042*	.010	51	76
Family commitments.	-.040	.296*	52	19
To live or work in a country where this language is spoken.	.036*	-.022	53	65
I enjoy language learning.	.036	-.111*	54	33
Learning environment and facilities.	.034	-.126*	55	28
Problems with daily travel.	-.034	.254*	56	20
Support from fellow students.	.032	-.103*	57	35
Teachers' teaching skills.	.029	-.121*	58	31
Approachability and availability of teachers.	.024	-.090*	59	41
My friends are discontinuing.	-.021	.544*	60	2
What languages do you speak with your relative?	.021	-.024*	61	64
To communicate with native speakers of the language.	.019	-.063*	62	47
Workload associated with learning to write the language.	.018	.096*	63	38
How well I learned to read the language.	.015*	-.002	64	79
How well I learned to understand other speakers.	-.015	-.109*	65	34
Index of family knowledge of languages.	.014	-.045*	66	56
How much freedom did you have to choose whether or not you study a language as part of your degree?	-.014	-.018*	67	67

3. SPLITTING THE MASSES

	Function		Rank of Variables in	
Variables	F1	F2	Func 1	Func 2
To travel to where this language is spoken.	.014	-.033*	68	58
I have a family background in this language.	-.014	-.030*	69	60
Because I have previously spent time in a country where the language is spoken.	-.012	-.064*	70	46
How much I learned about the culture of the language.	.011	-.053*	71	50
To complete my degree.	.009	.054*	72	49
Index of extended family knowledge of languages.	.009	-.015*	73	73
How well I learned to speak the language.	.009	-.126*	74	29
Overall difficulty of the course.	.009	.152*	75	27
Advice and feedback from teachers.	.008	-.125*	76	30
Health reasons.	-.006	.243*	77	21
My friends are studying this language.	.005	.052*	78	51
Does your degree require compulsory language study?	-.001*	.000	79	80
Difficulty learning the grammar in particular.	.001	.094*	80	40

Source: Discriminant Analysis of Phase 2 Questionnaire Data.
*Largest absolute correlation between each variable and any discriminant function.

Before exploring how well the discriminant function works for the Phase 2 sample, it is important to consider the graphical representation of the Canonical Discriminant Functions (Figure 3.2). Here we can see how the whole sample is distributed in the two-dimensional space by plotting each respondent score in the space created by the two functions. Figure 3.2.a shows the plotting of the three groups under analysis together. Figure 3.2.b plots those students who reported that they seriously thought of discontinuing L&C studies, but continued (Doubters). Figure 3.2.c plots those students who discontinued L&C studies (Quitters). Figure 3.2.d plots those students who did not think of discontinuing L&C studies (Committed Students).

Table 3.IX.a. Standardised Canonical Discriminant Function Coefficients (ranked by Function 1)

Variables	Function 1	Function 2	Rank of Variables in Func 1	Rank of Variables in Func 2
I think knowing more than one language is important.	.459	.166	1	13
I enjoy learning the language.	.457	.300	2	3
People are discouraging me from continuing language study.	-.274	.393	3	1
No better study alternatives are available.	.265	.082	4	20
I get good marks/grades.	.156	-.118	5	16
It would be a shame to give up at this stage.	.139	.225	6	6
Other study commitments.	-.139	.174	7	11
Paid work commitments.	-.130	-.010	8	23
I enjoy language learning.	-.130	-.163	9	14
My friends are discontinuing.	.129	.290	10	4
For employment reasons.	-.121	.011	11	22
I like the learning materials.	.118	-.095	12	17
Timetable clash.	-.115	.049	13	21
Difficulty learning the grammar in particular.	.090	-.085	14	18
Enjoyment of language learning.	-.085	.082	15	19
I feel I am progressing well with the language.	.076	-.168	16	12
Not enough class time is spent on speaking the language.	-.071	.193	17	8
I didn't think I would get to use the language outside university.	-.049	.200	18	7
Age of respondents.	-.046	.149	19	15
To communicate with native speakers of the language.	-.045	-.186	20	10
I'm thinking of terminating all of my studies.	-.033	.263	21	5
I'm not enjoying the course content.	.013	.186	22	9
I'm finding the workload too high.	.009	.345	23	2

Table 3.IX.b. Standardised Canonical Discriminant Function Coefficients (ranked by Function 2)

Variables	Function 1	Function 2	Rank of Variables in Func 1	Rank of Variables in Func 2
People are discouraging me from continuing language study.	-.274	.393	3	1
I'm finding the workload too high.	.009	.345	23	2
I enjoy learning the language.	.457	.300	2	3
My friends are discontinuing.	.129	.290	10	4
I'm thinking of terminating all of my studies.	-.033	.263	21	5
It would be a shame to give up at this stage.	.139	.225	6	6
I didn't think I would get to use the language outside university.	-.049	.200	18	7
Not enough class time is spent on speaking the language.	-.071	.193	17	8
I'm not enjoying the course content.	.013	.186	22	9
To communicate with native speakers of the language.	-.045	-.186	20	10
Other study commitments.	-.139	.174	7	11
I feel I am progressing well with the language.	.076	-.168	16	12
I think knowing more than one language is important.	.459	.166	1	13
I enjoy language learning.	-.130	-.163	9	14
Age of respondents.	-.046	.149	19	15
I get good marks/grades.	.156	-.118	5	16
I like the learning materials.	.118	-.095	12	17
Difficulty learning the grammar in particular.	.090	-.085	14	18
Enjoyment of language learning.	-.085	.082	15	19
No better study alternatives are available.	.265	.082	4	20
Timetable clash.	-.115	.049	13	21
For employment reasons.	-.121	.011	11	22
Paid work commitments.	-.130	-.010	8	23

Source: Discriminant Analysis of Phase 2 Questionnaire Data.

It can be seen that the classification into three groups allows plotting respondents of the survey into three clearly defined clouds, as defined by the dependent variable (that is the three-way distinction between Quitters, Doubters and Committed Students). While the clouds for Committed Students and Quitters are relatively compact, and there is little spread of respondents' scores over the other categories, the cloud of Doubters is more dispersed in the plot, and also shows considerable more overlap with the other categories.

Table 3.X shows the Classification Results of a cross-validation classification of the three groups in the dependent variable. The cross-validation of scores for each case is used to assess how well the discriminant function works, and if it works equally well for each group of the dependent variable. Here it correctly classifies about 96 per cent of the cases, which validates using the three groups in the rest of the data analysis. However, the classification is not equally good for each of the groups. The Classification Results procedure correctly classifies all the Quitters (100 per cent), and almost all Committed Students (97.3 per cent), but only 86.7 per cent of the Doubters in the Canonical Discriminant Functions. This confirms what the observation of the plotting of scores (Figure 3.2) allowed us to predict, as it misclassifies some of the Doubters as Committed Students (7.6 per cent) and Quitters (5.7 per cent). This points to the need to characterise the Doubters in contrast to the other two categories with other techniques, something which we have carried out and report in detail in Chapter 5.

3. SPLITTING THE MASSES

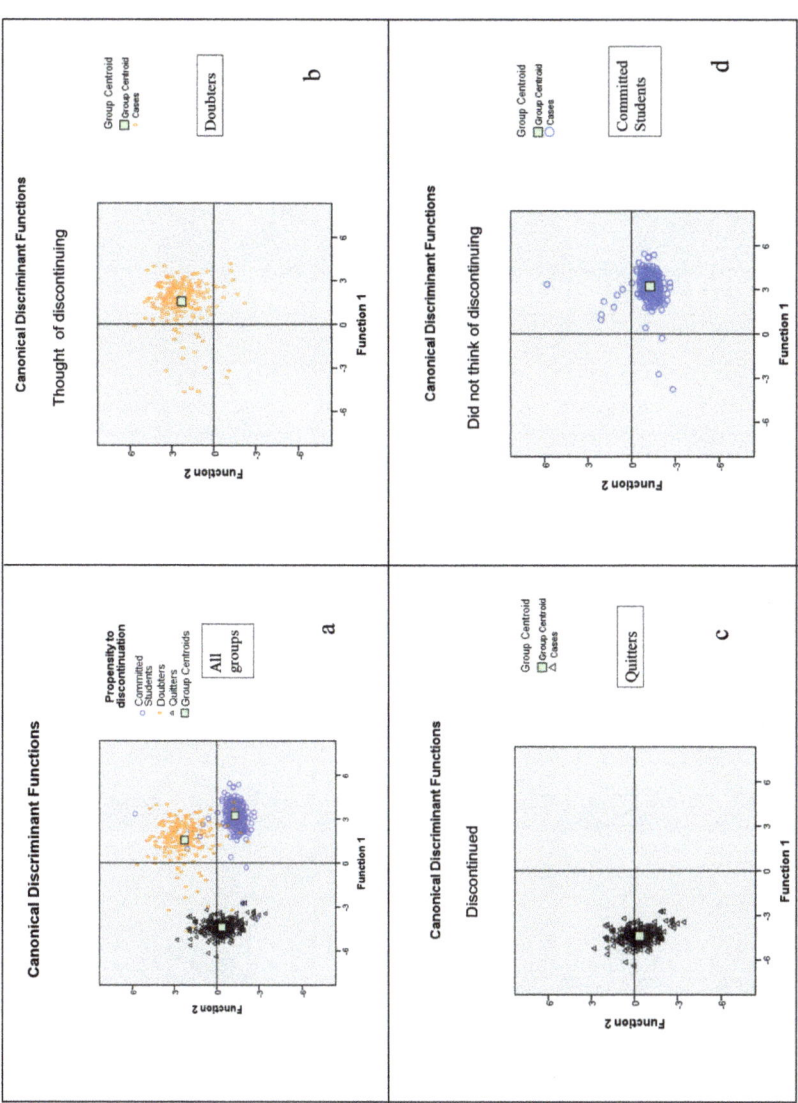

Figure 3.2. Graphical representation of the Canonical Discriminant Functions—Full ANU study sample
Source: Discriminant Analysis of Phase 2 Questionnaire Data.

THE DOUBTERS' DILEMMA

Table 3.X. Classification Results[b,c] for the Canonical Discriminant Functions

		Group membership	Values of the variable "Propensity to discontinuation"	Predicted Group Membership			Total
				Committed Students Did not think of discontinuing and continued	Doubters Thought of discontinuing but continued	Quitters Discontinued	
Original	Count	Committed Students	Did not think of discontinuing and continued	293	6	2	301
		Doubters	Thought of discontinuing but continued	14	186	10	210
		Quitters	Discontinued	0	0	297	297
	%	Committed Students	Did not think of discontinuing and continued	97.3	2.0	0.7	100.0
		Doubters	Thought of discontinuing but continued	6.7	88.6	4.8	100.0
		Quitters	Discontinued	0.0	0.0	100.0	100.0
Cross-validated[a]	Count	Committed Students	Did not think of discontinuing and continued	293	6	2	301
		Doubters	Thought of discontinuing but continued	16	182	12	210
		Quitters	Discontinued	0	0	297	297
	%	Committed Students	Did not think of discontinuing and continued	97.3	2.0	0.7	100
		Doubters	Thought of discontinuing but continued	7.6	86.7	5.7	100
		Quitters	Discontinued	0.0	0.0	100.0	100

a. Cross validation is done only for those cases in the analysis. In cross validation, each case is classified by the functions derived from all cases other than that case.
b. 96.0% of original grouped cases correctly classified.
c. 95.5% of cross-validated grouped cases correctly classified.
Source: Discriminant Analysis of Phase 2 Questionnaire Data.

Figure 3.2 and Tables 3.IX.a and 3.IX.b allow us also to propose a preliminary overall interpretation of the differences among the groups, based on the projection of the centroids of the clouds over each of the axes. Function 1 in Figure 3.2 orders the groups in the following sequence: Quitters, Doubters and Committed Students. An exploration of the positive and negative correlations in Table 3.IX.a allows for the uncontroversial and straightforward interpretation that Function 1 stands for commitment and ability to undertake L&C studies.

Function 2 in Figure 3.2 orders the groups in the following sequence: Committed Students, Quitters and Doubters. This function, as well as the ordering of variables in Table 3.IX.b, is more difficult to interpret. As we will explain in detail in Chapter 5, we propose that this function can be interpreted with a construct called 'Language Capital'. However, before doing this, we require a full characterisation of each of the groups of students.

3.5. Summary

In conclusion, the Discriminant Analysis performed on the full ANU sample indicated that the three groups in the dependent variable were maximally separated by 79 independent variables, of which 23 were more important than others in explaining the variance of each axis of the Discriminant Analysis plot (Figure 3.2). What the plot did not reveal, however, were the details needed to characterise inter-group differences between Committed Students, Quitters and Doubters in function 2, which is where Chapter 4 will take up the story, using individual variables that we reported as significant in this chapter.

4

Some Detective Work: Comparing Committed Students, Quitters and Doubters

4.1. Overview

The ANU case study has provided a great deal of univariate, bivariate and multivariate data. However, we believe that the primary contribution of this case study to the broader field of research on retention in L&C courses is in the detailed and robust characterisation of three groupings—which we view as archetypes—of L&C students, derived from the Canonical Discriminant Analysis of the data (as described in Chapter 3). In this chapter, we focus on detailing the characteristics of these archetypes—Committed Students, Doubters and Quitters—and explore how these groups differ from one another across a range of demographic, attitudinal and education variables. We also consider variables that distinguish between any two of the three groups in terms of students' motivations for continuing or discontinuing studying a language. This will allow us to show how we have understood the implications of these archetypal groupings of our L&C students at ANU—a finding we hope future research will confirm is generalisable across the sector. In Chapter 5, we will explain our hypothesis that the existence of these archetypes can best be understood in the context of a construct related to language capital as a form of social capital, but first we must explain in detail the salient characteristics of these three archetypes.

4.2. A detailed interpretation of the cross-tabulated variables that characterise Committed Students, Doubters and Quitters

In this section, we reconceptualise and extend the analysis reported by Martín and Jansen (2012) to present a thorough description of the cross-tabulated variables relevant in characterising the three groups of students identified in Chapter 3. To avoid extraneous detail, and having already shown that the variables are statistically significant in the Discriminant Analysis that identified the three groups, we will dispense with the need to re-establish the statistical significance of correlations of each individual variable with the variable that defines the three groups of students, as elaborated in Chapter 3, section 3.4.3.

The variables we consider in this section involve (1) general basic characteristics, such as the student's year of study, their age and nationality. Then we investigate (2) the degree of freedom in their studies; (3) their perceptions about being forced to study or discontinue a language; and (4) their reasons for studying a language. We then explore factors such as students' exposure to languages through (5) the language background of their family and peers, and (6) their own language learning. This is followed by students' (7) perceptions of difficulty of language study and sense of progress; (8) perceptions of workload with respect to the four basic language skills; and (9) perceptions of teachers and the learning environment. Finally we look at (10) the effects of students' grades/marks, and explore other factors that differentiate only pairs of the groups under analysis, namely reasons for continuing with language study (11), and reasons for discontinuing language study (12). The latter involve a re-analysis of the factors explored by Jansen and Schmidt (2011). In all cases, we have excluded 'not applicable' answers.[1]

For consistency and readability, in Figures 4.1 to 4.13 the three groups being characterised (Committed Students, Doubters and Quitters) in Table 3.VI are presented in the same order on the horizontal axis, with the names and values of the relevant variables in the upper right corner of each figure. The labels under the bars in the figures correspond to the

---

1 Except in Figure 4.6.a, where this is relevant.

values of the 'propensity to discontinuation' variable defined in Table 3.VI, as follows: Committed Students (did not think of discontinuing and continued), Doubters (thought of discontinuing but continued) and Quitters (discontinued). Percentages have been used instead of actual values to facilitate comparisons among the three groups. For each variable, or set of variables, we describe the contrast among the three groups, if any, and highlight prominent group characteristics. (In Chapter 5 we will summarise all the characteristics of these three student archetypes, first on the basis of the prominent characteristics, then on the basis of additional relevant characteristics that contribute to a fuller differentiation of the three groups. Readers who would prefer to understand the characterisation before seeing the detailed analyses may skip straight to Chapter 5.)

4.2.1. Student characteristics

As expected, those students who discontinued L&C studies (Quitters) are those who have been at ANU for longer (Figure 4.1.a). This implies that some of them have discontinued L&C studies because they have completed their language major or have completed their studies altogether: the category 'fourth year or later year (including postgraduate)' shown in black in Figure 4.1.a thus includes those who have completed their ANU degree and answered the questionnaire. We also include here those students who discontinued because their degree does not allow for many electives, as usually electives are not always available in the early years, and those who attended just one or two L&C courses near the end of their degree (identified as 'Late Starters'), who would also be included as Quitters. A similar situation is found in the case of students' age (Figure 4.1.b): those who have discontinued L&C studies are older than those who have continued.

THE DOUBTERS' DILEMMA

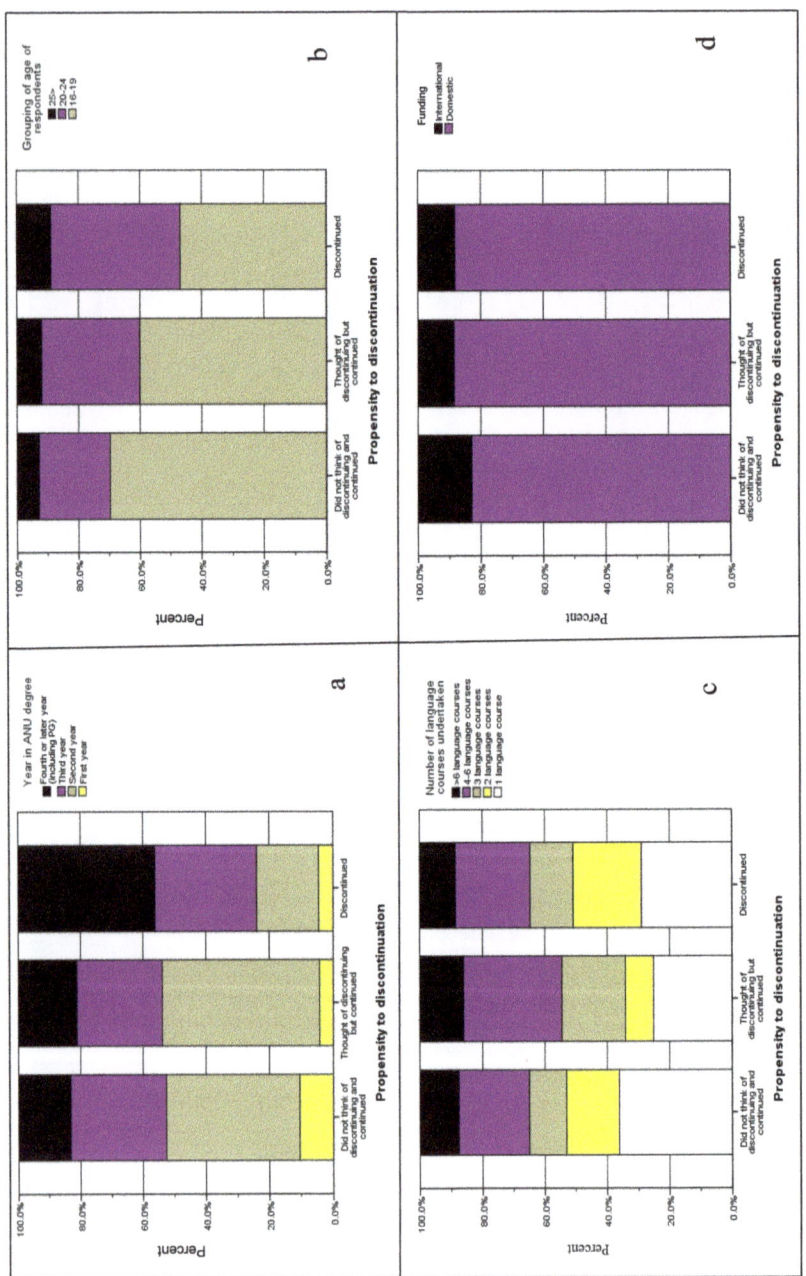

Figure 4.1. Basic characteristics—Student characteristics
Source: Phase 2 Questionnaire Data.

Figure 4.1.c tells an interesting story. The group of Doubters (i.e. those students who have doubts about continuing their language study) includes a larger proportion of students who have completed three or more language courses than the other two groups. This shows that retention is not only an issue for Beginner students. There is a large proportion of students who doubt whether they will continue L&C studies at the stage when they have to decide whether or not to complete the L&C major, or, if they have already completed a major, to complete extra courses out of interest, or to qualify for Honours. Notably, there is a large proportion of students who had only completed one course at the time of the data collection among the Committed Students (Figure 4.1.c), with some 40 per cent of those that quit having completed more than four L&C courses. This confirms our characterisation of the Quitters described above, namely that some simply discontinued because they could not study languages any longer because the degree did not allow them to do so or they had completed the degree (Reluctant Quitters). In addition, we note that there is a higher proportion of international students among the Committed Students than among the Quitters and Doubters (Figure 4.1.d).

4.2.2. Freedom to study languages

In general, students who have less compulsion to study languages quit more frequently, although some 35 per cent of Quitters discontinued even though they were enrolled in degrees which require compulsory language study (Figure 4.2.a). This could suggest that some students began to study more than one language towards a major and later discontinued studying one of them, or that they changed degrees to avoid compulsory L&C studies, or that they chose different majors within degrees with less strict language compulsion. (In relation to the latter, there were at the time 'escape routes' for students studying the BA International Relations, allowing them to substitute a language major for an international communication major, the latter only requiring four language courses plus linguistic courses.)

THE DOUBTERS' DILEMMA

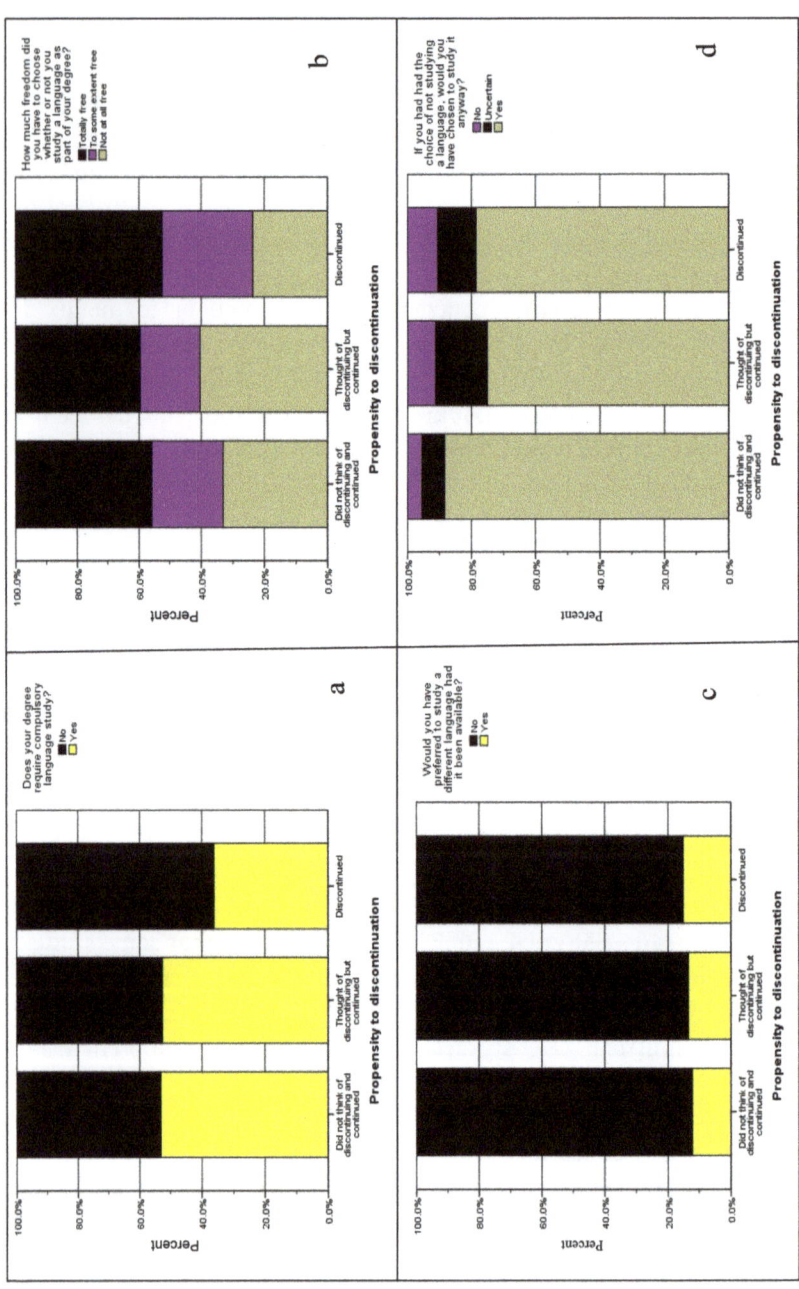

Figure 4.2. Basic characteristics—Freedom to study languages
Source: Phase 2 Questionnaire Data.

Figure 4.2.b shows that the proportion of those who are, to some extent or entirely, free to study a language or not is highest among the Quitters, and lowest among the Doubters, with the latter reporting the highest proportion. The lack of availability of the language that students really wanted to study appears not to have been an issue for any of the groups, even though the figure is slightly higher for the Quitters (Figure 4.2.c): this is not surprising given that ANU teaches the greatest diversity of languages of any Australian university (Nettelbeck et al., 2007; Dunne and Pavlyshyn, 2012).

Students were asked whether they would have studied a language even if they had had the choice of not studying one. The difference between Committed Students and the other two groups is clear, with some 90 per cent of the Committed Students reporting that they would have studied a language anyway as opposed to around 75 per cent in the other two groups (Figure 4.2.d). The Doubters are those who proportionally report most often that they would not have studied it, or are uncertain.

4.2.3. Perceptions of being compelled to study, or to discontinue studying, a language

Figure 4.3 reports students' perceptions of being compelled or forced to study a language or to discontinue it. When the question is asked in general, that is, when students are asked if there is anything that requires them to study a language, there are no big differences between the groups, although Doubters express more uncertainty about the question (Figure 4.3.a). There are not big differences either in the proportion of each of the groups reporting that they are studying more than one language (Figure 4.3.b). However, when a question is asked about the importance of being discouraged to study a language, it is clear that for Committed Students this is not very important, but that it is for Doubters, and even more so for Quitters (Figure 4.3.c). Quitters are also most likely to report that other study commitments are more important (Figure 4.3.d).

THE DOUBTERS' DILEMMA

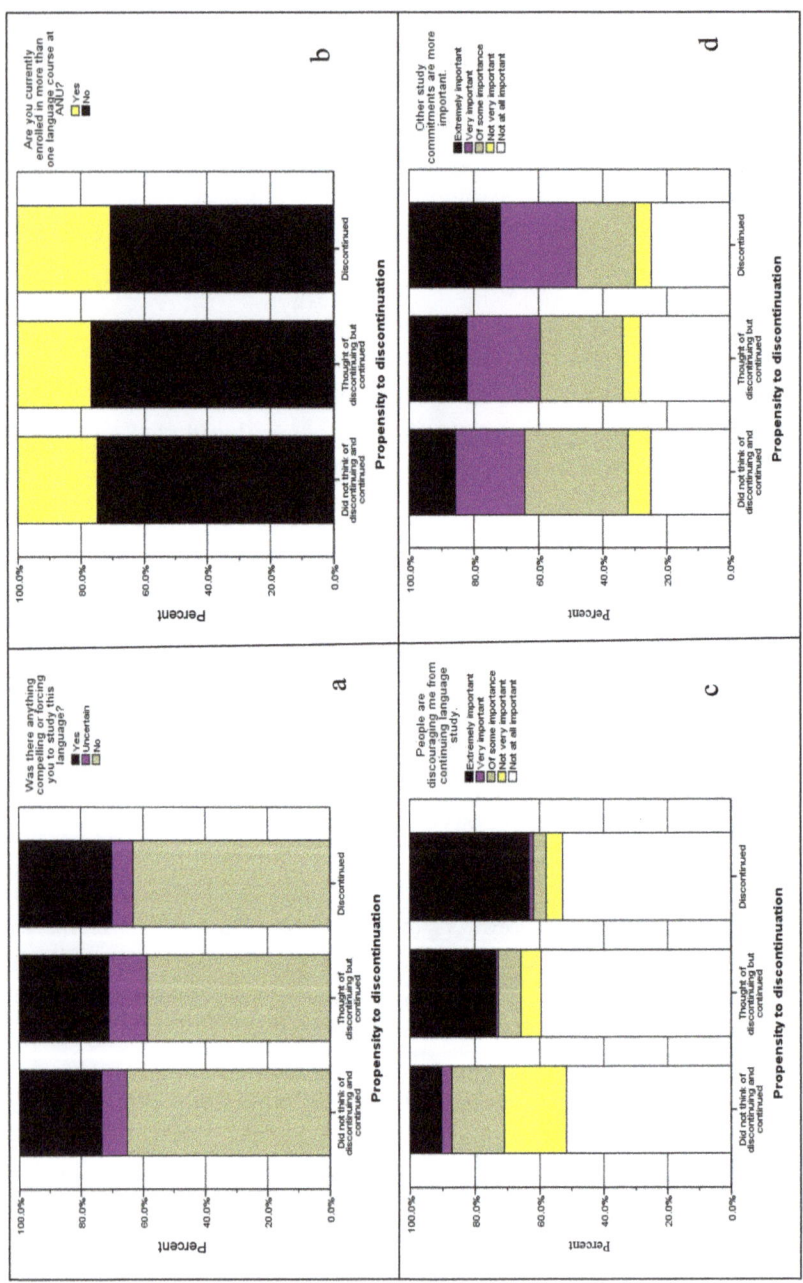

Figure 4.3. Basic characteristics—Perceptions of being forced to study or to discontinue studying a language

Source: Phase 2 Questionnaire Data.

4.2.4. Reasons for studying the language

We also explored the reasons respondents gave for studying the language they had chosen (Figures 4.4 and 4.5). Quitters rate studying a language 'in order to complete their degree' as slightly less important than the other two groups (Figure 4.4.a): this is surely connected with the relative freedom to study a language that Quitters tended to report (Figure 4.2). A very high proportion of students in all three groups report that to 'travel or to live or work in a country where the language they are studying is spoken' is very important (Figures 4.4b and 4.4.c). This contrasts with a less prominent proportion of students declaring 'employment reasons' as very important (Figure 4.4.d). Overall, Committed Students rate this set of reasons as more important than Doubters, and Doubters, in turn, rate them more important than Quitters (Figure 4.4).

Committed Students were more likely to rate the reason that they were 'studying their chosen language to help them with other studies' higher than the other two groups (Figure 4.5.a). This could be a reflection of their rating more highly other reasons such as 'to communicate with native speakers of the language', 'interest in the history and culture of the language being studied' and 'interest in understanding people and cultures outside their own' (Figures 4.5.b–d).

4.2.5. Family and peers

The 'importance of having a family background in the language' is reported as more pertinent by Committed Students, while Doubters had the highest proportion of 'not applicable' answers to the relevant question (Figure 4.6.a). When 'family encouragement to study the language' is explored, there are mixed results, but the proportion of Committed Students reporting that this is 'very important' or 'extremely important' is higher than for the other two groups, while for the Doubters it is the lowest (Figure 4.6.b). This is surely connected with the relative knowledge of languages in the students' families and peer groups (Figures 4.6.c and 4.6.d). Knowledge of languages is likewise more prominent in the families and peer groups of Committed Students.

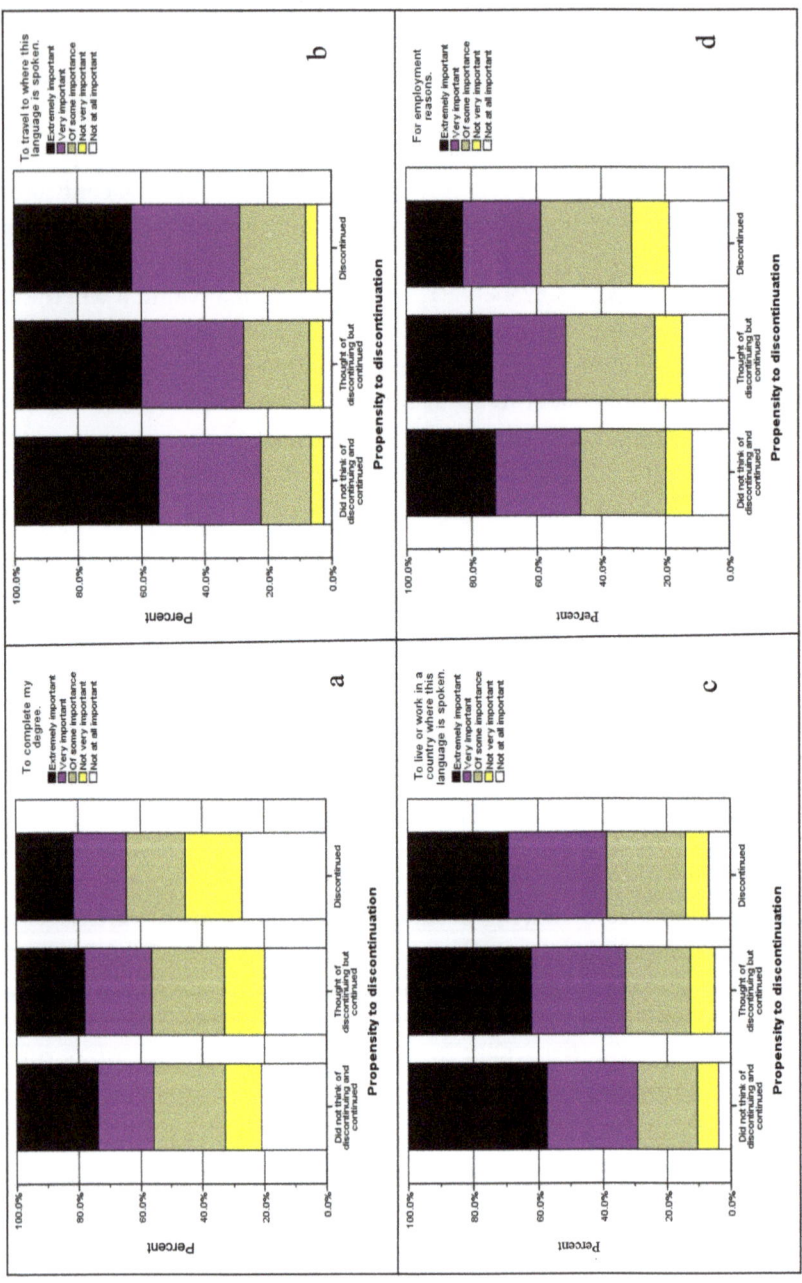

Figure 4.4. Reasons for studying the language 1
Source: Phase 2 Questionnaire Data.

4. SOME DETECTIVE WORK

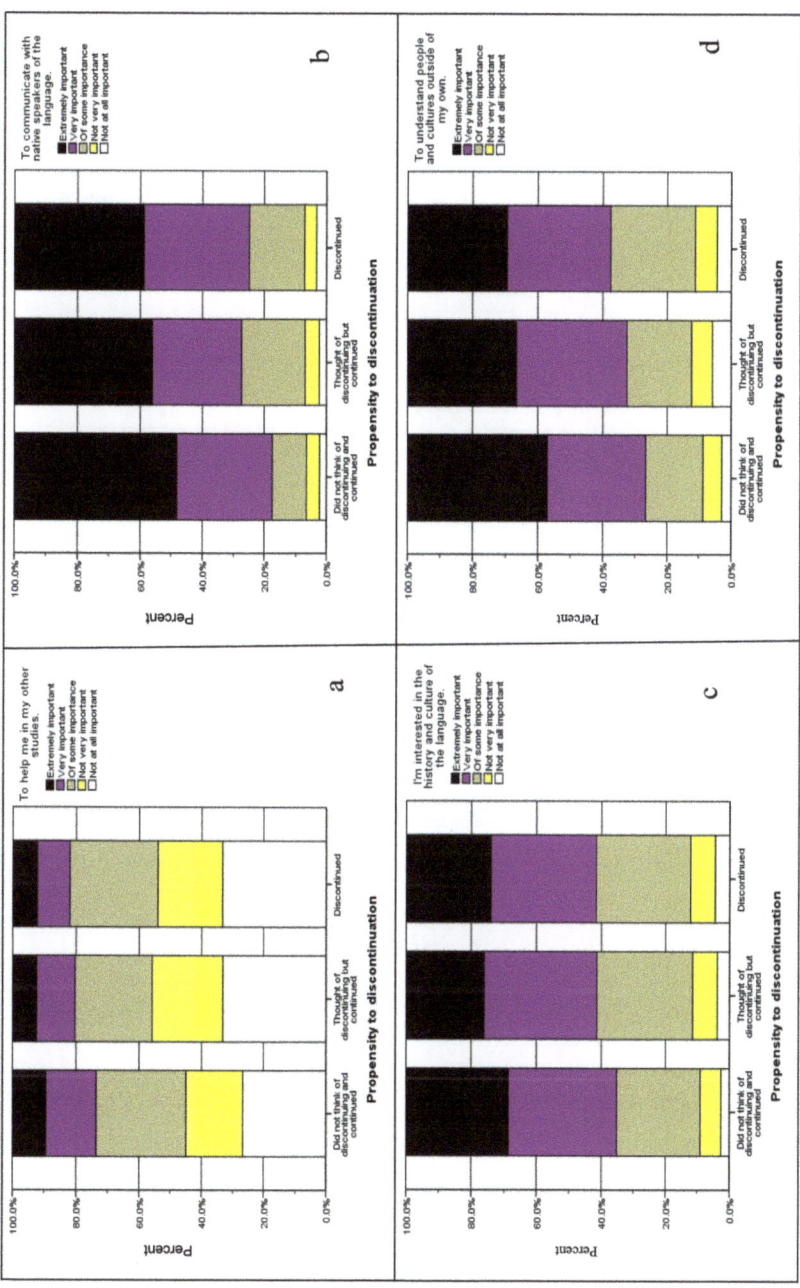

Figure 4.5. Reasons for studying the language 2
Source: Phase 2 Questionnaire Data.

THE DOUBTERS' DILEMMA

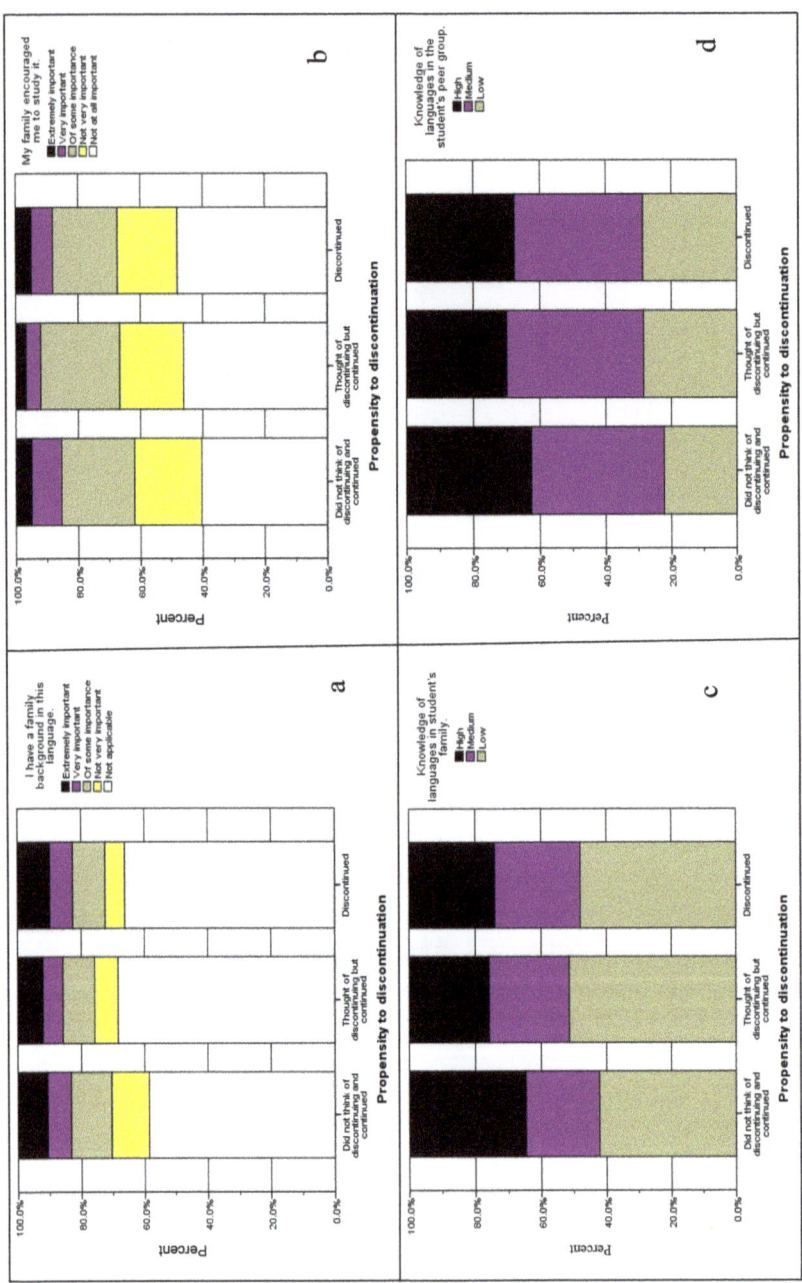

Figure 4.6. Family and peers
Source: Phase 2 Questionnaire Data.

4.2.6. Previous exposure to language learning

Previous exposure to language learning is reported in Figure 4.7. There is a higher proportion of Quitters who have been exchange students (Figure 4.7.a), probably reflecting that these students either completed their majors overseas (if they did their exchange as university students), or that they completed this exchange before entering university, and thus are likely to belong to the group of Advanced Starters. Among the Quitters in this group are also included exchange students *to* ANU, who are likely to have quit because they had to go back to study in their own university. The 'importance of having studied the language before' is lowest for Doubters (Figure 4.7.b). There are considerable differences between the three groups in 'how rewarding' they found studying languages before entering university: 60 per cent of Committed Students describe the experience as 'extremely' or 'very rewarding', while more than 50 per cent of Doubters report the experience to have been only 'somewhat' or 'not very rewarding', or 'not rewarding at all' (Figure 4.7.c). A similar pattern is found in regard to the importance of having 'spent some time in the country where the language being studied', reported less frequently as important by Doubters (Figure 4.7.d).

4.2.7. Perceptions of difficulty

The perception of 'how difficult it is to study languages' is reported in Figures 4.8 and 4.9. Doubters report the highest proportion (almost 60 per cent) of students finding the process 'more difficult than expected' (Figure 4.8a). 'Learning grammar' in particular is perceived as 'more difficult than expected' by more than 50 per cent of the Doubters, while a much lower proportion of Committed Students report that 'overall course difficulty' and 'learning grammar' are 'more difficult than expected' (Figures 4.8.a and 4.8.b). Nearly 40 per cent of Committed Students report that they have 'learned more than they expected' about the 'culture associated with the language' they were learning, while Doubters show the highest proportion of students who report that they learned 'less' or 'much less than expected' about culture (Figure 4.8.c). Committed Students are most prominent in reporting that they learnt to write the language better than expected (Figure 4.8.d).

THE DOUBTERS' DILEMMA

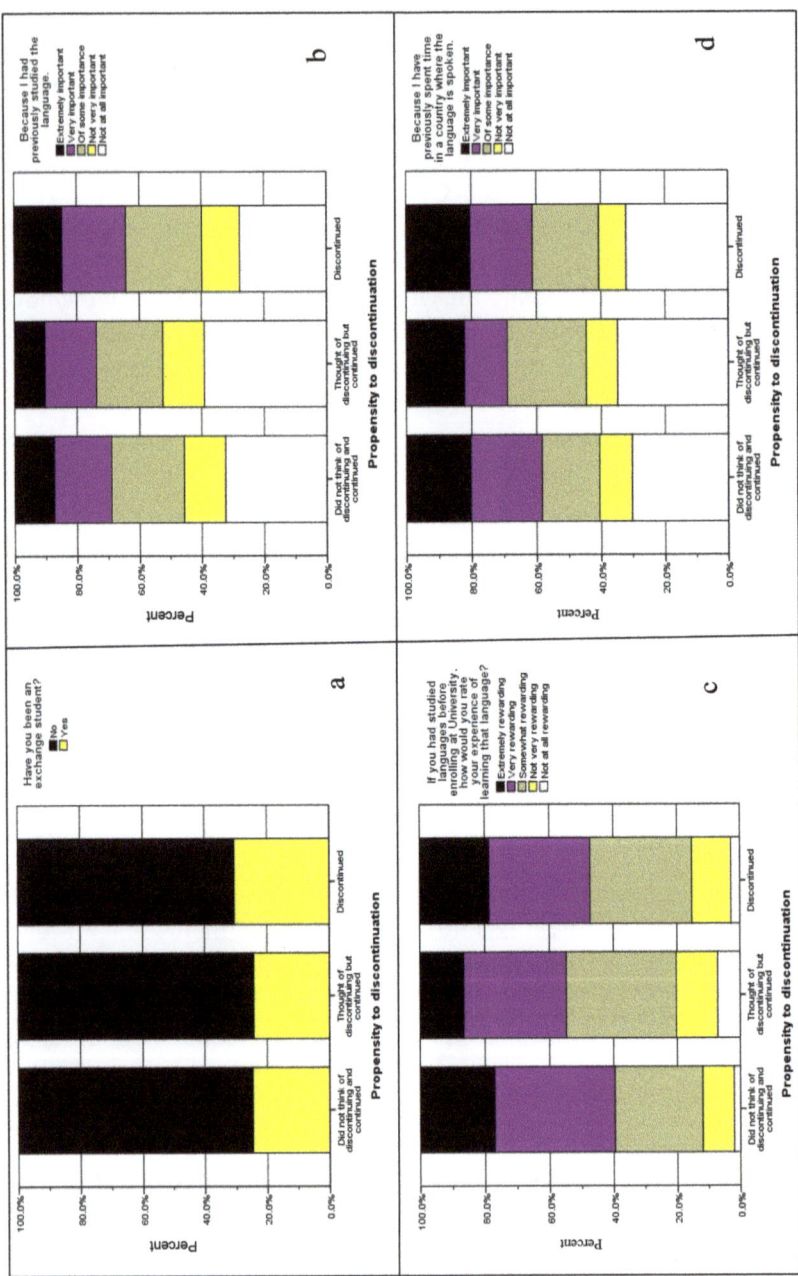

Figure 4.7. Previous exposure to language learning
Source: Phase 2 Questionnaire Data.

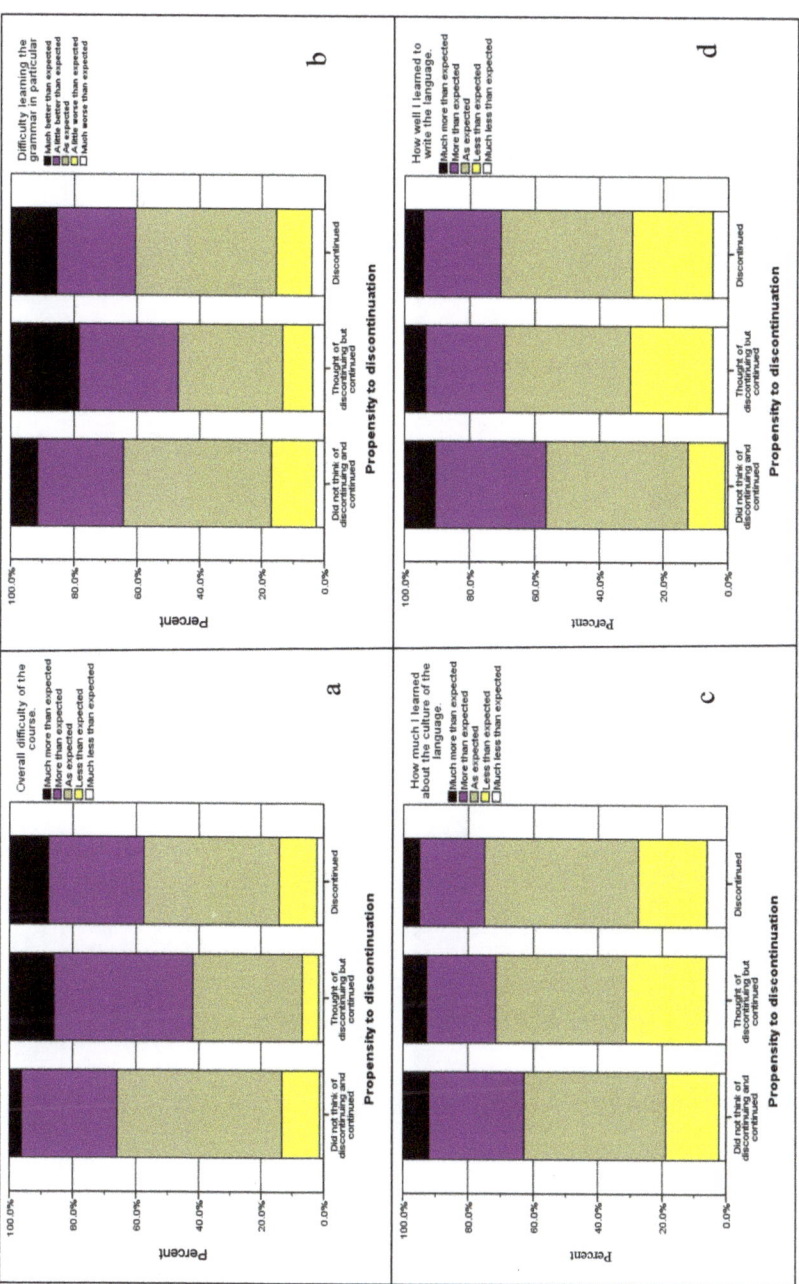

Figure 4.8. Perceptions of difficulty of language studies
Source: Phase 2 Questionnaire Data.

THE DOUBTERS' DILEMMA

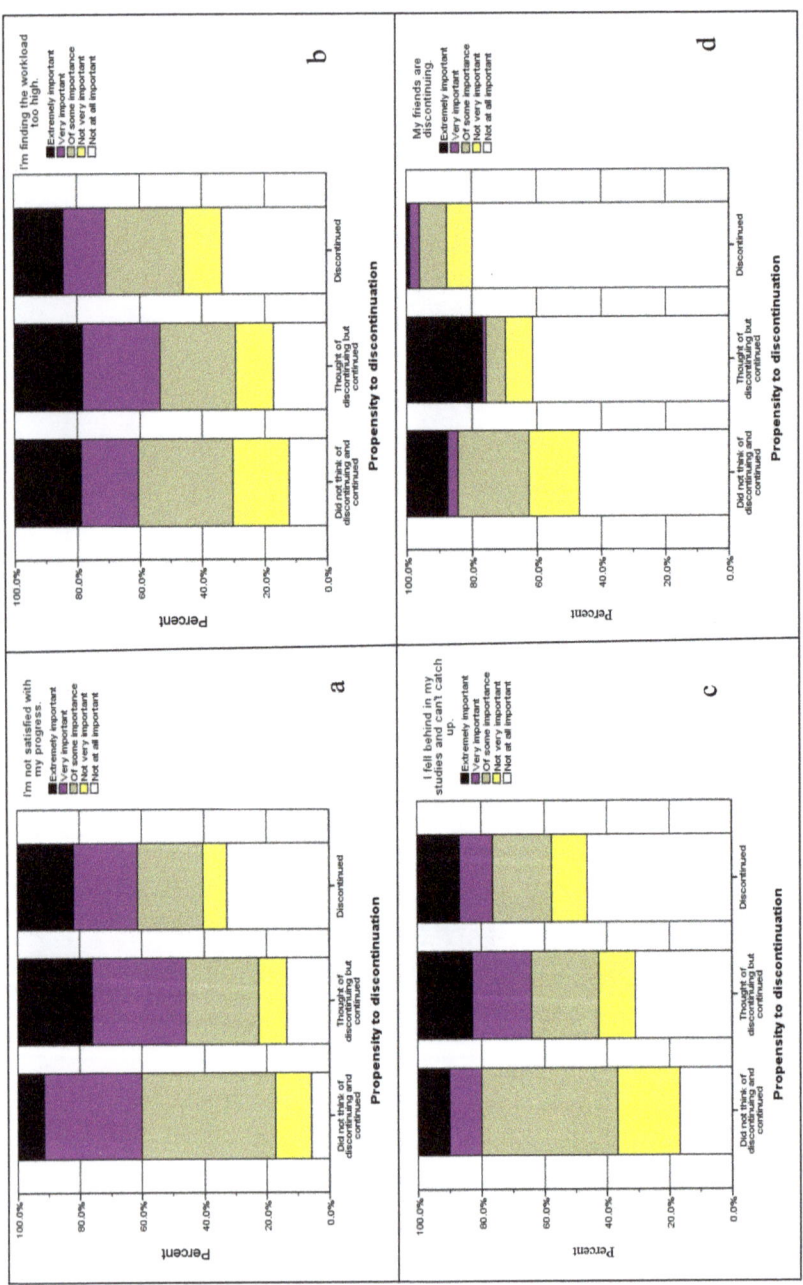

Figure 4.9. Difficulties in the language learning process
Source: Phase 2 Questionnaire Data.

A higher proportion of Doubters than the other two groups report serious problems regarding progress in their language studies (Figure 4.9.a), and especially the feeling that they had 'fallen behind in their language studies and could not catch up' (Figure 4.9.c). Doubters are also substantially more affected by their friends discontinuing language studies than Committed Students and Quitters (Figure 4.9.d). More than 40 per cent of Doubters also have the perception that the workload associated with language learning is too high (Figure 4.9.b; further explored below and in Figure 4.10).

4.2.8. Perceptions of workload

The perception of workload associated with learning the four basic language skills is reported in Figure 4.10, with a breakdown in terms of reading (Figure 4.10.a), writing (Figure 4.10.b), speaking (Figure 4.10.c), and understanding (Figure 4.10.d). For all four aspects, a higher proportion of Doubters report that the workload involved is 'more' or 'much more' than they expected.

4.2.9. Perceptions of teachers and the learning environment

Students' perceptions of language teachers are reported with regard to teachers' knowledge (Figure 4.11.a), teaching skills (Figure 4.11.b), advice and feedback received (Figure 4.11.c) and approachability and availability (Figure 4.11.d): in all cases, teachers are consistently perceived more positively by Committed Students than by Doubters, and more positively by Doubters than by Quitters.

The same pattern is found in the context of students' perceptions of learning environments, with Committed Students consistently perceiving this as better than Doubters, who in turn perceive learning environments better than Quitters (4.12.a and 4.12.b). Notably, Committed Students report having more 'support from fellow students' than both Doubters and Quitters (Figure 4.12.c), which suggests that Committed Students cluster in class activities and group work, and this may extend to social activities outside class. Committed Students are also considerably more worried than Doubters and Quitters about the size of language classes (Figure 4.12.d).

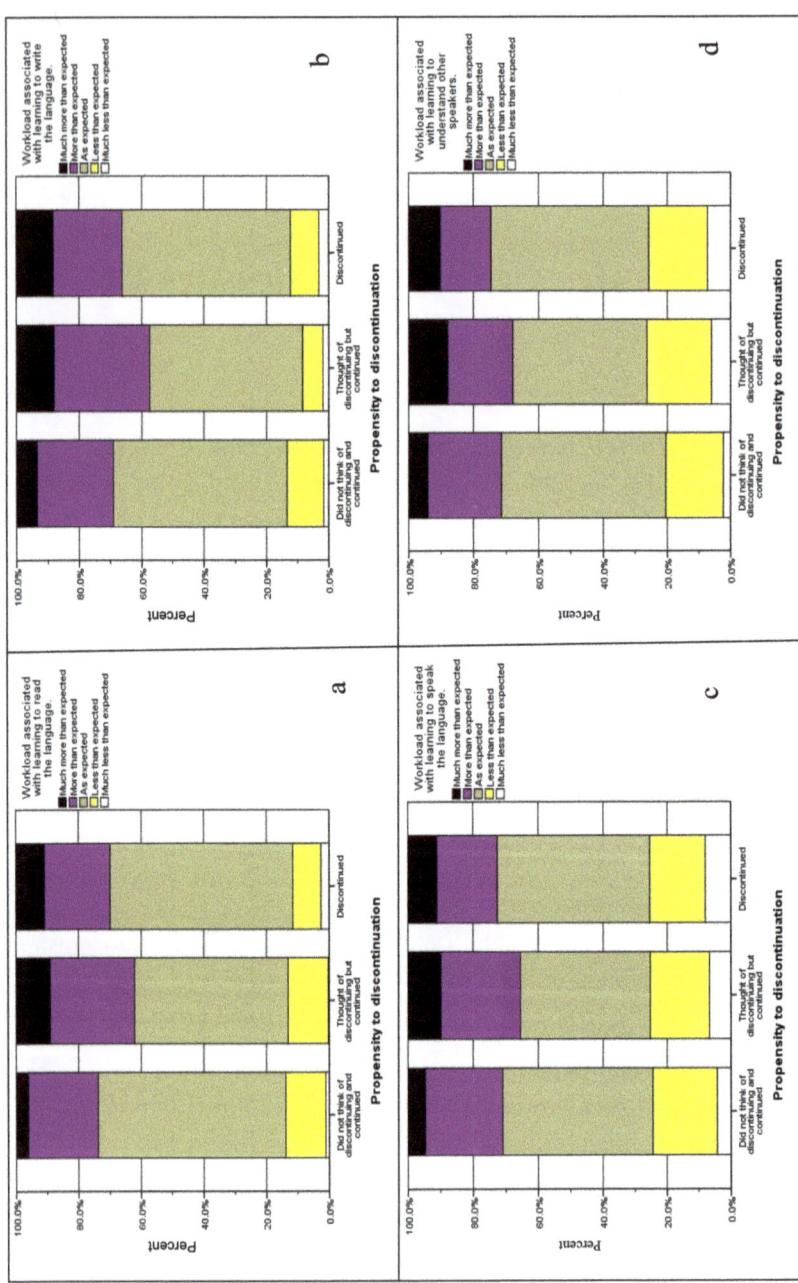

Figure 4.10. Perception of workload in learning the four basic skills
Source: Phase 2 Questionnaire Data.

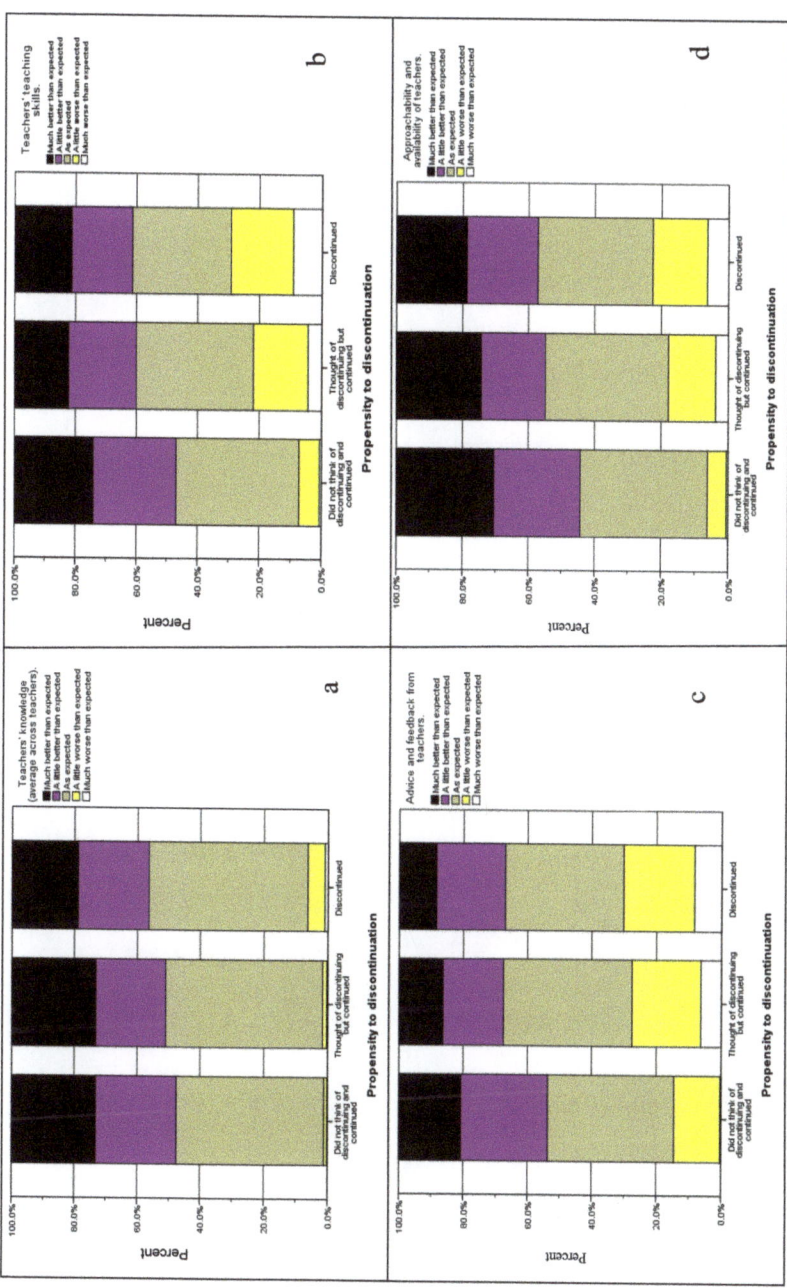

Figure 4.11. Perception of teachers
Source: Phase 2 Questionnaire Data.

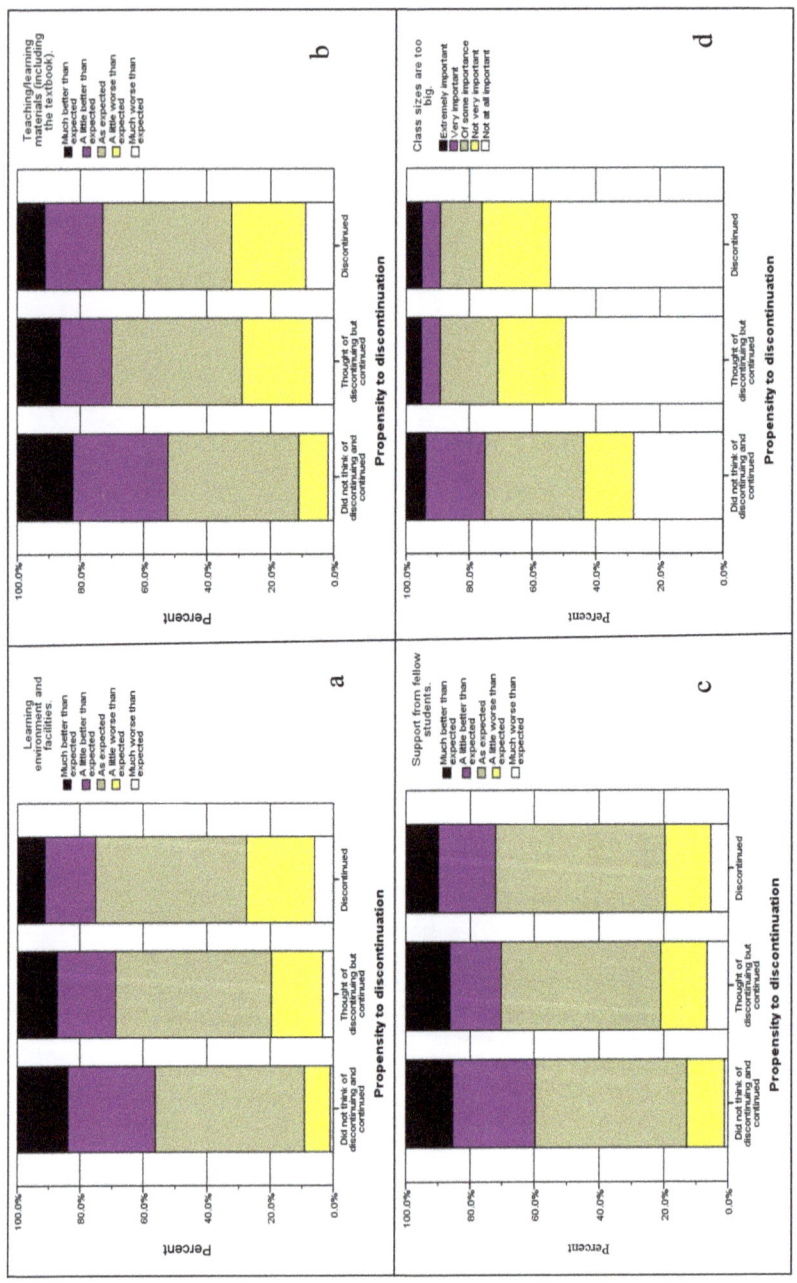

Figure 4.12. Perception of the learning environment
Source: Phase 2 Questionnaire Data.

4. SOME DETECTIVE WORK

4.2.10. The effect of grades/marks

The impact of grades obtained in L&C courses as a possible reason to discontinue, or to seriously consider discontinuing, those courses is reported in Figure 4.13, with Figures 4.13.a and 4.13.b pertaining to the reasons students indicated as to why they had discontinued or were planning to discontinue the study of a second language. No group reported thinking that the L&C course in which they had enrolled was going to be an easy subject (Figure 4.13.a). 'Not obtaining good grades' was more of a concern for Committed Students than for Doubters and Quitters, but no less than 30 per cent of Doubters were 'very' or 'extremely concerned' about the grades they were achieving (Figure 4.13.b).

When the actual grades obtained in language classes are considered, we find an interesting correlation between 'average grade obtained in language courses' and 'propensity to discontinue studying languages': the averages of Committed Students are systematically higher than those of Doubters, and those of Doubters are systematically higher than those of Quitters (Figure 4.13.c). The effect is most pronounced when we consider the maximum grade obtained in L&C courses attended: almost 90 per cent of Committed Students have in the past obtained a Distinction or High Distinction in a L&C course, but this proportion is considerably lower for Doubters and Quitters (Figure 4.13.d).

4.2.11. Reasons for continuing to study the language

Figures 4.14 to 4.16 present additional reasons for continuing language studies: as these questions were not asked in the questionnaire for discontinuing students (i.e. Quitters), this data shows only the contrast between Committed Students (did not think of discontinuing and continued) and Doubters (thought of discontinuing but continued). Committed Students are more likely than Doubters to report that they think that 'knowing more than one language' is important, although it is very important for both groups (Figure 4.14.a). The data confirm what we already know from the previous data analysis, namely that Committed Students are more likely than Doubters to i) report that they enjoy learning the language (Figure 4.14.b); ii) feel that they are progressing well in their language learning (Figure 4.14.c); and iii) report that the workload of learning a language is manageable (Figure 4.14.d).

THE DOUBTERS' DILEMMA

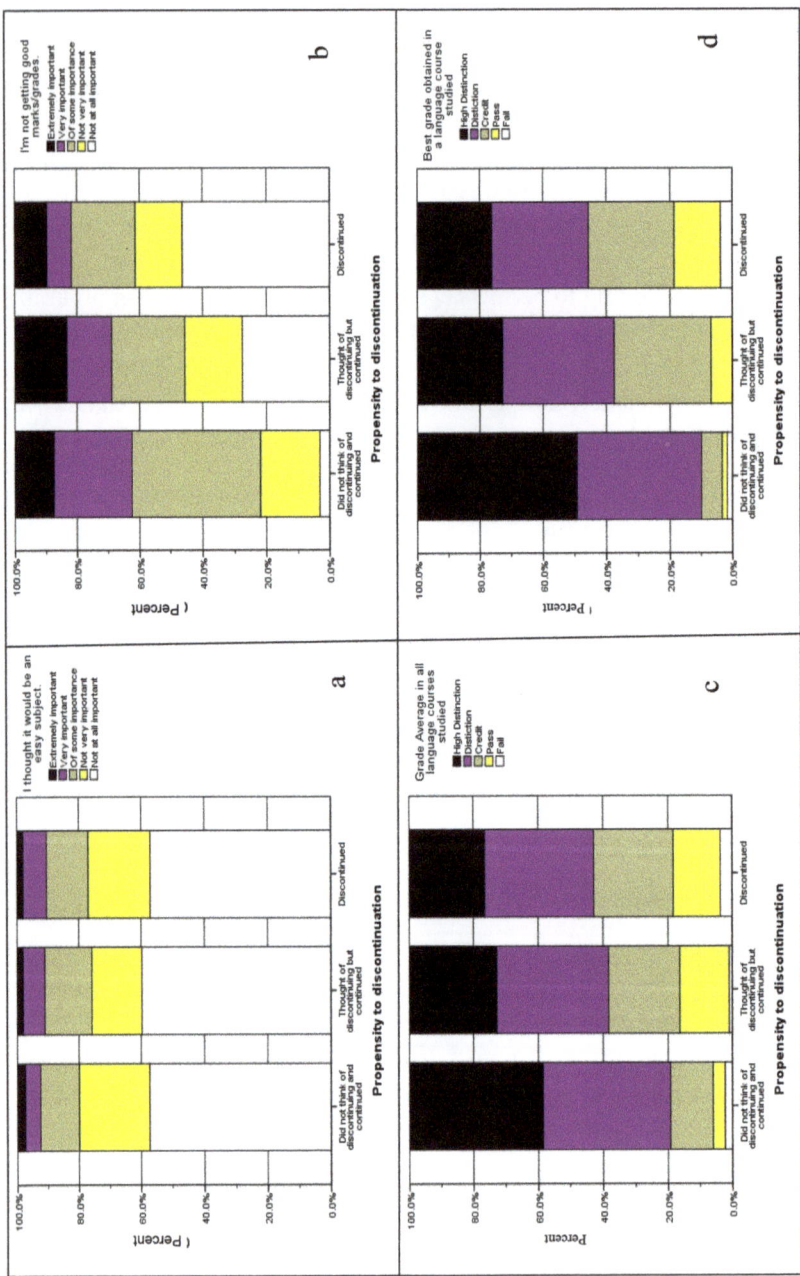

Figure 4.13. The effect of grades/marks
Source: Phase 2 Questionnaire Data.

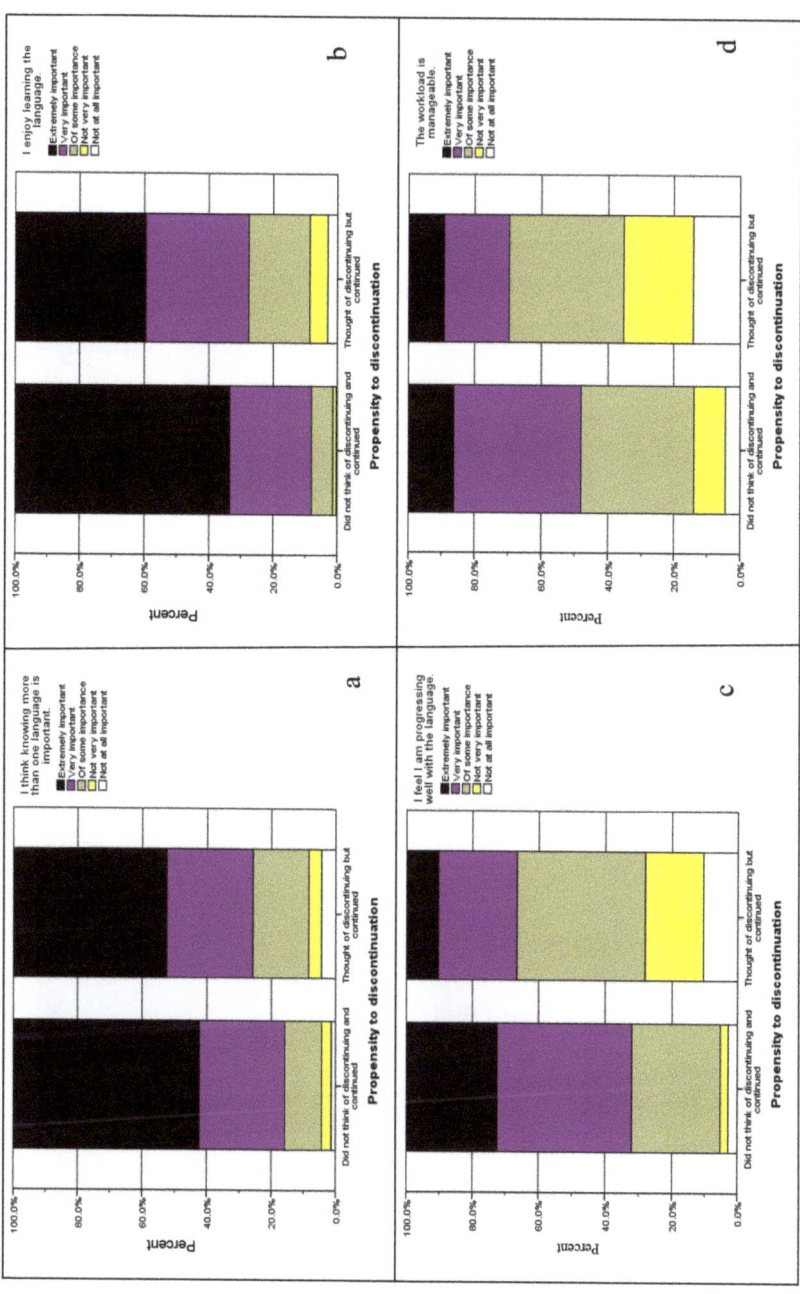

Figure 4.14. Reasons to continue studying the language 1
Source: Phase 2 Questionnaire Data.

THE DOUBTERS' DILEMMA

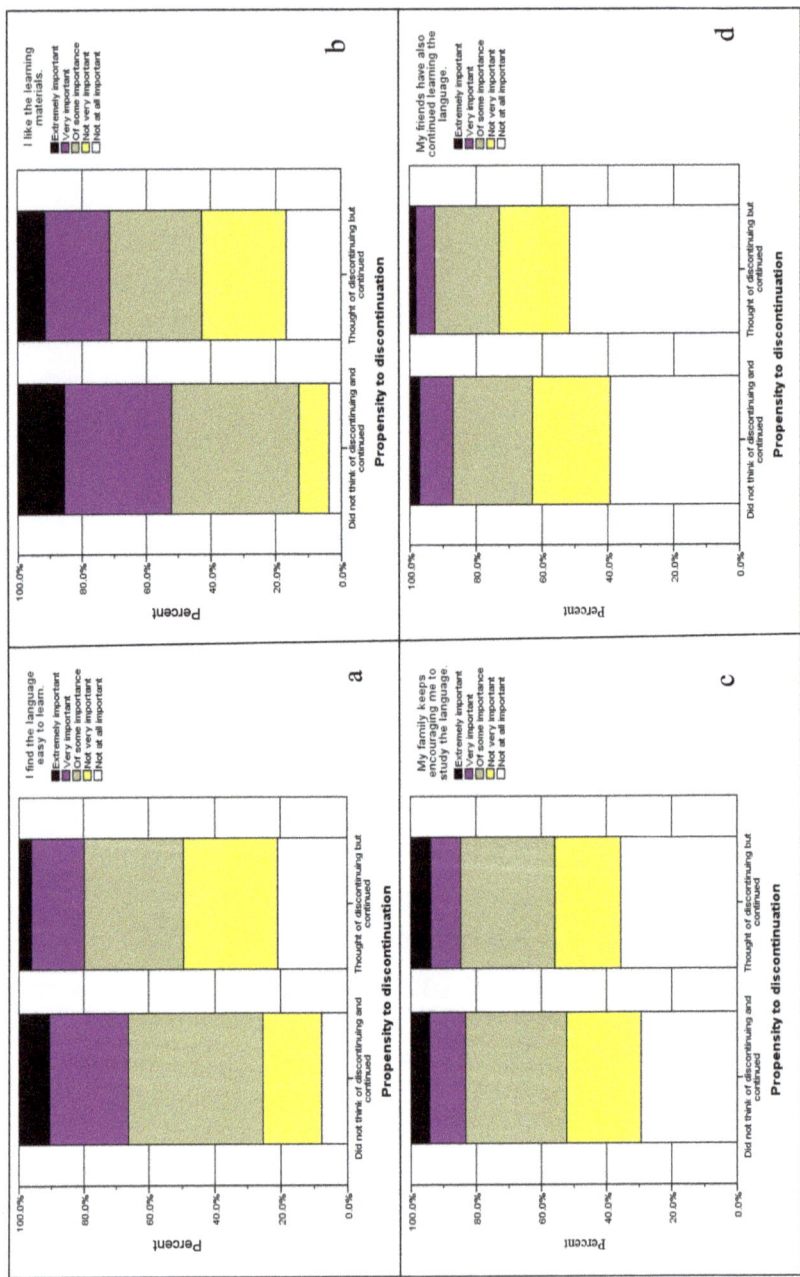

Figure 4.15. Reasons to continue studying the language 2
Source: Phase 2 Questionnaire Data.

Committed Students find their language of study 'easier to learn' than Doubters (Figure 4.15.a). A similar pattern is found in responses other questions such as 'I like the learning materials' (Figure 4.15.b); 'my family keeps encouraging me to study the language' (Figure 4.15.c); and 'my friends have also continued learning the language' (Figure 4.15.d), although the last two reasons are less obviously different.

Committed Students are more likely to report that they 'need to use the language they are studying in their work' (Figure 4.16.a). Doubters are more likely to report that they 'keep studying a language because there are no better study alternatives available' to them (Figure 4.16.b) and that it 'would be a shame to give up language studies at the stage they are at' (Figure 4.16.c). This could mean that Doubters are already committed to completing a major or a degree that requires language study, and that they will continue in spite of not being satisfied with their language learning experience.

As expected, the main contrast between Committed Students and Doubters are their plans for future language studies: Committed Students are considerably more likely to report that they want to complete a major in the language, or to go on and do Honours in the language, while more than 40 per cent of Doubters report that they are planning to complete only two years of study in the language, or just complete the course in which they were presently enrolled (Figure 4.16.d). This confirms the status of Doubters as students 'at risk of discontinuing'.

4.2.12. Reasons for discontinuing to study the language

In the questionnaire for Continuing students, those who reported that they were considering discontinuing L&C studies (Doubters) were asked to consider additional reasons not previously explored. The same questions were asked of Discontinuing students (Quitters), and shown in Figures 4.17 to 4.20 (variables not previously shown in Figures 4.1 to 4.13). The figures, then, present only the contrast between Doubters (thought of discontinuing but continued) and Quitters (discontinued). In regards to questions relating to difficulties with L&C studies (Figure 4.17), Doubters are more likely than Quitters to report that they are 'finding the course too difficult' (Figure 4.17.a); that they are 'finding the workload too high' (Figure 4.17.b); and that it worries them that other students seem to speak better' than they do (Figure 4.17.c).

THE DOUBTERS' DILEMMA

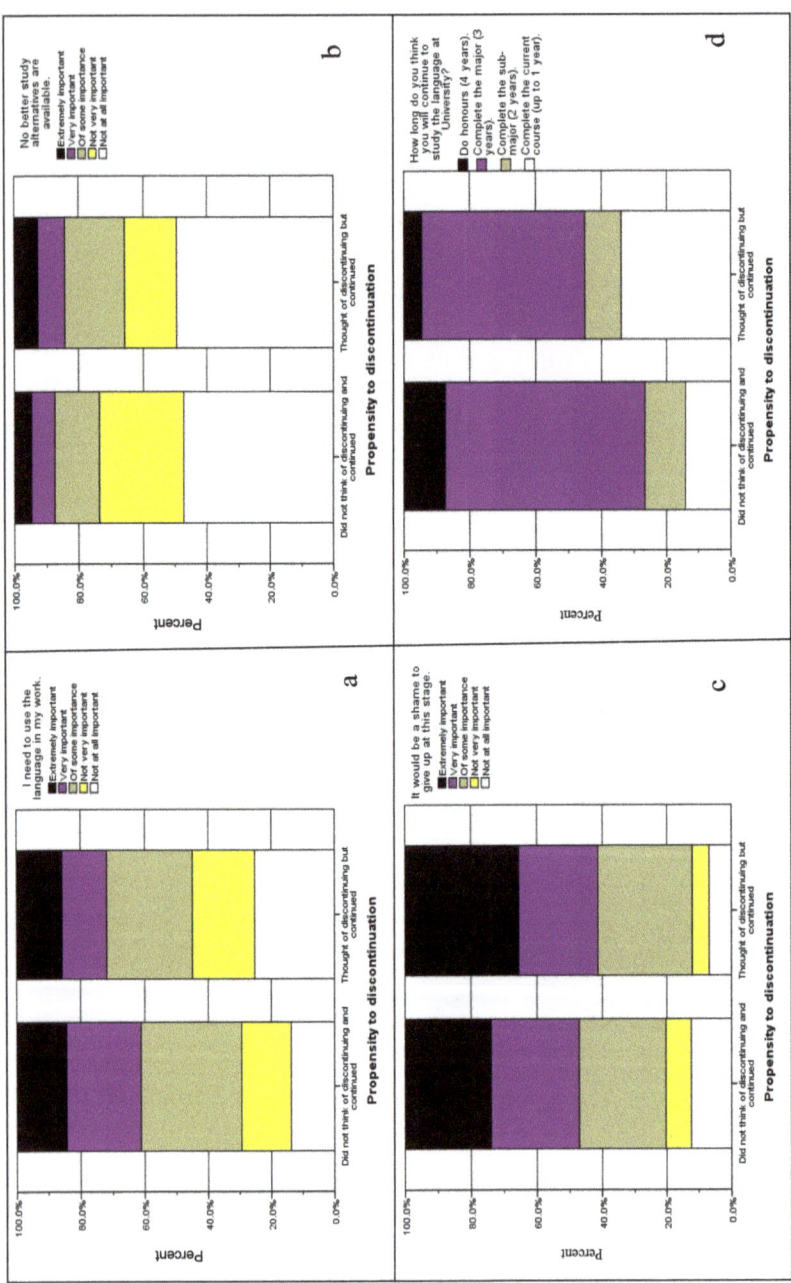

Figure 4.16. Reasons to continue studying the language 3
Source: Phase 2 Questionnaire Data.

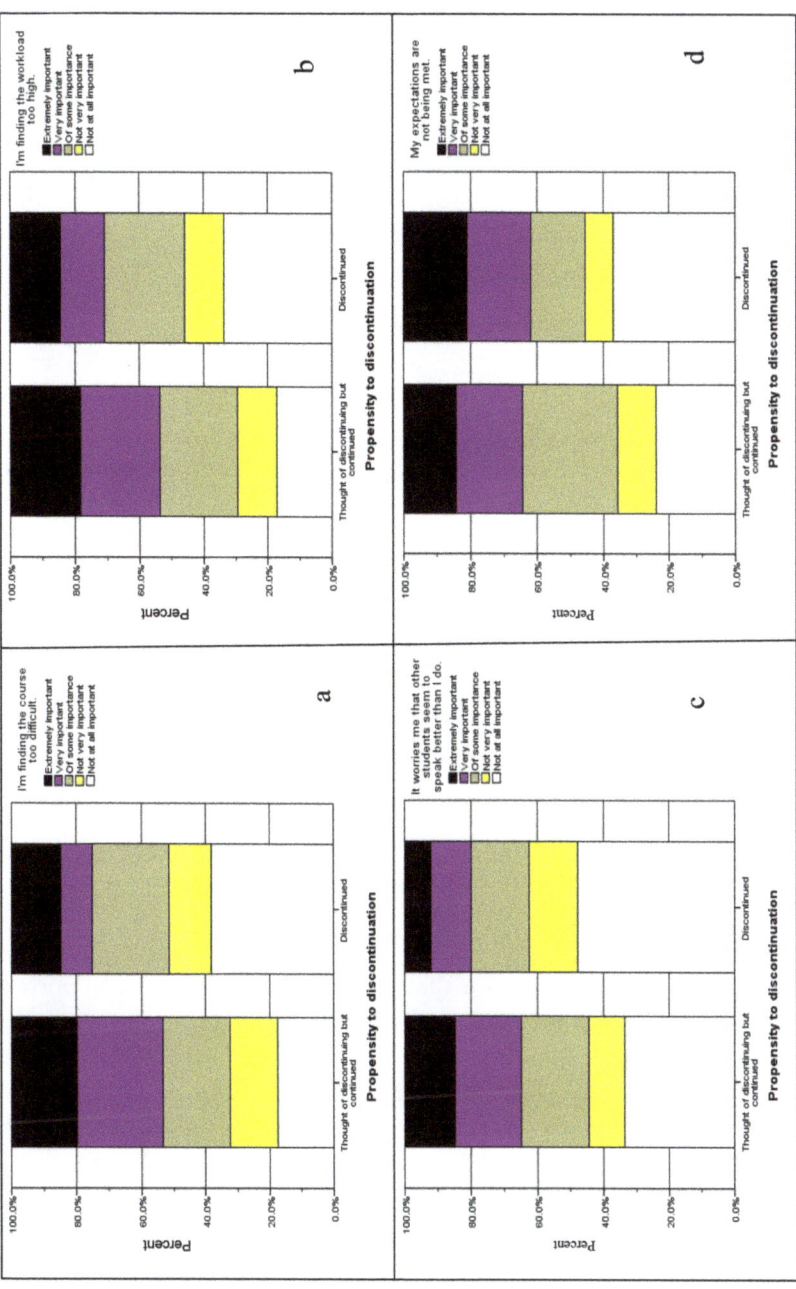

Figure 4.17. Reasons to discontinue 1
Source: Phase 2 Questionnaire Data

For the reason 'my expectations are not being met', we find mixed results (Figure 4.17.d): Quitters are as likely as Doubters to consider this reason as 'very important' or 'extremely important', but Doubters are more likely to consider this reason 'of some importance' (that is, they are less likely than Quitters to consider this reason as 'not very important' or 'not at all important'). This distribution reflects not only the ambivalent situation of Doubters, but also their relatively lesser freedom to quit L&C studies.

In regard to questions relating to negative perceptions of language learning (Figure 4.18), Doubters are more likely than Quitters to report that they are 'not enjoying the course content' (Figure 4.18.a); that they don't like 'the way the language is taught' (Figure 4.18.b); that they consider that 'not enough time is spent speaking the language' (Figure 4.18.c); and that they 'feel uncomfortable speaking the language in front of others' (Figure 4.18.d). The response that 'not enough time is spent speaking the language' (Figure 4.18.c) confirms a finding made by Nettelbeck et al. (2009, 19) that suggested that students are interested in learning to speak the language but that teachers offer other types of content rather than speaking practice. Overall, the data in Figure 4.18 strongly encourages a reconsideration of the particular needs of Doubters with regard to L&C curricula.

In terms of questions related to practical and external reasons for discontinuing language studies (Figure 4.19), Quitters are more likely than Doubters to report 'timetable clashes' as a reason for discontinuing L&C studies (Figure 4.19.a). This also reflects Quitters' relatively higher freedom to study or not to study a language, and the already explored perception that 'other studies' are more important to them (Figure 4.3.d). 'Paid work commitments' appear to be equally important reasons for discontinuing for both Quitters and Doubters (Figure 4.19.b), whereas 'financial reasons' seem to be slightly more important for Doubters (Figure 4.19.c). Other external reasons, such as 'problems with daily travel', seem to be of relatively little importance for the two groups (Figure 4.19.d), and the same is true for reasons such as 'family commitments' or 'health issues' (explored in the data, but not shown here).

4. SOME DETECTIVE WORK

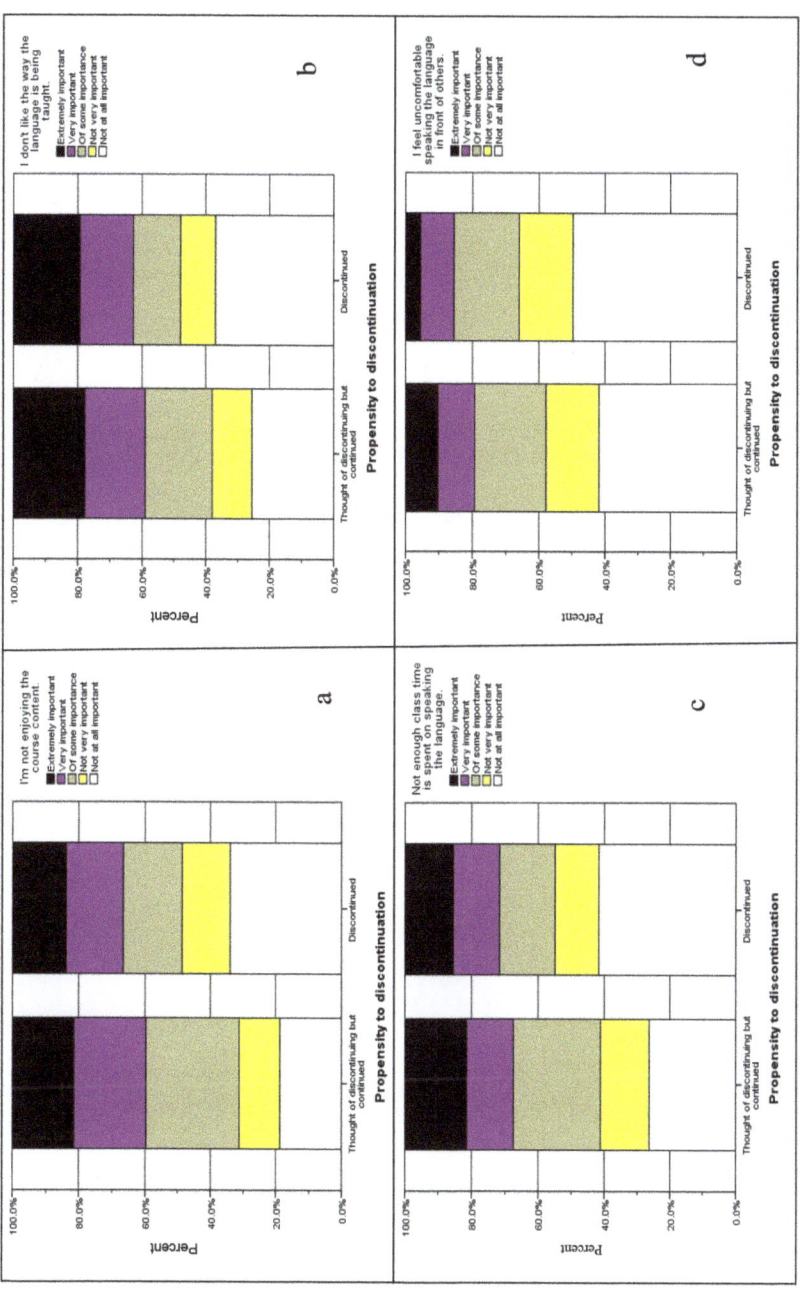

Figure 4.18. Reasons to discontinue 2
Source: Phase 2 Questionnaire Data.

THE DOUBTERS' DILEMMA

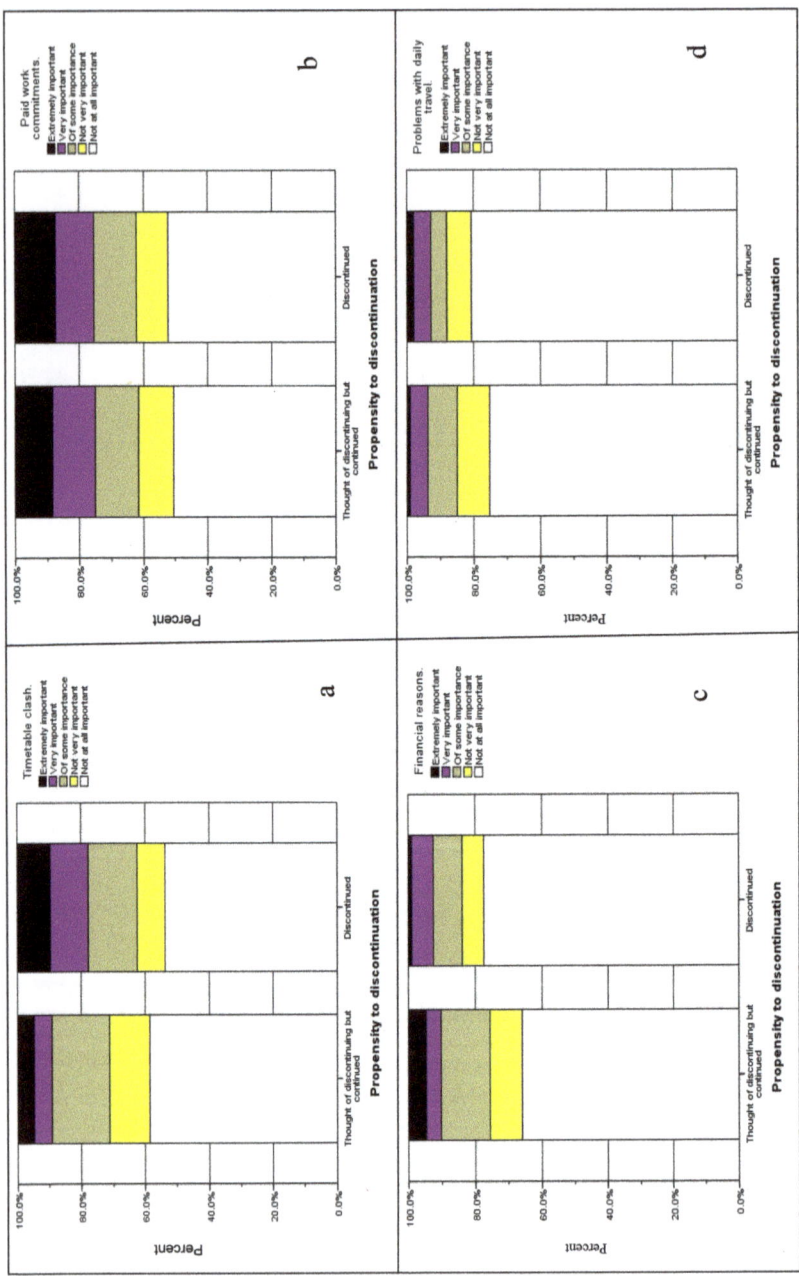

Figure 4.19. Reasons to discontinue 3
Source: Phase 2 Questionnaire Data.

4. SOME DETECTIVE WORK

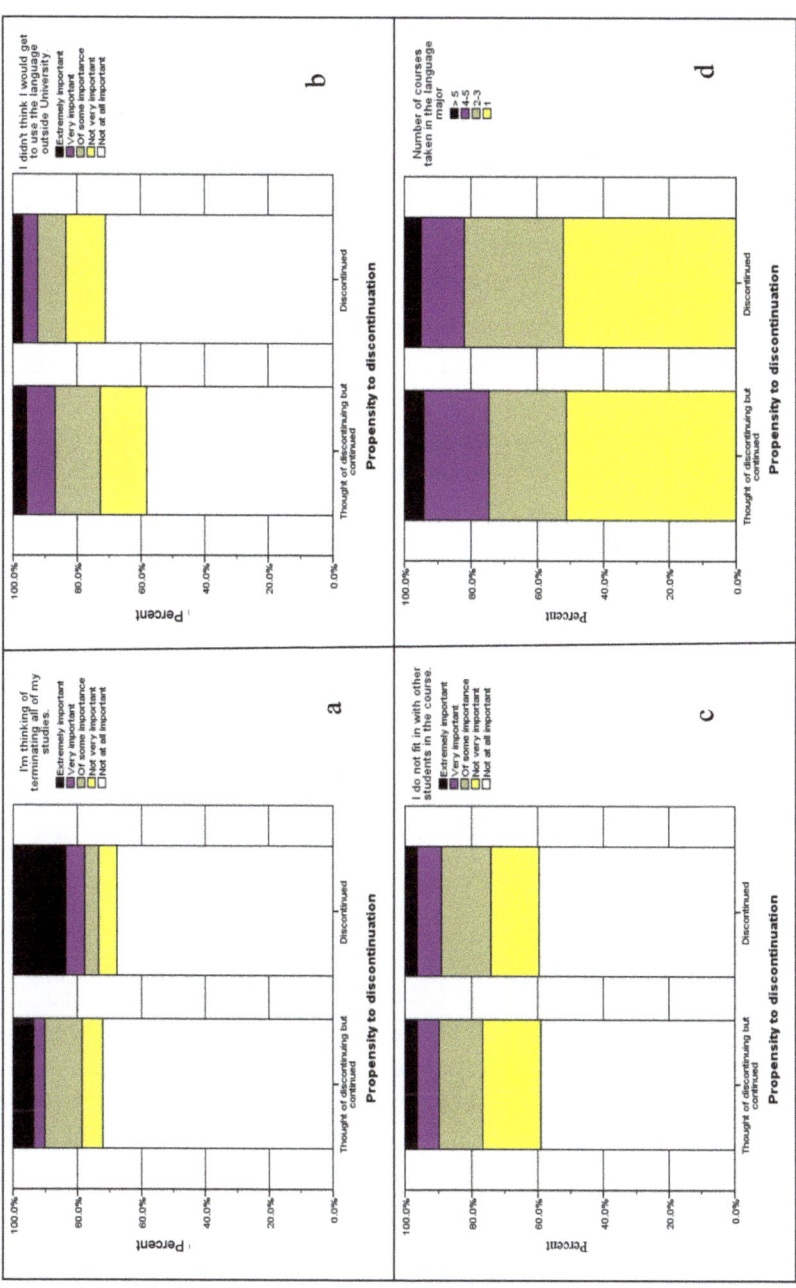

Figure 4.20. Reasons to discontinue 4
Source: Phase 2 Questionnaire Data.

Affective reasons for discontinuing were also explored (Figure 4.20). Quitters are more likely to report that they were 'thinking of terminating their university studies' as a reason for discontinuing L&C studies (Figure 4.20.a), but the latter could, for some, be a simple consequence of approaching the end of their degree. Doubters are slightly more likely than Quitters to perceive that they 'would not use the language outside university' (Figure 4.20.b).

Doubters and Quitters do not differ in their reported perception that they 'don't fit with other students in the class' (Figure 4.20.c), but this perception is of 'some importance' or 'very important' for more than 20 per cent of both groups, again pointing to the need to examine L&C curricula to accommodate both groups effectively. Finally, when the numbers of courses completed in the language major are compared in Figure 4.20.d, we confirm that Doubters stay longer in the major than Quitters, and that the risk of discontinuation in Language & Culture courses is not restricted to the initial years of language learning, as the bulk of the per cent difference between Doubters and Quitters is found in the period between two and four language courses being completed. When contrasted with Figure 4.16.d, this reflects the pressure on Doubters to complete the language major.

4.3. Summary

In this chapter we have presented a detailed analysis of the characteristics of the three groups of students we identified in the Discriminant Analysis carried out in Chapter 3. This detailed analysis forms the basis of the characterisations of the three groups that we present in Chapter 5, although the student characteristics are presented in a different order to that followed in this chapter to allow for a more coherent characterisation of the groups under analysis. In Chapter 5 we will also introduce the concept of language capital and illustrate how it can be used to explore students' perceptions about learning the spoken language, as the latter proved a key differentiating characteristic between Doubters and Quitters.

5
The Road to Language Capital: Interpreting the findings

5.1. Characterising the three student archetypes

In Chapter 3 we identified three groups of students—Committed Students, Doubters and Quitters—which we described in Table 3.VI, reproduced here as Table 5.I for the convenience of the reader. In Chapter 4 we reported more detailed analyses (Figures 4.1 to 4.20) that allow us, in this chapter, to characterise each of the three groups, first on the basis of their most prominent characteristics (i.e. those found to be prominent and unique to one of the groups when compared to the other two), and then on the basis of additional relevant characteristics that contribute to a fuller, more rounded description. First, we summarise the student characteristics from section 4.2, grouping them in a way conducive to characterising the three student archetypes, as a foundation for the more theoretical analysis presented in the latter part of this chapter.

Table 5.I. Classification of students' commitment to language study used to characterise the student groups

Commitment to language studies	Continuing Students	Discontinuing Students
High	**Commited Students** Did not think of discontinuing and continued	**Quitters** Discontinued. Include both: 1. Wanted to continue, but had had no choice but to discontinue (Reluctant Quitters) and 2. Thought of discontinuing and had discontinued (Voluntary Quitters)
Low	**Doubters** Thought of discontinuing but continued (or had to continue)	

Corresponds to Table 3.VI.
Source: Extrapolated from an analysis of Phase 2 Questionnaire Data.

5.1.1. Committed Students

The group we call Committed Students comprises those students who reported never having given serious thought to discontinuing their L&C studies. These are the students that language teachers consider 'ideal': confident and successful in their learning, self-motivated, appreciative of their past and present language learning experiences, yet discerning. These students stand out uniquely as a group in their positive perceptions of their language learning experiences, their teachers and the wider learning environment.

Committed Students show the following prominent characteristics:

- They would have chosen to study a language whether or not it was a compulsory element of their degree programs.
- They feel that studying the chosen language helps them with their other studies.
- They perceive teachers' skills, feedback, approachability and availability as better than expected.
- They perceive the teaching materials, and the language learning environment in general, as better than expected.
- They find that the support they receive from fellow students is at the appropriate level or better than expected.
- They are satisfied with their progress in language learning.

- They report that they have learned more than expected about both the culture(s) and the writing of the language being studied.
- They achieve higher marks, and are more concerned about receiving poor marks, than the other groups.
- They are concerned when language classes are 'too big'.

Compared with the other two groups, Committed Students also show the following characteristics:

- They rate their previous experiences of language learning as rewarding.
- Their expectations about the degree of difficulty of learning a language are more realistic than those of the other two groups—most Committed Students report the overall level of difficulty, and the specific difficulty of learning grammar, as the same, or even less, than expected.
- The reported knowledge of language learning in their families and peer group is higher than in the other groups. Committed Students are more likely to have a family background in the language they are studying, or to have studied the language previously. Moreover, if they have previously spent time in the country where the target language is spoken, they consider this important.
- Committed Students are more likely than the other two groups to rate highly certain reasons for studying a language, such as interest in the culture(s) associated with the language, a desire to communicate with native speakers of the language, and a general interest to understand people and cultures outside their own.
- They are more likely to be international students.
- They are more likely than Doubters to report an intention to complete a major in the language they are studying or to do Honours.
- They are more likely than Doubters to feel that knowing more than one language is very important, and to consider the language they are studying as easy to learn.
- They are more likely than Doubters to report that their friends have also continued learning the target language.
- They are more likely than Doubters to report that they need to use the target language in their work life.

5.1.2. Quitters

The group we have termed Quitters comprises those students who have already discontinued L&C studies. From the analysis reported in section 3.4.3, we know that this group includes both students who had wanted to continue their language study, but had to quit because they had no other choice ('Reluctant Quitters'), and students who quit voluntarily, either because they had chosen to complete a major in another discipline or because they were dissatisfied with their L&C learning experience. ('Voluntary Quitters'). This diversity potentially confounds any attempt to characterise the group. Nevertheless, we found that Quitters stand out uniquely as a group because of the following characteristics:

- They are more advanced in their undergraduate degree, or have completed their degree.
- They tend to be older.
- Language study is less frequently a compulsory requirement in their degree, so they have more freedom to choose whether or not to study a language.
- They consider it extremely important if people are discouraging them from studying the language.
- They consider their other study commitments more important than their L&C studies.

Compared with the other two groups, Quitters also show the following characteristics:

- They receive lower marks than the other two groups.
- They are less concerned about receiving poor marks than the other groups.
- They consistently rate lower than the other two groups their teachers' skills, feedback, approachability and availability, as well as the teaching materials and the language learning environment in general.
- They are less likely than the other two groups to report that studying a language to complete their degree is an important reason to study a language.
- Compared with Doubters, they are more likely to report that practical reasons—timetable clashes, thinking of discontinuing

university studies altogether, or work commitments—interfere with continuing their L&C studies.
- They are as likely as Doubters to report that their expectations of L&C studies had not been met.

5.1.3. Doubters

The group we term Doubters comprise those students who reported having seriously considered discontinuing their L&C studies, but who nonetheless were still enrolled in an L&C course at the time of data collection. Typically, these were the students who reported struggling with their L&C studies: they had either not studied a language before, or had done so but reported not having gained much from the experience. They stand out uniquely as a group because of their negative learning experiences (in direct contrast to reports by Committed Students).

As a group Doubters display some prominent characteristics:

- They find the workload for language learning is 'too high'.
- They are not satisfied with their progress in language learning.
- They perceive that they have fallen behind in their study and cannot catch up.
- They feel that having friends who are discontinuing L&C studies is a very important influence on their own thinking about discontinuing.

Compared with both the other two groups, Doubters also show the following characteristics:

- They are less likely to have previously studied the language.
- If they have previously studied a language, they are less likely to rate that previous experience of language learning as having been a rewarding one than either Committed Students or Quitters.
- They perceive the degree of difficulty of both learning a language in general, and learning grammar in particular, as higher than expected.
- The reported knowledge of language learning in the Doubters' families and peer group is lower than for both Committed Students or Quitters.

- They are less likely to have a family background in the language they are studying, or to have studied that language previously.
- They receive less encouragement from their family to study languages.
- They are less likely than Committed Students or Quitters to report that they were free to choose whether or not they study a language.
- When asked if they would have chosen to study a language regardless of whether this was compulsory in their degree program, Doubters were the most uncertain in their responses.

Doubters also show characteristics that distinguish them from the other two groups in different ways. For example:

- Some 25 per cent of Doubters reported that it was extremely important if people discouraged them from studying languages. This was even more relevant to Quitters (40 per cent).
- Doubters receive lower marks than Committed Students, and only slightly higher marks than Quitters. However, Doubters are less concerned about receiving poor marks than are Committed Students, but more likely to perceive poor marks as important than are Quitters.
- Doubters are more likely than Committed Students to report that it would be a shame to give up language studies at the stage they are at, and/or to report that they keep studying a language because there are no better alternatives.
- Doubters are more likely than Quitters to report that they are finding the course too difficult, that they don't like the way the language is taught, and/or that they are not enjoying the course content.
- Doubters are more likely than Quitters to report worry about other students speaking better than they do, and/or that they feel uncomfortable speaking the language in front of others. This appears linked to a common perception by Doubters that not enough time in class is spent speaking the language, which is less commonly found among Quitters.

5.2. Doubters as 'students at risk'

The methodologies described in Chapter 3, notably our extensive data collection and our statistical analyses, have allowed us to provide the detailed summary above of the characteristics of Committed Students, Doubters and Quitters. These characterisations are sufficiently evidence-based and robust to form the basis for our interpretation of the general findings using the construct of language capital, which we will discuss in this section in the context of 'students at risk'.

We can differentiate as two groups—Committed Students and Doubters—the students who enrolled in L&C courses at ANU in 2008 and were still enrolled in at least one L&C course in 2009. Our data suggest that Doubters are likely to discontinue their L&C studies unless they are compelled to study a language by their degree structure or they are subjected to other external pressures—for example from family or work situations—that influence them to continue. Given these characteristics, we therefore consider the Doubters analogous to the 'at risk' group identified in various general attrition studies of the first year university experience in Australia and elsewhere (e.g. Baik et al., 2015; Krause, 2005; Krause, Hartley, James and McInnis, 2005; James et al., 2010; Lobo and Matas, 2010; Long, Ferrier and Heagney, 2006; Longden, 2006; McInnis et al., 2000; Nelson et al., 2009; Nelson, Quinn, Marrington and Clarke, 2012; Pitkethly and Prosser, 2001; Taylor and Bedford, 2004; Tinto, 1999, 2009; Weston, 1998; Yorke and Longden, 2008). Importantly from a teaching perspective, Doubters are also the students who are most likely to be sensitive to negative influences arising from being in mixed proficiency groups, from actual or perceived high study workloads, or from external pressures to discontinue L&C studies. The latter may include implicit as well as explicit pressures: stemming, for example, from an awareness that English-dominant language contexts are the norm in Australian business and social life, or from input from career advisors who do not sufficiently value L&C knowledge or capabilities.

We feel that the statistical identification and characterisation of Doubters is one of the most important outcomes of this study, as it allows for a clearer understanding of, and focus on, the typifying features of students who are at risk of discontinuing. This outcome is even more important as, to our knowledge, this subgroup of continuing students has not previously been identified in studies of retention in Australian L&C programs, yet would seem a key target for proactive policies and strategies designed to maximise retention, especially from a learner-centred perspective (e.g. as suggested by Baik et al., 2015; Lobo and Matas, 2010; Tinto, 2015; Zepke, Leach and Prebble, 2006). Moreover, the level of understanding of students' motivations and concerns provided through this case study will allow researchers in the field to reconceptualise the nature of retention in L&C programs: in particular, the issues that Doubters find important could be investigated in retention studies that explore 'at risk' students in other disciplines. This is of notable importance because Doubters are not primarily *ab-initio* students nor are they students in their first year at university, as has been the focus of many retention studies.

5.3. The concept of 'language capital'

Crucially, the above conceptualisation of student archetypes requires a theoretically motivated interpretation. In keeping with Bourdieu's argument that 'all speech is produced for and through the market to which it owes its existence and its most specific properties' (Bourdieu, 1991, 76), we hypothesise that a useful way of thinking about the three groups we have identified—Committed Students, Doubters and Quitters—could be to consider that students enter university with a certain amount of 'language capital'. In our context, the speech or writing produced by students in a 'foreign' language will be evaluated in the market of university language studies. Those students endowed with more language capital will be able to obtain more profit (e.g. greater enjoyment of the language learning experience, higher marks) and more opportunities (e.g. scholarships to study abroad, invitations to study at Honours level). Our suggestion is not intended to encourage an over-economic interpretation of language capital, such as those described by Chiswick and Miller (2003) or Pendakur and Pendakur (2002). Rather we seek to develop a social interpretation of the language learning setting at universities, in a similar vein to the notional use of 'cultural capital' in some other retention and attrition studies (e.g. Lawrence, 2005; Luzeckyj, King, Scutter and Brinkworth, 2011).

In our conceptualisation, language capital can be acquired and appropriated via a diverse set of life experiences. Thus we argue that a student in Australia who speaks a language other than English

(LOTE) at home, or who has a partner or parents who speak a LOTE, would have more language capital than one who speaks only English. Similarly, students who have travelled abroad, or who are in constant contact with native speakers of the language they study, or who have parents or peers who have learnt foreign languages, would have more language capital than those who have never travelled to a non-English-speaking country, or who primarily have contact with monolingual English speakers, or who have monolingual English-speaking parents. On the same basis, students who had enjoyed a fruitful experience of language learning before entering university, or who had successfully participated as an exchange student in a non-English-speaking country, would have more language capital than those with no, or a frustrating, prior exposure to language learning (which may itself be related to low levels of language capital to start with), or those who have never travelled and never had a student exchange experience. Similarly, we would argue that students with previous experience of one language who, as Beginners, started study of a cognate language (e.g. students who start to learn Spanish when they already know French) would have more language capital than those who begin to study a language without prior exposure to a cognate language. One can imagine many more circumstances in which the language capital of students, and other individuals, would be enriched or impoverished.

In the context of this proposed conceptualisation, we believe that the amount of language capital that L&C students bring with them when they enter university could be the crucial influence as to whether they will become Committed Students or Doubters. As the Quitters category includes both Reluctant and Voluntary Quitters (see Chapter 3, section 3.4.3), we would expect this group as a whole to fall between the other two groups in terms of language capital: unfortunately we do not have enough data to explore how much the language capital concept influences the composition of the two subgroups of Quitters at ANU. However, this is an important issue that we believe would bear fruit if addressed in future studies (as we discuss in Chapter 6).

5.4. The concept of language capital as a means of interpreting the classroom context

Given that our interpretation of the ANU data leads us to argue that commitment to continuing L&C study is a function of both pre-existing and developing language capital, how could this new characterisation of students be applied to improving retention in L&C programs? One key factor in our characterisation of Doubters (section 5.3) is related to students' perceptions of speaking the language they are studying in class. This is not the only characteristic that differentiates Doubters from the other two groups, but because it is a very important one in terms of its implications for curriculum design, we will explore it in detail here to exemplify how the concept of language capital could help not only in understanding the three identified groups but in more effectively meeting their needs as learners.

If we consider student interest in learning the four language skills according to four groupings of languages, it is clear that for all languages, except Classics, oral skills (understanding and speaking the language) are perceived as more important than writing and reading skills (Figure 5.1). This is also less relevant for students studying languages such as Sanskrit. Comparing the data in Figure 5.1 with that in Figure 5.2, which shows the students' perceptions of how well they have learned the four skills, it is clear that students perceive that they have been less successful in learning the skills they are most interested in (i.e. oral skills) than they have in learning the skills of reading and writing the language studied. It is interesting to observe that students in Classics, while not as interested in oral skills, perceive that they have learnt these skills more than students in the other three language groups.

The difference between literacy skills (reading and writing) and oral skills is very pronounced in Classics, as it should be expected. However, in the other three groupings of languages, where oral skills are an integral part of the teaching, we also find the same contrast, even more pronounced in the Middle Eastern and Central Asian languages.

5. THE ROAD TO LANGUAGE CAPITAL

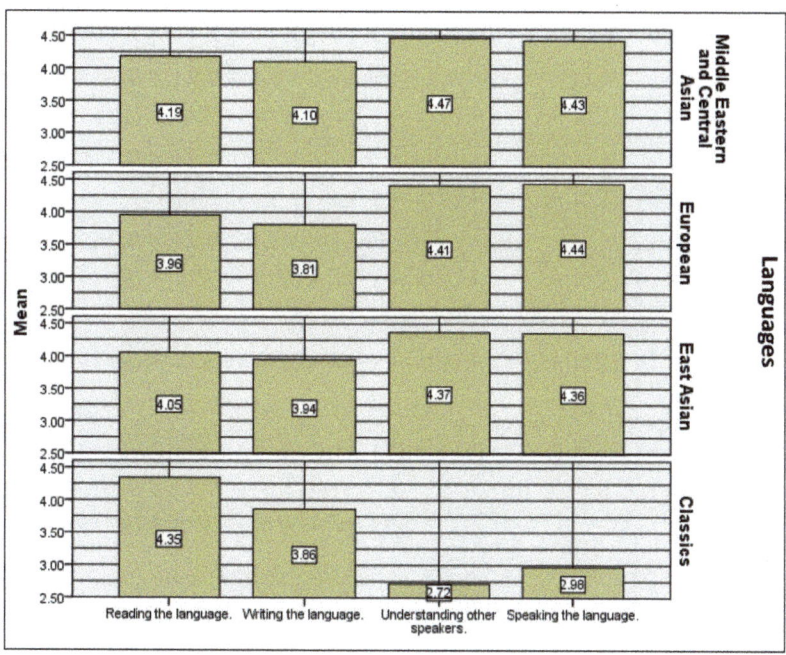

Figure 5.1. Interest in learning the four language skills—discriminated by grouping of languages

Source: Phase 2 Questionnaire Data.

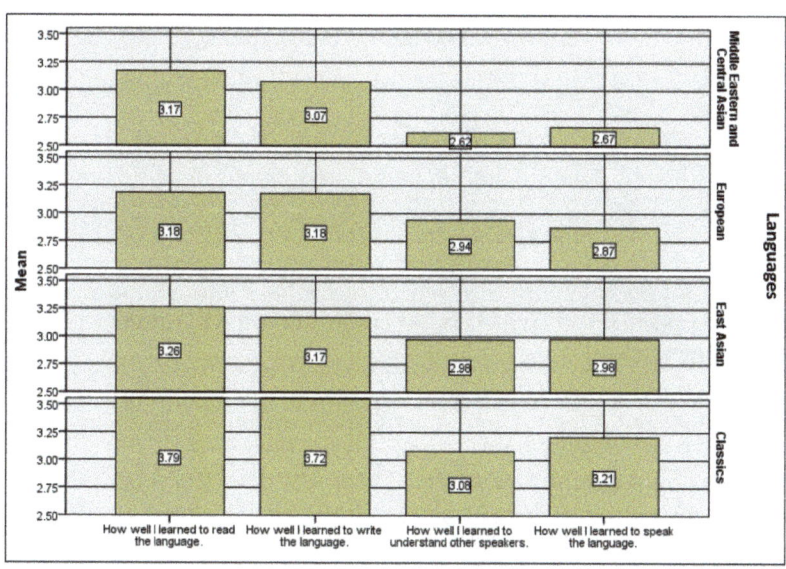

Figure 5.2. Perceptions of how well students report they have learned the four language skills at the time of the data collection. All students

Source: Phase 2 Questionnaire Data.

THE DOUBTERS' DILEMMA

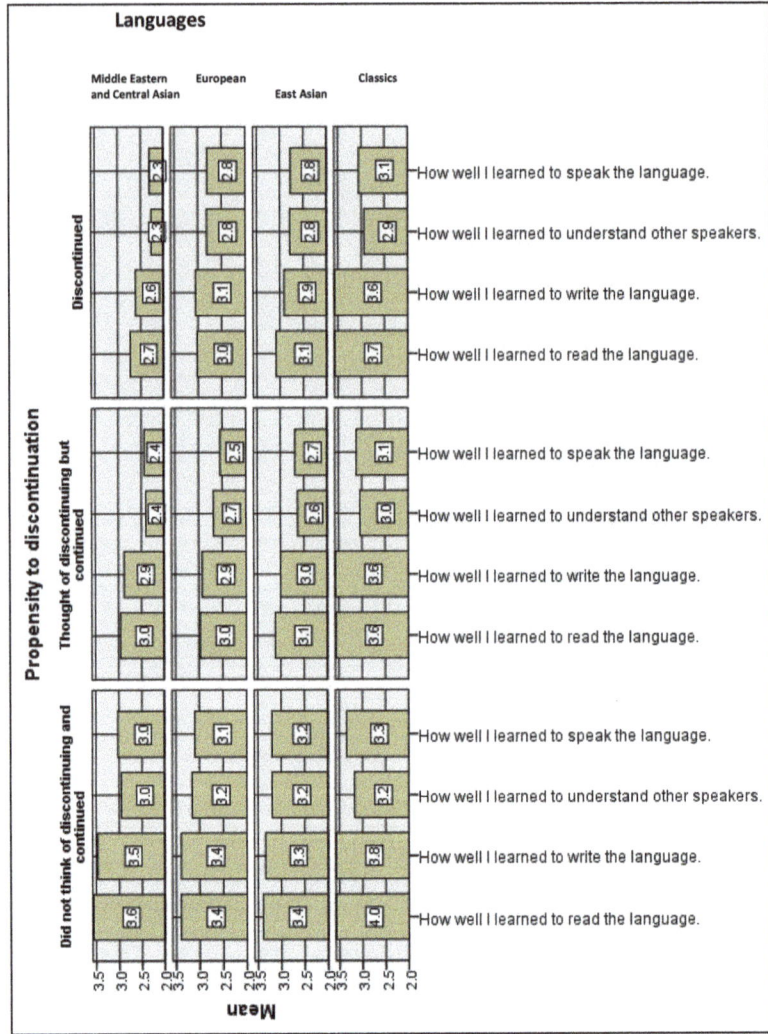

Figure 5.3. Perceptions of how well students have learned the four language skills, discriminated by language groups and propensity to discontinuation
Source: Phase 2 Questionnaire Data.

When we break down the perceptions reported in Figure 5.2 into the three groups of Committed Students, Doubters and Quitters (Figure 5.3), we find that, even for all groups and languages, there is still a differential in perceptions that reading and writing were learned more successfully than oral skills, as is evident in the considerable differences found across the three student groups. This is summarised in Figure 5.4, where, taking the whole respondent sample, we calculated means for the parameters related to students' reports of how much that they had learned about the culture associated with the language studied, and how much of the four language skills (reading, writing, understanding and speaking) they felt they had learned by the time they were responding to the survey. Culture was added because of the commonly held view (which we share, as does the Languages and Cultures Network for Australian Universities) that the teaching of language and culture cannot be separated.

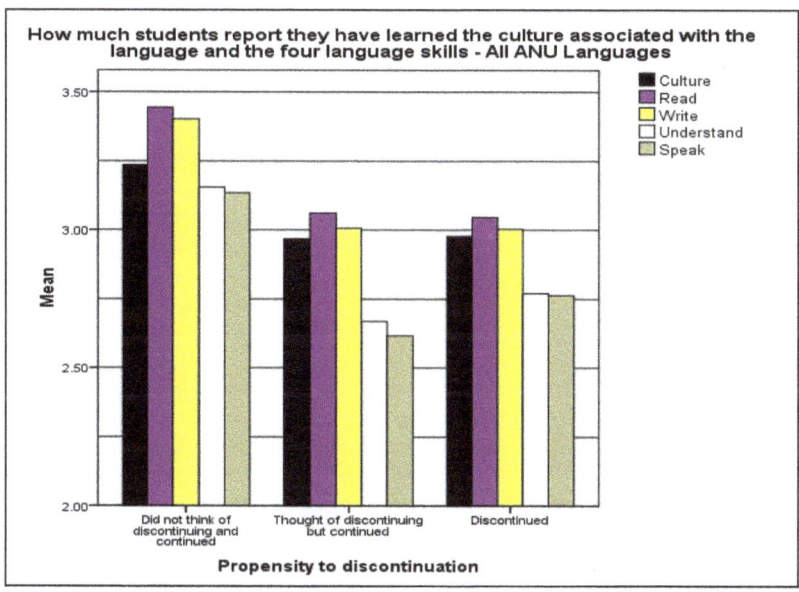

Figure 5.4. Perceptions of how much students have learned about the culture associated with the language and the four language skills, discriminated by propensity to discontinuation. All students
Source: Phase 2 Questionnaire Data.

On average, Committed Students reported more learning than the other two groups in each skill category: indeed, the means for all items reported by Committed Students are higher than the highest score in any skill category for Quitters or Doubters (Figures 5.3 and 5.4), except for Classics. Our interpretation of this undoubtedly interesting finding—which many teachers might see as indicating the nature of 'good' students—is that it reflects both the higher language capital that Committed Students have when they start at university, and their ability to use their language capital in the university L&C learning setting. Committed Students not only achieve higher marks, but are also able to derive more benefit from both the cultural components and the language skills-based content in their courses. This would then explain why Committed Students report that they have learned more grammar, or more culture, than they expected, and more than is reported by members of the other two groups (section 4.2.7, Figures 4.8.b and 4.8.c).

Quitters and Doubters can also potentially be differentiated in this context: while the two groups differ little in the average amount of learning they report for culture, reading and writing, they are noticeably different with respect to understanding and speaking the language (section 4.2.7, Figures 4.8.b and 4.8.c). However, this is possibly a sampling issue, because, as we discussed in Chapter 3, Quitters are actually a composite of two groups, Reluctant Quitters, who share characteristics with the Committed Students, and Voluntary Quitters, who are more like the Doubters. Therefore, we cannot convincingly say more about Quitters in relation to the issue at hand.

In contrast to the other two groups, Doubters are more likely to be sensitive to the presence in their classes of students with more language capital, and to worry that this differential in language capital will work to their disadvantage, especially in mixed-ability classes. Doubters are more likely to feel embarrassed speaking in front of other students who (because of their acquired language capital) are perceived to be better speakers of the language (section 4.2.12, Figures 4.17.c and 4.18.d). Moreover, Doubters share a perception that no amount of study could compensate for their lack of accumulated language capital. This perception appears to be confirmed as they progress in their L&C study and witness an increase in the proportion of students in their classes who speak the LOTE at home (section 2.6, Table 2.XV and Figure 2.15.b). Doubters are thus prone to feeling that not enough course time is being spent on speaking and understanding the language, because their deficits in this area provide the most noticeable evidence of their lack of language capital. Yet, because Doubters feel that they have no option but to continue studying in the relevant L&C program in which they are enrolled (because of degree requirements or external pressures), they worry about their grades (section 4.2.10, Figure 4.13.b).

Overall, therefore, Doubters are likely to feel that learning a language has proven more difficult than they expected. In an effort to compensate for their initial lack of language capital, they might focus more on learning language skills rather than on the cultural and other aspects of the course: in turn, this high level of effort could make them perceive the workload as unmanageable, and prevent them from enjoying the course content as a whole (sections 4.2.8 and 4.2.12, Figures 4.10 and 4.18.a). Notably, even if teachers try to cater for the whole class and take the Doubters' needs into consideration, experience tells us that the mere presence of students with more language capital creates a class dynamic that might be perceived by Doubters as working against their success.

Undoubtedly, this putative psychographic exploration of what might be happening in an L&C course—what we term the Doubters' Dilemma—needs refining in future studies that are designed to test the categorisation that we have found and to examine its nature in more depth. However, we feel that there is real value in using the construct of language capital to underpin more specific interpretations like those above, which purport to interpret how different students may be approaching and engaging with their language learning, almost irrespective of the nature of the actual teaching. We feel such interpretations of the collected data provide valuable insights, for teachers and curriculum design. Significantly, we could not have created this interpretation by simply listing the factors that contribute to discontinuation, or by considering the simple dichotomy of Continuers versus Discontinuers.

We believe that the Doubters' Dilemma is a situation well known to experienced L&C teachers at universities. More importantly, our interpretation shows *why* Doubters may feel that they have not learned sufficient speaking and comprehension skills in the same classes that seem to satisfy other students. Our interpretation of the ANU data also provides a cogent explanation of why, survey after survey, researchers report that a considerable proportion of L&C students are dissatisfied with the amount of class time devoted to speaking, except in languages like Classics, where this is not pertinent (e.g. Bowden et al., 1989, 131; Leal et al., 1991, 141; Nettelbeck et al., 2009, 19).

5.5. Summary

In this chapter we characterised the student groups of Committed Students, Doubters and Quitters in detail and introduced the construct of language capital. We also explored an issue frequently reported in the language retention literature—perceptions about learning the spoken language—using the construct of language capital to illustrate how it could be apply in understanding the doubters' dilemma. In the final chapter we will summarise the case study, reflect on methodological issues and implications of the use of the language capital construct, and explore other potential applications or uses of this construct.

6

Where to from Here? Conclusions and suggestions

The intention of this monograph has been to contribute to the research and debate on retention and attrition in L&C programs in Australian universities by providing the full details of an in-depth single-institution case study. By considering retention as a social phenomenon as well as an educational phenomenon, we have been able to provide an evidence-based framework for reconceptualising retention and attrition in L&C programs as a function of students' language capital at the commencement of their university language studies.

Guided methodologically and philosophically by ideas expressed by Bourdieu (2010) and Lo Bianco (2009) (see Chapter 1), and largely contemporaneously with the most significant research focused specifically on retention in L&C programs in Australian universities (Lobo and Matas, 2010; Nettelbeck et al., 2007, 2009), the ANU case study was developed through a data-driven approach. This involved thorough statistical analyses of both an extensive set of institutional enrolment information, and of the detailed student data collected through a comprehensive questionnaire across multiple L&C programs.

The outcomes achieved with these methodologies, and their accessibility to theory-guided interpretation, indicate the potential for future similar studies across multiple institutions to guide the development of new, more effective policies related to student retention in university L&C programs. In particular, five key findings from the case study, once replicated and debated across the sector, could be expected to contribute significantly to future policy development.

First, it has become clear that using a retention/attrition dichotomy, which simply compares 'continuing' to 'discontinuing' students, results in an incomplete, and relatively unhelpful, understanding of the retention/attrition profiles of L&C programs. Instead, the case study has shown that at least three—and ideally four—groups of students need to be differentiated. The evidence-based characterisation of students as falling into the groups of Committed Students, Doubters and Quitters (comprising Reluctant Quitters and Voluntary Quitters) accounts for the phenomenon of attrition much more effectively than the traditional dichotomy of Continuers versus Discontinuers.

Second, the case study data show clearly that research into student retention in L&C programs cannot be based on the assumptions that all first year university students enrol in Beginner level courses, or that all students who enrol in Beginner level courses are in their first year at university. Similarly, researchers and administrators cannot assume that all students in higher level L&C courses are beyond first year, that is, that they are already accustomed to university studies (and therefore perhaps no longer need as much in the way of academic and other support services).

Instead, we have to acknowledge that the real picture is much more complex: in at least some universities, significant numbers of students (including international students) who are already in the middle—or even in the last year—of their degree may still choose to enrol in Beginner L&C courses, and thus become Late Starters. Conversely, many students in their first year of university who have a background in a LOTE (including international students and local background speakers), or have studied a language before, may start their L&C studies beyond Beginner levels, and thus become Advanced Starters. These cohort-based phenomena not only confound many aspects of attrition calculations, but also create significant complexity for teachers, as they must work with classes of students with potentially very diverse levels of pre-existing knowledge of the language, and diverse status in terms of their relative experience in a university setting.

Moreover, students who are background LOTE speakers and/or international students appear to have a significant impact on attrition and retention rates, both through their enrolment as Advanced Starters, and, indirectly, by their presence in mixed-ability classes, through their unintended influence on other students with less language capital, who may perceive the Advanced Starters as having an unfair advantage. The mix of cohorts created by student enrolment patterns may be further complicated by institutional funding constraints that reduce the capacity for staff to stream L&C courses effectively.

This finding from the case study is extremely important, as it means that the complexities of retention and attrition issues in L&C programs will never be understood through data collection and analysis that focuses solely on Beginner students. In this context, the finding not only identifies an unexpected methodological limitation of both LASP studies (Nettelbeck et al., 2007, 2009), which was confined to Beginner students, but also presents an important facet of L&C student behaviour for future in-depth exploration.

Undoubtedly, L&C programs can be considered to be at a structural disadvantage when compared with other humanities or social sciences majors because a substantial proportion of L&C budgets must be devoted to helping students develop the language skills required for more content-oriented courses. The range of electives and subject choices for students in L&C programs is therefore always going to be significantly more limited than in humanities or social sciences programs.

However, the third case-study finding of significance is that student retention rates in L&C programs may not be as low as previously thought. This has become evident through the more refined methodology and analyses—the Global Retention Rate and Semester Level Retention Rate measures (Chapter 2)—developed as part of the case study research. These measures show that similar—even comparatively lower—retention rates are found in some groupings of science disciplines that have degree majors structurally similar to L&C majors. Real attrition rates are, however, difficult to determine because effective collection of the appropriate data requires contact with students who are no longer enrolled at the university, and who may therefore not be contactable, or not interested in providing feedback even if they can be contacted.

The fourth key finding of the case study hinges on those students who fit the characterisation of Doubters, namely those students who doubt the benefits of continuing their L&C studies, and who are therefore the students at greatest risk of giving up. While it is not surprising that 25 per cent of students in ANU Beginner (Level 1) courses were Doubters—as this is comparable to the proportion of at-risk students among Beginners identified in the LASP1 study (Nettelbeck et al., 2007, 11)—it is of some concern that no less than 40 per cent of students in the ANU Intermediate or Advanced courses (Levels 2 and 3) were also identifiable as Doubters. The issue of learning anxiety—for languages and in general (see Chapter 1)—may prove a worthwhile contribution to the description of Doubters in this context.

This finding is of significance as it contrasts substantially with the traditional perception that retention efforts have to be concentrated on first year students as those most at risk of giving up. If the implications of this finding gain acceptance, as we think they should, they will have a major bearing on the design of future interventions aimed at improving student retention in L&C programs in Australian universities. For example, while Lobo and Matas (2010) achieved success in improving retention by means of early identification of Beginner students at potential risk of discontinuing, this benefit could be lost in the students' subsequent years of study, as we do not yet understand the drivers for later-year Doubters and potential Voluntary Quitters.

Our case study results thus raise a concern that retention strategies that focus solely on students at Beginner level may turn out to be relatively unsuccessful in the long term in their impact on overall numbers of students completing L&C programs. Moreover, such an emphasis on Beginners would also fail the more advanced students on whom L&C programs ultimately depend. Losing students who are already in Intermediate or Advanced courses seriously compromises the overall number of students available to complete majors or move into Honours programs, and it is from this group that Australia's future language teachers and scholars will come.

The final key finding from the case study relates to the relevance of language capital as a construct that facilitates a deeper understanding of the uniqueness of retention issues among L&C students. We believe that such a construct—once replicated, tested and debated across the sector—may provide valuable guidance for curriculum- and program-level interventions, such as those already suggested by Nettelbeck et al. (2009, 18–19). In particular, the importance of needs-based design for different groups of L&C students becomes paramount: language curricula, and the design of majors and minors, should cater to the needs, at all levels, not only of Committed Students, but also to those of the other identifiable groups—Doubters, potential Voluntary Quitters, Late Starters, international students, background speakers of a LOTE, and all students at risk of discontinuing L&C courses.

In this context, we can only echo the most recently published view of the most prolific and long-term researcher on student retention in the world, Professor Vincent Tinto of Syracuse University:

> Our prevailing view of student retention has been shaped by theories that view student retention through the lens of institutional action and ask what institutions can do to retain their students. Students, however, do not seek to be retained. They seek to persist. The two perspectives, though necessarily related, are not the same. Their interests are different. While the institution's interest is to increase the proportion of their students who graduate from the institution, the student's interest is to complete a degree often without regard to the institution in which it is earned. Although there has been much written from the former point of view, much less has been written from the latter … For institutions, an understanding of student perceptions, not simply their behavioural manifestation, and their impact upon student decisions to stay or leave is a pre-requisite for the development of a more comprehensive strategy to further enhance the persistence and completion of all, not just some, students. Only when institutions understand how student perceptions shape decisions to persist and how their actions influence those perceptions can institutions move to impact those decisions in ways that enhance the likelihood of greater persistence … (Tinto, 2015).

What are the implications of all the ANU case study findings for future research in this field? Potentially, we can imagine the characteristics of the three identified student cohorts—Committed Students, Doubters, and Quitters—being generalised across other L&C programs in Australian tertiary institutions. However, we first advocate replication of the case study methodology with more defined institutional or jurisdictional foci.

We see an urgent need to refine and test, in the broader sector, our reconceptualisation of retention in L&C programs, with a particular focus on the dilemma faced by the students we characterise as Doubters. While we consider that the psychographic characteristics of Doubters are an excellent starting point for distinguishing students at risk of discontinuing their L&C studies, more cross-sectional studies involving different types of universities would allow a detailed refinement of the relevant cohort profiles. (A study encompassing all universities in one of the Australian state capitals could be ideal, as it would contrast diversity of institution and language capital profiles within the student population.)

Replication of the research methodology would also allow a revisiting of the characterisation of Voluntary versus Reluctant Quitters, which we could not explore in depth in the ANU case study because of sampling issues. In particular, we were unable to investigate factors that may influence motivation to continue or discontinue L&C studies in tertiary settings, such as the teaching programs, mode of delivery, or proportion of native/background speakers or international students in the class mix, or students' socio-economic background, rural or urban backgrounds, or Australian Tertiary Admission Rank (ATAR) score.[1] We also suspect that the experiences of students in the transition period from high school to university would be a crucial focus for exploration in the context of the concepts we have raised, such as language capital, degree structure, and Advanced and Late Starters.

We have hypothesised that the construct of language capital provides a crucial, and potentially causative, basis to the many issues previously identified in L&C research as individual retention problems (such as mixed proficiency groups, perceptions of high workloads, frustrations with slow progress, and perceptions that not enough time in class is spent on learning to speak the language). In both the LASP1 and LASP2 studies (respectively Nettelbeck et al., 2007; Nettelbeck et al., 2009), and in our preliminary treatment of the ANU case study data using the dichotomy of Continuers versus Discontinuers, all the above factors were considered as separate issues.

---

1   The Australian First Year Experience Study 2014 found that studying a language was less common among respondent students with a disability, part-time students, students from regional backgrounds, students with low socio-economic status, and low ATAR students (Baik, Naylor and Arkoudis, 2015).

We now believe that the methodological failing of using such a simple dichotomy masked the much more integrated issues related to both the language setting and the identity of students participating in mixed-ability classes. We are now convinced that a more effective use of theoretical frameworks and perspectives, and especially a more open consideration of frameworks derived from diverse academic disciplines (for example, as advocated by Wesely, 2010, and by Forsman, Linder, Moll, Fraser and Andersson, 2014), and of students' perceptions (as advocated by Tinto, 2015) may generate new ways of understanding the concepts of retention and attrition, certainly in the context of L&C programs, and potentially in more general contexts.

In particular, the concept of language capital that we propose in this book appears to be independent of the social factors known to influence attrition and retention in other disciplines, and is thus a construct we believe could be useful in developing a more complete understanding of the realities of student retention and attrition in L&C programs. If this approach were to be combined with current trends for 'big data' analysis (Daniel, 2015; Ram, Wang, Currim and Currim, 2015; Tickle, 2015), and data reduction methods and complexity thinking as an approach to calculating retention (Forsman et al., 2014), the concept, more broadly defined as cultural capital (Bourdieu, 1986), could be potentially applied to other disciplines as well (especially those comparable to L&C, such as the sciences and Mathematics).

We believe that future research in this field is vital. Even though the empirical methodologies described in this book were limited to a single institution, we believe that the findings, and especially the tools developed to interpret those findings, can provide valuable insights into retention and attrition in other university L&C programs. As such, we hope this case study will serve as a springboard for future studies and policy formation.

We especially advocate combining the methodologies of the in-depth approach reported in this book with a cross-sectoral approach such as that used by Nettelbeck et al. (2009). By analysing new data in the context of the four characteristic segments of the student body that we have identified, we believe that other areas of focus, such as language aptitude or differences in learning styles, could also provide an enriched source of guidance for language teachers in developing curricula and strategies to meet student needs.

Future research that is based on the national collation of accurate Australia-wide retention and attrition data, and used to inform debate through the more rigorous calculations suggested in this book, could provide a firm platform from which an evidence-based Australia-wide retention policy for university L&C programs could be developed, ideally informing a broader national policy on tertiary language teaching. The policy we envisage would be 'bottom-up', and, ideally, would be planned, conceived and proposed within the framework of activities overseen by the Languages and Cultures Network for Australian Universities (LCNAU). Such a policy should be based both on empirical data gathered by Australia-wide and longitudinal retention studies and reconsideration of Australia's future L&C learning needs as a society, for example as envisaged and debated by Liddicoat and Scarino (2010).

Participants in this policy-making would ideally include all Australian universities, the secondary language-teaching associations, the Australian Government department responsible for higher and schools education (currently the Department of Education and Training), and other relevant federal and state government departments, as well as other stakeholder sectors such as Chambers of Commerce, and representatives of major export industries and tourism.

We hope that the methodologies, outcomes and interpretations in this book can provide insights of practical value to language teaching practitioners and educational policymakers as they attempt to address the Doubters' Dilemma, that is, the decision that many students face every year, perhaps every day, as to whether or not to continue their L&C studies at university.

Appendices:
Online Questionnaires Used in the ANU Study

Appendix 1: Questionnaire 1. Language Retention Study: First year students 2009

Section 1. BACKGROUND INFORMATION

(Questions marked * are mandatory)

Please complete a SEPARATE questionnaire for EACH language studied.

Q1. Please give your student ID.*

(Your ID will be deleted from the database after responses are analysed to protect your anonymity.)

Q2. Are you currently enrolled in more than one language course at ANU?

Yes
No

Q3. If yes, please specify which language(s):

(AND *please complete another questionnaire for each language studied.*)

Q4. Which language are you completing this questionnaire for?

(Please select ONE option from the pull-down list.)

Arabic	*Latin*	*Korean*	*Turkish*
Chinese	*Hindi*	*Persian*	*Urdu*
French	*Indonesian*	*Sanskrit*	*Vietnamese*
German	*Italian*	*Spanish*	*Other (please*
Greek	*Japanese*	*Thai*	*specify)*

Q5. Would you have preferred to study a different language had it been available?

Yes
No

Q6. If yes, please specify the language(s):

Q7. Does your degree require compulsory language study?

Yes
No

Q8. How much freedom did you have to choose whether or not you study a language as part of your degree?

Not at all free
To some extent free
Totally free

Q9. Have you studied (formally or informally) any languages (*including English as a second language*) before enrolling in university?

Yes
No

Q10. If *yes*, please specify which language(s) and at what level (primary school, secondary school, community centre, overseas experience etc.):

Q11. If you had studied languages before enrolling at university, how would you rate your experience of learning that language?

Not at all rewarding
Not very rewarding
Somewhat rewarding
Very rewarding
Extremely rewarding

Q12. Have you been an exchange student?

Yes
No

Q13. If *yes*, please specify when, where, how long and which language(s) were spoken:

Q14. What languages do you speak with your immediate family?

Please provide the following information with respect to your family and friends' experiences of other languages (*Please tick the relevant circles and leave the rest blank*):

○   *Speaks a language (native or non-native) other than English.*
○   *Converses regularly with you in a language other than English.*
○   *Has learned a second (non-native) language well enough to get by in a country where it is spoken.*

Q15. Partner.

Q16. Children.

Q17. Parents.

Q18. Siblings.

Q19. Grandparents.

Q20. Other relatives.

Q21. Close friends.

Q22. Other friends.

Q23. Acquaintances.

Section 2. REASONS FOR STUDYING A LANGUAGE

(Answer ONLY for the language that you specified in Q4)

How important are the following reasons for your decision to commence language study at university?

Not at all important   *Very important*
Not very important   *Extremely important*
Of some importance   *Not applicable*

Q24. I have a family background in this language.

Q25. I'm interested in the history and culture of the language.

Q26. My friends are studying this language.

Q27. To travel to where this language is spoken.

Q28. To live or work in a country where this language is spoken.

Q29. To communicate with native speakers of the language.

Q30. To participate in cultural activities of the language group.

Q31. For religious reasons.

Q32. For employment reasons.

Q33. To complete my degree.

Q34. To help me in my other studies.

Q35. My family encouraged me to study it.

Q36. Because I had previously studied the language.

Q37. Because I have previously spent time in a country where the language is spoken.

Q38. Because of the reputation of this language at ANU.

Q39. I thought it would be an easy subject.

Q40. I enjoy language learning.

Q41. To understand people and cultures outside of my own.

Q42. Other reasons (please specify and rate them, eg. '*I like the sound of the language—very important*'):

APPENDIX 1

Section 3. EXPERIENCE OF LANGUAGE STUDY

(Answer ONLY for the language that you specified in Q4)

How interested were you in the following aspects of the language when you first enrolled at university?

Not at all interested
Not very interested
Somewhat interested
Very interested
Extremely interested

Q43. Reading the language.

Q44. Writing the language.

Q45. Speaking the language.

Q46. Understanding other speakers.

Q47. The culture of the language.

To what extent has your first-year language course been meeting your expectations in the following areas?

Much worse than expected
A little worse than expected
As expected
A little better than expected
Much better than expected

Q48. Teachers' knowledge (*average across teachers*).

Q49. Teachers' teaching skills.

Q50. Teaching/learning materials (*including the textbook*).

Q51. Learning environment and facilities.

Q52. Advice and feedback from teachers.

Q53. Approachability and availability of teachers.

Q54. Support from fellow students.

And to what extent has the language course met your expectations in the following additional areas?

Much less than expected
Less than expected
As expected
More than expected
Much more than expected

Q55. Workload associated with learning to <u>read</u> the language.

Q56. Workload associated with learning to <u>write</u> the language.

Q57. Workload associated with learning to <u>speak</u> the language.

Q58. Workload associated with learning to <u>understand</u> other speakers.

Q59. Overall difficulty of the course.

Q60. Difficulty learning the grammar in particular.

Q61. Enjoyment of language learning.

Q62. How well I learned to <u>read</u> the language.

Q63. How well I learned to <u>write</u> the language.

Q64. How well I learned to <u>speak</u> the language.

Q65. How well I learned to <u>understand</u> other speakers.

Q66. How much I learned about the <u>culture</u> of the language.

Q67. Others (please specify and rate them):

Q68. Please comment on any expectations that are not being met:

APPENDIX 1

Q69. If you are studying the Bachelor of International Relations (BIR), Bachelor of International Commerce (BIC) or any other degree where a language component is compulsory, to what extent has your languages study supported your other BIR or BIC studies, especially in terms of cross-cultural understandings?

Much less than expected
Less than expected
As expected
More than expected
Much more than expected
Not applicable

Q70. If you are studying an International Relations (IR) or International Commerce (IC) or any other course as major within the BA, to what extent has your languages study supported your interest in IR or IC or others, especially in terms of cross-cultural understanding?

Much less than expected
Less than expected
As expected
More than expected
Much more than expected
Not applicable

Section 4. THOUGHTS ON DISCONTINUING LANGUAGE STUDY

Q71. How much freedom do you have in continuing to study this language and not another?

Not at all free
To some extent free
Totally free

Q72. Was there anything compelling or forcing you to study this language?

Yes
No
Uncertain

Q73. Please expand on the reasons for your answer in Q72. (e.g. family, religion, career track, degree only, etc.)

Q74. If you had had the choice of not studying a language, would you have chosen to study it anyway?

Yes
No
Uncertain

Q75. Please expand on the reasons for your answer in Q74.

Q76. Are you now seriously considering (or have you in the past) discontinuing or deferring your language studies?

Yes
No

Comments

If no, please mention why not in the comment box above and go to Q102.

If yes, please indicate the importance of the following reasons for thinking of discontinuing/deferring.

Not at all important
Not very important
Of some importance
Very important
Extremely important
Not applicable

Q77. Health reasons.

Q78. Financial reasons.

Q79. My expectations are not being met.

Q80. I'm not satisfied with my progress.

Q81. I'm not enjoying the course content.

APPENDIX 1

Q82. I don't like the way the language is being taught.

Q83. Class sizes are too big.

Q84. I'm finding the course too difficult.

Q85. I'm finding the workload too high.

Q86. Not enough class time is spent on speaking the language.

Q87. I'm not getting good marks/grades.

Q88. My friends are discontinuing.

Q89. People are discouraging me from continuing language study.

Q90. I fell behind in my studies and can't catch up.

Q91. Problems with daily travel.

Q92. Timetable clash.

Q93. Other study commitments.

Q94. Paid work commitments.

Q95. Family commitments.

Q96. I feel uncomfortable speaking the language in front of others.

Q97. I do not fit in with other students in the course.

Q98. It worries me that other students seem to speak better than I do.

Q99. I didn't think I would get to use the language outside university.

Q100. I'm thinking of terminating all of my studies.

Q101. Other reasons (please specify and rate them):

Plans for continuing language study

Q102. How long do you think you will continue to study the language at university? (*Please select ONE option from the pull-down list.*)

Complete the current course (up to 1 year).
Complete the sub-major (2 years).
Complete the major (3 years).
Do honours (4 years).
Do postgraduate study.
Other (please specify)

Q103. Do you plan to keep learning the language informally after you complete university study?

Yes
No
Uncertain

Q104. Which aspects of language study do you enjoy <u>least</u>?

Q105. Which aspects of language study do you enjoy <u>most</u>?

Q106. Is there anything else you would like to share about your experiences of language study?

Section 5. THE NEXT STAGE OF THE PROJECT

Q107. Would you like to receive a copy of the survey report when it is available?

Yes
No

Q108. If *yes*, please insert your <u>email address</u> so that we can contact you:

Q109. Would you be available for a follow-up interview about your experiences of language study?

Yes
No

APPENDIX 1

Q110. If yes, please insert your <u>email address</u> and <u>telephone number</u> so that we can contact you (if you already provided your email address in the previous question, then write 'as above' in the email box):

Email
Phone number

THANK YOU FOR TAKING YOUR TIME TO COMPLETE
THIS QUESTIONNAIRE.

Please press the 'Submit' button only when you are satisfied with your responses as you will not be able to change your answers once the survey is submitted.

Appendix 2: Questionnaire: Continuing intermediate and advanced level students 2009

Section 1. BACKGROUND INFORMATION

(Questions marked * are mandatory)

Please complete a SEPARATE questionnaire for EACH language studied.

Q1. Please give your student ID.*

(Your ID will be deleted from the survey database after responses are analysed to better protect your anonymity.)

Q2. Which year of your ANU degree (full-time equivalent) are you in at the moment?

(Please select ONE option from the pull-down list.)

First year
Second year
Third year
Other (please specify)

Q3. Does your degree require compulsory language study?

Yes
No

Q4. How much freedom did you have to choose whether or not you study a language as part of your degree?

Not at all free
To some extent free
Totally free

Q5. Are you currently enrolled in more than one language course at ANU?

Yes
No

Q6. If yes, please specify the language(s):

(AND *please complete another questionnaire for each language studied.*)

Q7. Which language are you completing this questionnaire for?

(Please select ONE option from the pull-down list.)

Arabic
Chinese
French
German
Greek
Latin
Hindi
Indonesian
Italian
Japanese
Korean
Persian
Sanskrit
Spanish
Thai
Turkish
Urdu
Vietnamese
Other (please specify)

Q8. Would you have preferred to study a different language had it been available?

Yes
No

Q9. If *yes*, please specify which language:

Q10. Did you study (formally or informally) any languages (*including English as a second language*) before enrolling at university?

Yes
No

Q11. If *yes*, please specify which language(s) and at what level (primary school, secondary school, community centre, overseas experience, etc.):

Q12. If you had studied languages before enrolling at university, how would you rate your experience of learning that language?

Not at all rewarding
Not very rewarding
Somewhat rewarding
Very rewarding
Extremely rewarding

Q13. Have you been an exchange student?

Yes
No

Q14. If *yes*, please specify when, where, how long and which language(s) were spoken:

Q15. What languages do you speak with your immediate family?

Please provide the following information with respect to your family and friends' experiences of other languages (*Please tick the relevant circles and leave the rest blank*):

- ○ *Speaks a language (native or non-native) other than English.*
- ○ *Converses regularly with you in a language other than English.*
- ○ *Has learned a second (non-native) language well enough to get by in a country where it is spoken.*

Q16. Partner.

Q17. Children.

Q18. Parents.

Q19. Siblings.

Q20. Grandparents.

Q21. Other relatives.

Q22. Close friends.

Q23. Other friends.

Q24. Acquaintances.

Section 2. REASONS FOR STUDYING A LANGUAGE

(Answer ONLY for the language that you specified in Q6)

How important are the following reasons for your decision to commence language study at university?

Not at all important
Not very important
Of some importance
Very important
Extremely important
Not applicable

Q25. I have a family background in this language.

Q26. I'm interested in the history and culture of the language.

Q27. My friends are studying this language.

Q28. To travel to where this language is spoken.

Q29. To live or work in the country where this language is spoken.

Q30. To communicate with native speakers of the language.

Q31. To participate in cultural activities of the language group.

Q32. For religious reasons.

Q33. For employment reasons.

Q34. To complete my degree.

Q35. To help me in my other studies.

Q36. My family encouraged me to study it.

Q37. Because I had previously studied the language.

Q38. Because I have previously spent time in a country where the language is spoken.

Q39. Because of the reputation of this language at ANU.

Q40. I thought it would be an easy subject.

Q41. I enjoy language learning.

Q42. To understand people and cultures outside of my own.

Q43. Other reasons (please specify and rate them, eg. '*I like the sound of the language—very important*'):

Section 3. EXPERIENCE OF LANGUAGE STUDY

(Answer ONLY for the language that you specified in Q6)

How interested were you in the following aspects of the language when you first enrolled at university?

Not at all interested
Not very interested
Somewhat interested
Very interested
Extremely interested

Q44. Reading the language.

Q45. Writing the language.

Q46. Speaking the language.

Q47. Understanding other speakers.

Q48. The culture of the language.

Thinking back to your *first-year or second year language course,* to what extent did it meet your expectations in the following areas?

Much worse than expected
A little worse than expected
As expected
A little better than expected
Much better than expected

Q49. Teachers' knowledge (*average across teachers*).

Q50. Teachers' teaching skills.

Q51. Teaching/learning materials (*including the textbook*).

Q52. Learning environment and facilities.

Q53. Advice and feedback from teachers.

Q54. Approachability and availability of teachers.

Q55. Support from fellow students.

And to what extent did your *first-year or second year course* meet your expectations in the following additional areas?

Much less than expected
Less than expected
As expected
More than expected
Much more than expected

APPENDIX 2

Q56. Workload associated with learning to read the language.

Q57. Workload associated with learning to write the language.

Q58. Workload associated with learning to speak the language.

Q59. Workload associated with learning to understand other speakers.

Q60. Overall difficulty of the course.

Q61. Difficulty of learning grammar in particular.

Q62. Enjoyment of language learning.

Q63. How much I learned about reading the language.

Q64. How much I learned about writing the language.

Q65. How much I learned about speaking the language.

Q66. How much I learned to understand other speakers.

Q67. How much I learned about the culture of the language.

Q68. Others (please specify and rate them):

Q69. Please comment on any expectations that were not met:

Q70. If you are studying the Bachelor of International Relations (BIR) or Bachelor of International Commerce (BIC) or any other degree where a language component is compulsory, to what extent has your language study supported your other BIR or other studies, especially in terms of cross-cultural understanding?

Much less than expected
Less than expected
As expected
More than expected
Much more than expected
Not applicable

Q71. If you are studying any International Relations (IR) or International Commerce (IC) or any other course as major within BA where a language component is compulsory, to what extent has your language study supported your interest in IR or IC or others, especially in terms of cross-cultural understanding?

Much less than expected
Less than expected
As expected
More than expected
Much more than expected
Not applicable

Section 4. THOUGHTS ON DISCONTINUING LANGUAGE STUDY

(Answer ONLY for the language that you specified in Q6)

Q72. How much freedom do you have in continuing to study this language and not another?

Not at all free
To some extent free
Totally free

Q73. Was there anything compelling or forcing you to study this language?

Yes
No
Uncertain

Q74. Please expand on the reasons for your answer in Q73. (e.g. family, religion, career track, degree only, etc.)

Q75. If you had had the choice of not studying a language, would you have chosen to study it anyway?

Yes
No
Uncertain

If you answered 'Yes' or 'No' in this question, please mention the reason for 'Yes' or 'No' in the following question.

APPENDIX 2

Q76. Please expand on the reasons for your answer in Q75.

Q77. Even though you are currently continuing to study the language, have you ever seriously thought about discontinuing or deferring your language study, now or in the past?
Yes
No

Comments

If no, please explain why not in the comment box above and go to SECTION 5 by clicking either number '5' on the top left corner of this page or 'Next' at the end of this page.

If yes, please indicate the importance of the following reasons for thinking of discontinuing/deferring.

Not at all important
Not very important
Of some importance
Very important
Extremely important
Not applicable

Q78. Health reasons.

Q79. Financial reasons.

Q80. My expectations were not being met.

Q81. I wasn't satisfied with my progress.

Q82. I wasn't enjoying the course content.

Q83. I did not like the way the language was taught.

Q84. Class sizes were too big.

Q85. I was finding the course too difficult.

Q86. I was finding the workload too high.

Q87. Not enough class time was spent on speaking the language.

Q88. I did not get good marks/grades.

Q89. My friends were discontinuing.

Q90. People discouraged me from continuing language study.

Q91. I fell behind in my studies and couldn't catch up.

Q92. Problems with daily travel.

Q93. Timetable clash.

Q94. Other study commitments.

Q95. Paid work commitments.

Q96. Family commitments.

Q97. I felt uncomfortable speaking the language in front of others.

Q98. I did not fit in with other students in the course.

Q99. It worried me that other students in my class seemed to speak the language better than I did.

Q100. I didn't think I would get to use the language outside university.

Q101. I was thinking of terminating all of my studies.

Q102. Other reasons (please specify and rate them).

Section 5. REASONS FOR CONTINUING YOUR LANGUAGE STUDY

(Answer ONLY for the language that you specified in Q6)

Please indicate the importance of the following reasons for deciding to *continue* your language study at university this year:

Not at all important
Not very important
Of some importance
Very important
Extremely important
Not applicable

Q103. I enjoy learning the language.

Q104. I like the way it is taught.

Q105. I like the learning materials.

Q106. The workload is manageable.

Q107. I get good marks/grades.

Q108. I find the language easy to learn.

Q109. My friends have also continued learning the language.

Q110. My family keeps encouraging me to study the language.

Q111. I think knowing more than one language is important.

Q112. I need to use the language in my work.

Q113. I feel I am progressing well with the language.

Q114. No better study alternatives are available.

Q115. It would be a shame to give up at this stage.

Q116. Other reasons (please specify and rate them):

Q117. How long do you think you will continue to study the language at university?

(Please select ONE option from the pull-down list.)

Complete the current course.
Complete a sub-major.
Complete the major.
Do honours.
Do postgraduate study.
Other (please specify)

Q118. Do you plan to keep learning the language informally after you complete university study?

Yes
No

Q119. Which aspects of language study do you enjoy least?

Q120. Which aspects of language study do you enjoy most?

Q121. Is there anything else you would like to share about your experiences of language study?

Section 6. THE NEXT STAGE OF THE PROJECT

Q122. Would you like to receive a copy of the survey report when it is available?

Yes
No

Q123. If yes, please insert your email address so that we can contact you:

Q124. Would you be available for a follow-up interview about your experiences of language study?

Yes
No

APPENDIX 2

Q125. If *yes*, please insert your <u>email address</u> and <u>telephone number</u> so that we can contact you (if you already provided your email address in your previous answer, please write 'as above'):

Email

Phone number

THANK YOU FOR TAKING YOUR TIME TO COMPLETE THIS QUESTIONNAIRE.

Please press the 'Submit' button only when you are satisfied with your responses, as you will not be able to change your answers once the survey has been submitted.

Appendix 3: Questionnaire: Discontinuing students 2009

Section 1. BACKGROUND INFORMATION

(Questions marked * are mandatory)

Please complete a SEPARATE questionnaire for EACH language studied.

Q1. Please give your student ID.*

(Your ID will be deleted from the survey database after responses are analysed to better protect your anonymity.)

Q2. Which year of your ANU degree (full-time equivalent) are you in at the moment?

(Please select ONE option from the pull-down list.)

First year
Second year
Third year
I finished my degree
Have discontinued or deferred all ANU studies
Other (please specify)

Q3. Does/did your degree require compulsory language study?

Yes
No

Q4. How much freedom did you have to choose whether or not you study a language as part of your degree?

Not at all free
To some extent free
Totally free

Q5. Are you, or have you been, concurrently enrolled in more than one language course in your ANU degree?

Yes
No

Q6. If *yes*, please specify the language(s):

(AND *please complete another questionnaire for each language studied.*)

Q7. Which language that you studied at ANU are you completing this questionnaire for?

(Please select ONE option from the pull-down list.)

Arabic
Chinese
French
German
Greek
Latin
Hindi
Indonesian
Italian
Japanese
Korean
Persian
Sanskrit
Spanish
Thai
Turkish
Urdu
Vietnamese
Other (please specify)

APPENDIX 3

Q8. Would you have preferred to study a different language had it been available?

Yes
No

Q9. If *yes*, please specify which language:

Q10. Did you study (formally or informally) any languages (*including English as a second language*) before enrolling at university?

Yes
No

Q11. If *yes*, please specify which language(s) and at what level (primary school, secondary school, community centre, overseas experience, etc.):

Q12. If you had studied languages before enrolling at university, how would you rate your experience of learning that language?

Not at all rewarding
Not very rewarding
Somewhat rewarding
Very rewarding
Extremely rewarding

Q13. Have you been an exchange student?

Yes
No

Q14. If *yes*, please specify when, where, how long and which language(s) were spoken:

Q15. What languages do you speak with your immediate family?

Please provide the following information with respect to your family and friends' experiences of other languages (*Please tick the relevant circles and leave the rest blank*):

- ○ *Speaks a language (native or non-native) other than English.*
- ○ *Converses regularly with you in a language other than English.*
- ○ *Has learned a second (non-native) language well enough to get by in a country where it is spoken.*

Q16. Partner.

Q17. Children.

Q18. Parents.

Q19. Siblings.

Q20. Grandparents.

Q21. Other relatives.

Q22. Close friends.

Q23. Other friends.

Q24. Acquaintances.

Section 2. REASONS FOR STUDYING A LANGUAGE

(Answer ONLY for the language that you specified in Q6)

How important were the following reasons for your initial decision to study a language at university?

Not at all important
Not very important
Of some importance
Very important
Extremely important
Not applicable

Q25. I have a family background in this language.

Q26. I'm interested in the history and culture of the language.

Q27. My friends are studying this language.

Q28. To travel to where this language is spoken.

Q29. To live or work in the country where this language is spoken.

Q30. To communicate with native speakers of the language.

Q31. To participate in cultural activities of the language group.

Q32. For religious reasons.

Q33. For employment reasons.

Q34. To complete my degree.

Q35. To help me in my other studies.

Q36. My family encouraged me to study it.

Q37. Because I had previously studied the language.

Q38. Because I had previously spent time in a country where the language is spoken.

Q39. Because of the reputation of this language at ANU.

Q40. I thought it would be an easy subject.

Q41. I enjoy language learning.

Q42. To understand people and cultures outside of my own.

Q43. Other reasons (please specify and rate them, eg. '*I like the sound of the language—very important*'):

Section 3. EXPERIENCE OF LANGUAGE STUDY

(Answer ONLY for the language that you specified in Q6)

How interested were you in the following aspects of the language when you first enrolled at university?

Not at all interested
Not very interested
Somewhat interested
Very interested
Extremely interested

Q44. Reading the language.

Q45. Writing the language.

Q46. Speaking the language.

Q47. Understanding other speakers.

Q48. The culture of the language.

To what extent did your first-year or second-year language course meet your expectations in the following areas?

Much worse than expected
A little worse than expected
As expected
A little better than expected
Much better than expected

Q49. Teachers' knowledge (*average across teachers*).

Q50. Teachers' teaching skills.

Q51. Teaching/learning materials (*including the textbook*).

Q52. Learning environment and facilities.

Q53. Advice and feedback from teachers.

Q54. Approachability and availability of teachers.

Q55. Support from fellow students.

And to what extent did the language course meet your expectations in the following additional areas?

Much less than expected
Less than expected
As expected
More than expected
Much more than expected

APPENDIX 3

Q56. Workload associated with learning to <u>read</u> the language.

Q57. Workload associated with learning to <u>write</u> the language.

Q58. Workload associated with learning to <u>speak</u> the language.

Q59. Workload associated with learning to <u>understand</u> other speakers.

Q60. Overall difficulty of the course.

Q61. Difficulty of learning grammar in particular.

Q62. Enjoyment of language learning.

Q63. How much I learned about <u>reading</u> the language.

Q64. How much I learned about <u>writing</u> the language.

Q65. How much I learned about <u>speaking</u> the language.

Q66. How much I learned to <u>understand</u> other speakers.

Q67. How much I learned about the <u>culture</u> of the language.

Q68. Others (please specify and rate them):

Q69. Please comment on any expectations that were not met?

Q70. If you were studying the Bachelor of International Relations (BIR) or Bachelor of International Commerce (BIC) or any other degree where a language component was compulsory, to what extent had your language study supported your BIR or other studies, especially in terms of cross-cultural understanding?

Much less than expected
Less than expected
As expected
More than expected
Much more than expected
Not applicable

Q71. If you were studying any International Relations (IR) or International Commerce (IC) or any other course as major within BA where a language component was compulsory, to what extent had your language study supported your interest in IR or IC or other courses, especially in terms of cross-cultural understanding?

Much less than expected
Less than expected
As expected
More than expected
Much more than expected
Not applicable

Section 4. REASONS FOR DISCONTINUING LANGUAGE STUDY

(Answer ONLY for the language that you specified in Q6)

Q72. How much freedom did you have in continuing to study this language and not another?

Not at all free
To some extent free
Totally free

Q73. Was there anything compelling or forcing you to study this language?

Yes
No
Uncertain

Q74. Please expand on the reasons for your answer in Q73. (e.g. family, religion, career track, degree only, etc.)

Q75. If you had had the choice of not studying a language, would you have chosen to study it anyway?

Yes
No
Uncertain

APPENDIX 3

Q76. Please expand on the reasons for your answer in Q75.

Please indicate the importance of the following reasons in your decision *not to continue* studying the language this year:

Not at all important
Not very important
Of some importance
Very important
Extremely important
Not applicable

Q77. Health reasons.

Q78. Financial reasons.

Q79. I wasn't satisfied with my progress.

Q80. My expectations were not being met.

Q81. I did not enjoy the course content.

Q82. I did not like the way the language was taught.

Q83. Class sizes were too big.

Q84. I found the course too difficult.

Q85. I found the workload too high.

Q86. Not enough class time was spent on speaking the language.

Q87. I did not get good marks/grades.

Q88. My friends also discontinued the language course.

Q89. People discouraged me from continuing language study.

Q90. I fell behind in my studies and couldn't catch up.

Q91. Problems with daily travel.

Q92. Timetable clash.

Q93. Other study commitments.

Q94. Paid work commitments.

Q95. Family commitments.

Q96. I felt uncomfortable speaking the language in front of others.

Q97. I did not fit in with other students in the course.

Q98. It worried me that other students in the class seemed to speak better than I did.

Q99. I didn't think I would get to use the language outside university.

Q100. I ceased *all* my studies.

Q101. Other reasons (please specify and rate them):

Q102. Would you consider studying a language again?
Yes
No

Q103. Which aspects of language study do you enjoy least?

Q104. Which aspects of language study do you enjoy most?

Q105. Is there anything that would have made you continue with your language studies?

Q106. Please explain your answer:

Q107. Is there anything else you would like to share about your experience of language study?

APPENDIX 3

Section 5. THE NEXT STAGE OF THE PROJECT

Q108. Would you like to receive a copy of the survey report when it is available?

Yes

No

Q109. If *yes*, please insert your email address so that we can contact you:

Q110. Would you be available for a follow-up interview about your experiences of language study?

Yes

No

Q111. If *yes*, please insert your email address and telephone number so that we can contact you (if you already provided your email address in your previous answer, please write 'as above'):

Email

Phone number

THANK YOU FOR TAKING YOUR TIME TO COMPLETE THIS QUESTIONNAIRE.

Please press the 'Submit' button only when you are satisfied with your responses, as you will not be able to change your answers once the survey has been submitted.

Bibliography

Ashcraft, M.H. & Kirk, E.P. (2001). The relationships among working memory, math anxiety, and performance. *Journal of Experimental Psychology: General*, 130: 224–237.

Australia, Department of Employment, Education and Training (1991). *Australia's Language: The Australian language and literacy policy*. Canberra: Australian Government Publishing Service.

Australian Bureau of Statistics (2011). *4102.0. Australian Social Trends, December 2011—International students*. Retrieved from www.abs.gov.au/AUSSTATS/abs@.nsf/Lookup/4102.0Main+Features20Dec+2011, 5 January 2016.

Australian Government Department of Education and Training (2014). Higher education all student enrolment tables for the 2013 full year. Retrieved from docs.education.gov.au/node/35961, 5 January 2016.

Baik, C., Naylor, R. & Arkoudis, S. (2015). *The First Year Experience in Australian Universities: Findings from two decades, 1994-2014*. Melbourne: Centre for the Study of Higher Education, The University of Melbourne. Retrieved from melbourne-cshe.unimelb.edu.au/__data/assets/pdf_file/0016/1513123/FYE-2014-FULL-report-FINAL-web.pdf, 30 June 2016.

Bourdieu, P. (1986). The forms of capital. pp. 241–258. In: Richardson, J. (Ed.). *Handbook of Theory and Research for the Sociology of Education*. New York: Greenwood.

Bourdieu, P. (1991). *Language and Symbolic Power*. [Trans. G. Raymond and M. Adamson]. Cambridge: Polity Press.

Bourdieu, P. (2010) [1984]. *Distinction: A social critique of the judgement of taste*. [Translation first published 1984.] London: Routledge.

Bowden, J.A., Starrs, C.D. & Quinn, T.J. (1989). Modern language teaching in Australian universities. *Higher Education Research and Development*, 8(2): 129–146.

Byrne, N. [2005]. Information on the number of students studying languages in higher education for less than 50% of their degree, or as an extra curricular activity. European Network for the Promotion of Language Learning Among all Undergraduates. Unpublished. Retrieved from userpage.fu-berlin.de/~enlu/downloads/number_of_students.doc, 5 January 2015.

Chiswick, B.R. & Miller, P.W. (2003). The complementarity of language and other human capital: Immigrant earnings in Canada. *Economics of Education Review*, 22: 469–480.

Clyne, M. (1993). The role of language in Australian society. pp. 52–61. In: Schulz, G. (Ed.). *The Languages of Australia*. Canberra: Australian Academy of the Humanities.

Clyne, M. (1997). Language policy in Australia: Achievements, disappointments, prospects. *Journal of Intercultural Studies*, 18(1): 63–74.

Council of Australian Governments (1994). *Asian Languages and Australia's Economic Future: A report prepared for the Council of Australian Governments on a proposed National Asian Languages/Studies Strategy for Australian schools*. Brisbane: Queensland Government.

Curnow, T.J. & Kohler, M. (2007). Languages are important, but that's not why I am studying one. *Babel*, 42(2): 20–24.

Daniel, B. (2015). Big data and analytics in higher education: Opportunities and challenges. *British Journal of Educational Technology*, 46(5): 904–920.

Djité, P.G. (2011). Language policy in Australia: What goes up must come down? pp. 53–67. In Norrby, C. & Hajek, J. (Eds.), *Uniformity and Diversity in Language Policy: Global perspectives*. Bristol: Multilingual Matters.

Dobson, I. & Sharma, R. (1993). Student progress: A study of the experience in Victorian tertiary institutions. *Journal of Tertiary Education Administration*, 15(2): 203–211.

Dörnyei, Z. (2005). *The Psychology of the Language Learner: Individual differences in second language acquisition*. Mahwah: Lawrence Erlbaum.

Dunne, K.S. & Pavlyshyn, M. (2012). Swings and roundabouts: changes in language offerings at Australian universities 2005-2011. pp. 9–19. In Hajek, J., Nettelbeck, C. & Woods, A. (Eds.), *The Next Step: Introducing the Languages and Cultures Network for Australian universities. Selected Proceedings of LCNAU's Inaugural Colloquium*. Melbourne: Languages and Cultures Network for Australian Universities.

Education, Audiovisual and Culture Executive Agency (2012). *Key Data on Teaching Languages at School in Europe 2012*. Brussels: Education, Audiovisual and Culture Executive Agency. Retrieved from ec.europa.eu/eurostat/documents/3217494/5775673/EC-XA-12-001-EN.PDF/917d3746-886e-456a-8b01-1971013d1cef, 5 January 2016.

Forsman, J., Linder, C., Moll, R., Fraser, D. & Andersson, S. (2014). A new approach to modelling student retention through an application of complexity thinking. *Studies in Higher Education*, 39(1): 68–86.

Foster, G. (2010). Teacher effects on student attrition and performance in mass-market tertiary education. *Higher Education*, 60: 301–319.

Furman, N., Goldberg, D. & Lusin, N. (2010). *Enrollments in Languages Other than English in United States Institutions of Higher Education, Fall 2009*. Modern Languages Association of America. Retrieved from www.mla.org/pdf/2009_enrollment_survey.pdf, 5 January 2016.

Gabb, R., Milne, L. & Cao, Z. (2006). *Understanding Attrition and Improving Transition: A review of recent literature*. Melbourne: Postcompulsory Education Centre, Victoria University. Retrieved from www.researchgate.net/profile/Lisa_Milne3/publication/237632757_Understanding_attrition_and_improving_transition_A_review_of_recent_literature/links/543f06f10cf2eaec07e80d58.pdf, 5 January 2016.

Goldberg, D., Looney, D. & Lusin, N. (2015). *Enrollments in Languages Other than English in United States Institutions of Higher Education, Fall 2013*. Modern Languages Association of America. Retrieved from www.mla.org/content/download/31180/1452509/2013_enrollment_survey.pdf, 5 January 2016.

Group of Eight (2007). *Languages in Crisis: A rescue plan for Australia*. Manuka, ACT: Group of Eight.

Hajek, J. (2001). Languages and culture in Australia in the 21st century: Riding the multilingual tiger. pp. 87–96. In: M. Gillies, M. Carroll & J. Dash (Eds). *Humanities and Social Sciences Futures: Papers from the National Humanities and Social Sciences Summit, July 2001*. Canberra: Department of Education, Science and Training.

Hajek, J., Nettelbeck, C. & Woods, A. (2013). Leadership for Future Generations: A National Network for University Languages. Final Report to Australian Government Office for Learning and Teaching. Retrieved from lcnau.org/pdfs/LE10_1732_Hajek_Report_2013.pdf, 5 January 2016.

Hanley, J. & Brownlee, K. (2013). Investigating first year language students' decisions to continue: Design and implementation of student retention questionnaires. *Journal of the World Universities Forum*, 5(4): 11–20.

Hawley, D.S. (1982). *Foreign Language Study in Australian Tertiary Institutions 1974-1981*. Wollongong: University of Wollongong.

Horwitz, E.K. (2010). Foreign and second language anxiety. *Language Teaching*, 43(2): 154–167.

Horwitz, E.K., Horwitz, M.B. & Cope, J. (1986). Foreign language classroom anxiety. *The Modern Language Journal*, 70(2): 125–132.

James, R., Krause, K.-L. & Jennings, C. (2010). *The First Year Experience in Australian Universities: Findings from 1994 to 2009*. Centre for Study of Higher Education, University of Melbourne. Retrieved from melbourne-cshe.unimelb.edu.au/__data/assets/pdf_file/0003/1706403/FYE_Report_1994_to_2009-1.pdf, 30 June 2016.

Jansen, L., Åkerlind, G. & Maliangkay, R. (2011). Student motivation and retention in Language and Culture Programs at The Australian National University: Part 1: An overview of the project. Paper presented at ANU Educational Research Conference, Canberra, ANU, 15–16 November.

Jansen, L., Maliangkay, R., Martín, M.D. & Åkerlind, G. (2009). Student motivation and retention in Language and Culture Programs at the Australian National University: A pilot study. Paper presented at Beyond the Crisis: Revitalising Languages in Australian Universities, University of Melbourne, Melbourne, 16–18 February.

Jansen, L. & Martín, M.D. (2011). Identifying possible causes for high and low retention rates in language and culture programs at the ANU. Paper presented at Applied Linguistics as a Meeting Place: Second Combined Conference of the Applied Linguistics Association of Australia (ALAA) and Applied Linguistics Association of New Zealand (ALANZ), Canberra, 29 November–2 December.

Jansen, L., Martín, M.D. & Åkerlind, G. (2009). Student retention in Language and Culture Programs at the Australian National University: A pilot study. Paper presented at Participation and Acquisition: Exploring these Metaphors in Applied Linguistics, First Combined Conference of the Applied Linguistics Associations of New Zealand and of Australia. 2–4 December.

Jansen, L. & Schmidt, G. (2011). Das Auf und Ab im Deutschstudium: Gründe für die Aufnahme und den Abbruch eines Deutschstudiums in Australien. [The to and fro in German Studies: Reasons for starting and quitting the study of German in Australia.] *Deutsch als Fremsprache,* 3: 166–172.

Jones, R. (2008). *Student Retention and Success: A synthesis of research.* EvidenceNet. York: Higher Education Academy. Retrieved from www.heacademy.ac.uk/resources/detail/inclusion/wprs/WPRS_retention_synthesis, 5 January 2016.

Keckla, W.R. (1980). *Discriminant Analysis.* London: Sage.

Kleinsasser, R. (2000). A historical overview of six recurring issues in languages education throughout the 20th Century in the United States and Australia. *Babel,* 35(2): 20–26, 37–38.

Krause, K. (2005). Serious thoughts about dropping out in first year: Trends, patterns and implications for higher education. *Studies in Learning, Evaluation Innovation and Development*, 2(3): 55–68.

Krause, K., Hartley, R., James, J. & McInnis, C. (2005). *The First Year Experience in Australian Universities: Findings from a decade of national studies*. Final Report for Department of Education, Science and Training. Centre for the Study of Higher Education, University of Melbourne.

Lawrence, J. (2005). Re-conceptualising attrition and retention: Integrating theoretical, research and student perspectives. *Studies in Learning, Evaluation and Development*, 2(3): 16–33.

Leal, B., Bettoni, C. & Malcolm, I. (1991). *Widening our Horizons: Report of the Review of the Teaching of Modern Languages in Higher Education*. Canberra: Australian Government Publishing Service.

Leopold, K. (1986). Maintaining student numbers and academic standards in a small department. *Higher Education Research and Development*, 5(1): 3–14.

Liddicoat, A.J. (2010). Policy change and educational inertia: Language policy and language education in Australian schooling. pp. 11–24. In: Liddicoat, A.J. & Scarino, A. (Eds). *Languages in Australian Education: Problems, prospects and future directions*. Newcastle-on-Tyne: Cambridge Scholars.

Liddicoat, A.J. & Scarino, A. (Eds.) (2010). *Languages in Australian Education: Problems, prospects and future directions*. Newcastle-on-Tyne: Cambridge Scholars.

Liddicoat, A.J., Scarino, A., Curnow, T.J., Kohler, M., Scrimgeour, A. & Morgan, A. (2007). *An Investigation on the State and Nature of Language in Australian Schools*. Canberra: Department of Education, Employment and Workplace Relations.

Lo Bianco, J. (2009). *Second Languages and Australian Schooling*. Camberwell, Victoria: Australian Council for Education Research.

Lo Bianco, J. & Gvozdenko, I. (2006). *Collaboration and Innovation in the Provision of Languages Other than English in Australian Universities.* Melbourne: Faculty of Education, University of Melbourne. Retrieved from www.lcnau.org/pdfs/LO%20 BIANCO%20GVOZDENKO%20LOTES%20in%20Australian%20 Universities.pdf, 5 January 2016.

Lobo, A. (2012). Will we meet again? Examining the reasons why students are leaving first year university courses and moving towards an approach to stop them. *The International Journal of Learning,* 18(7): 199–212.

Lobo, A. & Matas, C.P. (2010). *War of Attrition: A prognostic remedial approach to student retention.* Saarbrücken, Germany: LAP Lambert Academic.

Lobo, A. & Matas, C.P. (2011). Towards the development of a prognostic approach to student retention in foreign language classes. *The International Journal of Learning,* 17(11): 305–316.

Lomax-Smith, J., Watson, L. & Webster, B. (2010). *The Higher Education Base Funding Review: Background Paper.* Canberra: Department of Education, Employment and Workplace Relations. Retrieved from www.canberra.edu.au/research/faculty-research-centres/edinstitute/ documents/HigherEd_FundingReviewReport1.pdf, 5 January 2016.

Long, M., Ferrier, F. & Heagney, M. (2006). *Stay, Play or Give It Away? Students continuing, changing or leaving university study in first year.* Melbourne: Centre for the Economics of Education and Training, Monash University.

Longden, B. (2006). An institutional response to changing student expectations and their impact on retention rates. *Journal of Higher Education Policy and Management,* 28(2): 173–187.

Lukic, T., Broadbent, A. & Maclachlan, M. (2004). *Higher Education Attrition Rates 1994-2002: A brief overview.* Strategic Analysis and Evaluation Group, Research Note No. 1. Canberra: Department of Education, Science and Training. Retrieved from pandora.nla. gov.au/pan/43490/20050122-0000/www.dest.gov.au/research/ publications/research_notes/1.htm, 5 January 2016.

Lusin, N. (2012). *The MLA Survey of Postsecondary Entrance and Degree Requirements for Languages Other Than English, 2009-10.* New York: Modern Languages Association. Retrieved from www.mla.org/Resources/Research/Surveys-Reports-and-Other-Documents/Teaching-Enrollments-and-Programs/The-MLA-Survey-of-Postsecondary-Entrance-and-Degree-Requirements-for-Languages-Other-Than-English-2009-10, 5 January 2016.

Luzeckyj, A., King, S., Scutter, S. & Brinkworth, R. (2011). The significance of being first: A consideration of cultural capital in relation to 'first in family' student's choices of university and program. A Practice Report. *The International Journal of the First Year in Higher Education*, 2(2): 91–96.

Ma, X. & Xu, J. (2003). The causal ordering of mathematics anxiety and mathematics achievement: A longitudinal panel analysis. *Journal of Adolescence*, 27(2): 165–179.

Macdonald, E. (2015). Staff and budget cuts at esteemed ANU College of Asia and the Pacific. *The Canberra Times*, 3 November. Retrieved from www.canberratimes.com.au/act-news/staff-and-budget-cuts-at-esteemed-anu-college-of-asia-and-the-pacific-20151102-gkojpp.html, 5 January 2016.

Martín, M.D. (2004). Who is to blame? The position of foreign languages in Australian society. pp. 75–91. In: Wigglesworth, G. (Ed.). *Marking our Difference: Languages in Australian and New Zealand universities.* Melbourne: University of Melbourne.

Martín, M.D. (2005). Permanent crisis, tenuous persistence: Foreign languages in Australian universities. *Arts & Humanities in Higher Education*, 4(1): 53–75.

Martín, M.D. & Jansen, L. (2011). Student motivation and retention in Language and Culture Programs at The Australian National University. Part 2: Core findings. Paper presented at ANU Educational Research Conference, Canberra, 15–16 November.

Martín, M.D. & Jansen, L. (2012). Identifying possible causes for high and low retention rates in language and culture programs at the ANU: A characterisation of three groups of students crucial for understanding student attrition. pp. 175–219. In: Hajek, J., Nettelbeck, C. & Woods, A. (Eds). *The Next Step: Introducing the Languages and Cultures Network for Australian Universities, Selected proceedings of the Inaugural LCNAU Colloquium, Melbourne, 26–28 September 2011*. Melbourne: Languages & Cultures Network for Australian Universities.

Martín, M.D., Jansen, L. & Beckmann, E.A. (2015). Calming down the bean counters: Comparing language and culture student retention rates with those of other disciplines. Paper presented at Tertiary Language and Culture Programs: Directions in Research, Teaching and Policy, LCNAU 2015 National Colloquium, Macquarie University, Sydney, 25–27 November. Abstract. Retrieved from www.mq.edu.au/pubstatic/public/download.jsp?id=270333, 5 January 2016.

McGroarty, M. (1997). Language policy in the USA: National values, local loyalties, pragmatic pressures. pp. 67–90. In: Eggington, W. & Wren, H. (Eds). *Language Policy: Dominant English, pluralist challenges*. Amsterdam: John Benjamins.

McInnis, C. (2001). Researching the first year experience: Where to from here? *Higher Education Research and Development*, 20(2): 105–114.

McInnis, C., Hartley, R., Polesel, J. & Teese, R. (2000). *Non-Completion in Vocational Education and Training and Higher Education: A literature review*. Commissioned by Department of Education, Training and Youth Affairs. Melbourne: Centre for the Study of Higher Education, University of Melbourne.

McInnis, C. & James, R. (2004). Access and retention in Australian higher education. In: Yorke, M. & Longden, B. (Eds). *Retention and Student Success in Higher Education*. Berkshire: Society for Research into Higher Education & Open University Press.

McInnis, C., James, R. & Hartley, R. (2000). *Trends in the First Year Experience*. Canberra: Australian Government Publishing Service.

Murray, N. (2010). Discussion—Languages education in Australia: Shaky data, disjointed policy, and a chicken and egg problem. pp. 87–96. In: Liddicoat, A.J. & Scarino, A. (Eds). *Languages in Australian Education: Problems, prospects and future directions*. Newcastle-on-Tyne: Cambridge Scholars.

Nelson, K., Duncan, M.E. & Clarke, J.A. (2009). Student success: The identification and support of first year university students at risk of attrition. *Studies in Learning, Evaluation and Development*, 6(1): 1–15.

Nelson, K.J., Quinn, C., Marrington, A.D. & Clarke, J.A. (2012). Good practice for enhancing the engagement and success of commencing students. *Higher Education*, 63(1): 83–96.

Nettelbeck, C., Byron, J., Clyne, M., Dunne, K., Hajek, J., Levy, M., Lo Bianco, J., McLaren, A., Möllering, M. & Wigglesworth, G. (2009). *An Analysis of Retention Strategies and Technology Enhanced Learning in Beginners' Languages Other than English (LOTE) at Australian Universities*. Canberra: Australian Academy of the Humanities.

Nettelbeck, C., Byron, J., Clyne, M., Hajek, J., Lo Bianco, J. & McLaren, A. (2007). *Beginners' LOTE (Languages Other than English) in Australian Universities: An audit survey and analysis*. Canberra: Australian Academy of the Humanities.

Nicholas, H. (2004). Looking backwards and sideways in order to go forward: A role for languages in shaping Australia's future. *Babel*, 39(2): 8–14, 38.

Nunez-Pena, M.I., Suarez-Pellicioni, M. & Bono, R. (2013). Effects of math anxiety on student success in higher education. *International Journal of Educational Research*, 58: 36–43.

Onwuegbuzie, A.J., Bailey, P. & Daley, C.E. (1999). Factors associated with foreign language anxiety. *Applied Psycholinguistics*, 20: 217–239.

Orton, J. (2008). *Chinese Language Education in Australian Schools*. Melbourne: University of Melbourne.

Ozga, J. & Sukhnandan, L. (1997). *Undergraduate Non-Completion in Higher Education in England. Report 2*. Bristol: Higher Education Funding Council for England.

Pascarella, E.T. & Chapman, D.W. (1983). Validation of a theoretical model of college withdrawal: Interaction effects in a multi-institutional sample. *Research in Higher Education*, 19: 25–48.

Pascarella, E.T. & Terenzini, P.T. (1991). *How College Affects Students: Findings and insights from twenty years*. San Francisco: Jossey-Bass.

Pascarella, E.T. & Terenzini, P.T. (2005). *How College Affects Students. Vol. 2: A third decade of research*. San Francisco: Jossey-Bass.

Pauwels, A. (2002). Languages in the university sector at the beginning of the 3rd millennium. *Babel*, 37(2): 16–20, 38.

Pendakur, K. & Pendakur, R. (2002). Language as both human capital and ethnicity. *International Migration Review*, 36(1): 147–177.

Pitkethly, A. & Prosser, M. (2001). The First Year Experience Project: A model for university wide change. *Higher Education Research and Development*, 20(2): 185–198.

Ram, S., Wang, Y., Currim, F. & Currim, S. (2015). Using big data for predicting freshmen retention. *Proceedings of International Conference on Information Systems 2015*. Retrieved from aisel.aisnet.org/icis2015/proceedings/DecisionAnalytics/13/, 5 January 2016.

Rover, C. & Duffy, L. (2005). Review of the Diploma in Modern Languages at the University of Melbourne. Unpublished.

Scarino, A. (2012). A rationale for acknowledging the diversity of learner achievements in learning particular languages in school education in Australia. *Australian Review of Applied Linguistics*, 35(3): 231–250.

Schmidt, G. (2011). *Motives for studying German in Australia: Re-examining the profile and motivation of German Studies students in Australian universities*. Frankfurt am Main: Peter Lang.

Scovel, T. (1978). The effect of affect on foreign language learning: A review of the anxiety research. *Language Learning*, 28(1): 129–142.

Shaw, B. (2008). *Investigating retention at Griffith University*. Brisbane: Office of Quality, Griffith University.

Sherman, B.F. & Wither, D.P. (2003). Mathematics anxiety and mathematics achievement. *Mathematics Education Research Journal*, 15(2): 138–150.

Stevens, J. (2002). *Applied Multivariate Statistics for the Social Sciences*. Mahwah, New Jersey: Lawrence Erlbaum.

Tabachnick, B.G. & Fidell. L.S. (2005). *Using Multivariate Statistics*. 5th edn. Boston: Pearson.

Taylor, J.A. & Bedford. T. (2004). Staff perceptions of factors related to non-completion in higher education. *Studies in Higher Education*, 29(3): 375–394.

Tickle, L. (2015). How universities are using data to stop students dropping out. *The Guardian*, 30 June. Retrieved from www.theguardian.com/guardian-professional/2015/jun/30/how-universities-are-using-data-to-stop-students-dropping-out, 5 January 2016.

Tinto, V. (1975). Dropout from higher education: A theoretical synthesis of recent research. *Review of Educational Research*, 45(1): 89–125.

Tinto, V. (1987). *Leaving College: Rethinking the causes and cures of student attrition*. Chicago: University of Chicago Press.

Tinto, V. (1993). *Leaving College: Rethinking the causes and cures of student attrition*. 2nd edn. Chicago: University of Chicago Press.

Tinto, V. (1999). Taking retention seriously: Rethinking the first year of college. *NACADA Journal*, 19(2): 5–9.

Tinto, V. (2002). Establishing conditions for student success: Lessons learned in the United States. Speech at 11th Annual Conference of the European Access Network, Monash University, Prato, Italy, 20 June 2002. Retrieved from vtinto.expressions.syr.edu/wp-content/uploads/2013/01/European-Access-Network-2002-Keynote.pdf, 5 January 2016.

Tinto, V. (2006). Research and practice of student retention: What next? *Journal of College Student Retention: Research, Theory & Practice* 8(1): 1–19.

Tinto, V. (2009). Taking student retention seriously: Rethinking the first year of university. Keynote address delivered at the Australian Learning and Teaching Council First Year Experience Curriculum Design Symposium, Brisbane, 5 February 2009. Retrieved from www.fyecd2009.qut.edu.au/resources/SPE_VincentTinto_5Feb09.pdf, 5 January 2016.

Tinto, V. (2015). Through the eyes of students. *Journal of College Student Retention: Research, Theory and Practice*. Pre-print online. doi: 10.1177/1521025115621917.

University of California, Berkeley (2015). Undergraduate Advising: Foreign language. Retrieved from ls-advise.berkeley.edu/requirement/fl.html, 5 January 2016.

Wesely, P.M. (2010). Student attrition from traditional and immersion foreign language programs. *Language and Linguistics Compass*, 4(9): 804–807.

Weston, J.M. (1998). *Higher Education and the Student Profile: A reconceptualised model of retention and attrition*. Toowoomba: University of Southern Queensland.

White, P. & Baldauf, R.B. (2006). *Re-examining Australia's Tertiary Language Programs: A five year retrospective on teaching and collaboration*. Brisbane: University of Queensland. Retrieved from www.murdoch.edu.au/ALTC-Fellowship/_document/whitebauldaufreport2006.pdf, December 2015.

Yale College (2015). Foreign Language Requirement. Retrieved from yalecollege.yale.edu/foreign-language-requirement, 5 January 2016.

Yorke, M. (1999). *Leaving Early: Undergraduate non-completion in higher education*. London: Falmer.

Yorke, M., Bell, R., Dove, A., Haslam, L., Hughes Jones, H., Longden, B., O'Connell, C., Typuszak, R. & Ward, J. (1997). *Undergraduate Non-completion in England. Report No. 1*. Bristol: Higher Education Funding Council for England.

Yorke, M. & Longden, B. (2008). *The First-Year Experience of Higher Education in the UK*. York: Higher Education Academy. Retrieved from www.heacademy.ac.uk/sites/default/files/fyefinalreport_0.pdf, 5 January 2016.

Zepke, N. & Leach. L. (2006). Improving retention and student outcomes? Some questions about the retention discourse. pp. 108–122. In: Walker, C. & McKegg, A. (Eds). *Engaging Students: Retention and success bridging education in New Zealand, Proceedings of the 6th Conference of the New Zealand Association of Bridging Educators*. Auckland: NZABE.

Zepke, N., Leach, L. & Prebble, T. (2006). Being learner centred: One way to improve student retention? *Studies in Higher Education*, 31(5): 587–600.

www.ingramcontent.com/pod-product-compliance
Lightning Source LLC
Chambersburg PA
CBHW040624240426
43666CB00029BA/2912